UFOs

UFOs

A Scientist Explains What We Know (And Don't Know)

Robert Powell

ROWMAN & LITTLEFIELD
Lanham • Boulder • New York • London

Published by Rowman & Littlefield
An imprint of The Rowman & Littlefield Publishing Group, Inc.
4501 Forbes Boulevard, Suite 200, Lanham, Maryland 20706
www.rowman.com

86-90 Paul Street, London EC2A 4NE

British Library Cataloguing in Publication Information Available

Library of Congress Cataloging-in-Publication Data Available

ISBN: 978-1-5381-7358-9 (cloth)
ISBN: 978-1-5381-7359-6 (electronic)

This book is dedicated to Dr. Michael Swords in appreciation for his mentorship, his collegial and personal friendship, and his decades of scientific pursuit of the subject of UFOs.

Contents

Preface

The impetus for this book comes from my sixteen years of studying the subject of unidentified flying objects as basically a full-time occupation. My college years were spent studying to obtain a BS in chemistry, while participating in intercollegiate debate. Chemistry nurtured my curiosity and scientific way of approaching a problem, while debate provided my framework for critical thinking through deductive and inductive reasoning. My work experience encompassed engineering, device physics, and statistical analysis as I spent most of my career in the semiconductor world of nanotechnologies. I enjoyed the challenges of the work and after twenty-eight years of corporate America, I was fortunate to have been able to retire at an early age. This provided me the opportunity to choose my next direction. One of the choices that I made was to look into the subject of UFOs. I was interested because of a book that I had read as a teenager, *The UFO Experience* by Dr. J. Allen Hynek. It was written in a scientific manner, which I appreciated. I returned to a subject that I had not thought about for the last thirty-five years, but that flame of curiosity was still there. I considered the possibility that the subject would be one that I would quickly dismiss after studying, and then move on to a different area of interest. Instead, the subject opened a new chapter in my life.

I joined an organization called MUFON (Mutual UFO Network) in 2006. I wanted to learn about the UFO subject firsthand. Within a few months of my joining MUFON, the organization posted an opening for a director of research. I read the expectations for the position, and I was appalled. They wanted to know where UFOs came from, what was their intention, and their method of propulsion. Nonetheless, I applied. I wrote that I would not address any of those questions because my first primary question was whether there was any reality to the phenomenon itself. I expected that my reply would eliminate me from the competition. I was shocked when I was contacted and awarded the position. I can only guess that my work experience as the manager of Advanced Micro Device's R&D lab, their chemistry lab, and my engineering manager experience must have caused MUFON to make me their director of research. My goal was to put more "science" into how MUFON operated.

My knowledge of the UFO phenomenon was born from a series of events that began in early 2007. The director of MUFON asked me to put together a team to study the history of the UFO phenomenon. He suggested that I contact an individual outside of MUFON by the name of Dr. Michael Swords. Mike had a BS and MS in chemistry with a PhD in science history. Furthermore, he had devoted his life to the study of UFOs. Mike was a member of CUFOS (Center for UFO Studies) and had known Dr. J. Allen Hynek personally. I could not have found a better mentor. Mike provided the rational, scientific view of the phenomenon that I needed to hear. He introduced me to the other no-nonsense researchers who were in the field. Our work culminated five years later in a collegiate-level book on the subject, *UFOs and Government: A Historical Inquiry.*

Meanwhile, I continued my role as the director of research for MUFON, and I also completed field investigations in a secondary role. I interviewed over 150 people in person during my investigations. I poured over thousands of cases within the MUFON database that had been collected from the 1970s through 2015. I read through the books that weren't as popular in the UFO community but that were written by scientists and historians: *Project Investigation, The UFO Enigma, Clear Intent, Anatomy of a Phenomenon, Grassroots UFOs,* and *Unconventional Flying Objects.* I established a Science Review Board made up of scientists to evaluate the best cases. There was a strong need for more scientists to be involved in the study of this phenomenon.

I hit a lot of obstacles promoting science within MUFON, but I was used to removing obstacles, as that was part of my role as an engineering manager in the manufacture of leading-edge computer chips using nanotechnology. I won't delve into the what/when/why of all those obstacles, but in 2017 I hit a brick wall of resistance. I resigned my position as director of research after eleven years in that role. Several other individuals within the organization also resigned at about the same time. It was time for a change.

I wanted to be part of a true science-based organization that studied the UFO phenomenon. Three others and I founded SCU (The Scientific Coalition for Ufology; later changed to The Scientific Coalition for UAP Studies) in August 2017 and registered the organization as a 501(c)(3) nonprofit a few months later. Today, SCU consists of over 250 members who include university professors, scientists, ex-military, individuals in intelligence, the high-tech industry, and the defense industry, and present/former members of NASA, the European Space Agency, and the Canadian Space Agency. There are multiple projects being run within SCU, papers have been published in journals, briefings have been given to government representatives, and more. Science has come to the study of the UFO phenomenon.

I hope this book will spark your curiosity to learn more about this mystery. And I hope that you will understand that one can contemplate the question of whether this mystery is driven by an unknown intelligence, while understanding and being open to the realization that there could be alternate explanations as well.

Introduction

I have been asked, "Why do you spend so much time studying UFOs?" This is a very valid question and one that I've thought about from time to time. The primary reason may be because of the wonderful people I've met along the way. Discussions about UFOs invoke a lot of strong human reactions by their very nature. There are those who have already decided exactly what UFOs are as well as their origin and purpose; there are those who have already decided that every UFO sighting has an explanation; and then there are those who are attracted to UFOs because of their innate human curiosity. It is in this latter group where I have met people who have taught me so much, have provided so many intriguing conversations, and usually have such a love for life. These friends and acquaintances are why I study the UFO phenomenon, and they are the type who are likely to ask me exactly what I mean by a UFO.

Why is the term *UFO* so difficult to define? Why are there so many hidden implications in the words *unidentified flying object*? Every object we see flying through the sky is a UFO for a split millisecond as our brain begins to characterize it as a bird, a bee, a balloon, an airplane, or something else. Sometimes we see an object that is not identified even after a few seconds. Once we have gone through our repertoire of possibilities and nothing matches, the tag *UFO* remains. But we've all seen this type of UFO: a far-off light, a small triangular shaped object in the distance, or a blurry object that zips by in the periphery of our eyesight. Our brain categorizes these instances as lacking sufficient information and we think no more about it as we go about our day. Let's take this one step further. We see a strange stationary object in the sky. It is cigar shaped. Could it be a side-view of an aircraft such that the wings are not visible? Suddenly the cigar rotates ninety degrees and it is clear that the shape is more disk-like as its spherical shape becomes evident. The disk suddenly moves vertically in what seems to be instantaneous movement to our eyes; it stops suddenly; and then it takes off horizontally and is gone from sight, within one to two, seconds. Either we just hallucinated, or we just witnessed an object perform feats that are beyond the capability of any human-made craft. If it was the latter, aren't we really saying this was alien technology? Isn't this what we mean by the term *UFO*? Yet so many of us would start the sentence by saying, "I'm not saying UFOs are alien . . ." But this is exactly why the subject of UFOs interests us, if we're being honest. Few of us are interested in studying UFOs because it was an object that was incorrectly identified or because there was insufficient information to draw any conclusion. We're interested in studying UFOs because of the possibility that they are alien craft. If true, this would be a watershed moment in the history of humanity. This book will discuss the reasons why such a hypothesis should be considered and the steps that need to be taken to investigate this hypothesis.

The first chapter of this book discusses the history of the UFO phenomenon so as to familiarize the reader with the modern beginnings of the phenomenon, some of the more enigmatic and interesting sightings, and how governments have reacted. Some readers may think that the history of the subject is not important, and that proper scientific research from a blank slate is all that is needed. This would be a mistake. Anyone versed in the liberal arts is aware of the value of history and the avoidance of previous mistakes. However, a reader well versed in the history of the subject may want to skip the first chapter.

The remainder of the book provides you with my perspective on the phenomenon after sixteen years steeped in the subject on a daily basis. It will include information never before released and provided by verified sources, off-the-record, regarding current military operations related to unidentified anomalous phenomena (UAP). I examine the phenomenon from a scientific and logical approach. Most reports are witness misidentifications, but there still remain thousands of reports from reputable and skilled observers. Occam's Razor can be invoked to explain some cases: select the solution with the fewer and more likely assumptions. But Occam's Razor can also be misused by piling unlikely assumption on top of unlikely assumption in order to create a solution so as to avoid a possible hypothesis that an investigator considers too unlikely. This is false logic that is known as an "argument from incredulity." This is the practice of rejecting an argument out of hand simply because it appears too incredible and violates one's own personal beliefs. This cynical fallacy falsely elevates the saying popularized by Carl Sagan, that "Extraordinary claims require extraordinary proof," to an absolute law of logic. "Because I don't believe a given hypothesis to be possible, I reserve the right to fiat any and all explanations necessary in order to negate any information supporting that hypothesis." This is not logical reasoning, and it is not science.

This book also makes important observational statements regarding what has been learned about the phenomenon over the last seventy-five years. It is important to reconcile some of the strangest aspects of the phenomenon such as electromagnetic interference, the bending of light, unusual spatio-temporal changes, and extreme acceleration. This is what Dr. Allen Hynek referred to when he discussed the "high strangeness" of a UFO report. Why would a reliable witness make a claim that was so strange that it endangered the credibility of his story, unless perhaps it was true? One must seriously consider the potential reality of these types of observations when they are reported over and over again.

Any modern review of the UFO subject cannot ignore the sudden change in attitude by the U.S. government and parts of the military. The December 2017 *New York Times* front-page article regarding the story of a Navy F/A-18F that engaged a Tic Tac–shaped object, was a large influence in the government's own new willingness to directly engage UFOs. More subtle and possibly buried within all our collective consciousness were the thousands of exoplanets discovered around other stars. We were not unique. This has also influenced how we now see the UFO phenomenon. Humanity has always seen itself as the center of all that is important. We are the one and only dominant, intelligent species on this planet, so it is only normal that we see reality as something that must revolve around us. This belief is also known as an anthropocentric view: the tendency to believe that human beings are the central and most important entity in the universe. We have lost a little of our anthropocentric character, but not much. We have given up the belief that the Earth was the center of the solar system, later the belief that our solar system was in the center of the galaxy, and more recently the belief that our solar system was created by a unique happenstance of events. We now protect our anthropocentrism with the view that due to distance, no other intelligence can reach us. Perhaps that view is also beginning to change.

Chapter One

The Beginnings of the
Modern UFO Phenomenon

The Romans saw phantom ships shining in the sky over 2,000 years ago. Residents of Nuremberg, Germany, described a large black triangle in the sky in 1561. Were these real UFOs? Think of what the acronym represents—an unidentified flying object. The acronym does not represent aliens from another world, flying by in a spaceship. Whatever those Romans and Germans were observing, the objects were unknown and unexplained to them. Yes, they were UFOs. Would they be UFOs to us? Perhaps, or perhaps not. It all depends on whether we could have identified those objects in the sky. People sometimes seeing objects in the sky that they cannot explain is not unusual; what is unusual is when that begins to happen frequently.

The modern UFO era began during the Second World War. The modern era did not begin with one or two sightings of an unexplained object in the sky. It began with many sightings from reliable American, British, and German pilots during the years 1942–1945. There are over 100 documented cases of objects that the pilots called Foo Fighters.[1] These incidents are documented in the reports that squadrons made after completing their missions. They usually reported plasma-like ovoid balls of light that were three to ten feet in size. Often, multiple Foo Fighters would fly alongside the aircraft for several minutes before racing away at speeds estimated to be thousands of miles per hour. A typical example of a Foo Fighter report was made by a British pilot while flying near Strasbourg, France, the night of December 23–24, 1944:

> At 0600 hrs., saw two lights coming towards a/c [aircraft] from the ground. Upon reaching altitude of [our] plane, they leveled off and stayed on my tail for approximately 2 minutes. Light appeared to be a large orange glow. After staying with a/c for approximately 2 minutes, they would peel off and turn away,

fly along level for a few minutes and then go out. They appeared to be under perfect control at all times.[2]

If there were just a few of these reports then it would be easier to dismiss them as pilot error, ball lightning, or the phenomenon known as St. Elmo's Fire. But with over 100 documented reports and likely many more undocumented reports, the evidence argues for an investigation into what the pilots were seeing. What we have here is much different than a UFO report here and there, made by ancient Romans and Germans and passed down as stories. We now have modern, documented reports by trained pilots.

Had these reports been limited to the war years, it is possible that no investigation would have been initiated. This was not the case. Reports continued after the Second World War had ended. Instead of 100 reports, there were hundreds of sightings reported each year and many of these came from military personnel. The United States Air Force (USAF) took these reports seriously and initiated a secret investigation in early 1948 with the code name Project SIGN.[3]

USAF PROJECTS 1947–1970

This new Air Force organization was investigating a phenomenon that had changed somewhat from the war years. There were still some reports of plasma-like objects, but the description provided in most of the sightings of the late 1940s was of a metallic disk. A new terminology was used to describe these objects. The disks were called flying saucers because their appearance and movement were similar to an inverted saucer that skimmed across the skies.

The USAF was concerned that these flying saucers were a new weapon developed by Russia, then known as the Soviet Union. They were concerned for a reason. The United States and the Soviet Union had grabbed every German scientist that they could find as the Second World War came to a close. The German scientists were the best in the world. They had invented jet aircraft, created V-2 rockets, and it was their scientists who had defected prior to the war and helped the United States build the first atomic bomb. Already, Werner Von Braun was developing rocket systems for the budding U.S. space program. German scientists, captured by the Soviets, were also developing rocket systems in Russia. Had they also developed a new disk-shaped flying aircraft? The USAF needed an answer, and quickly.

The Air Force created Project SIGN in early 1948. Its purpose was to investigate these unknown craft and determine if they posed a threat to our national security. Project SIGN provided an answer to the Commanding General of the USAF, Gen. Hoyt Vandenberg, in late 1948. The leaders of the project hypothesized in their report that the flying saucers might be from another world. The Pentagon ordered the Project SIGN leaders to Washington, D.C., on November 12, 1948, to discuss their report. The review did not go well. Their hypothesis was batted down as untenable. They were told to write up a final SIGN report, and without mention of an extraterrestrial hypothesis. The leaders of Project SIGN were disbanded.[4] Ironically, one of the most interesting reports of 1948 happened six days after the Project SIGN–Pentagon meeting.[5]

Two AF lieutenants sighted an oblong ball from their T-6 trainer at 1,700 feet. It was 11 p.m. on November 18 near Andrews AFB in the Washington, D.C., area. The object had a glowing light, no wings, and no exhaust. The pilots closed in on the object, but it quickly flew up and over their aircraft. The pilots continued their chase as the object increased and decreased altitude from 7,500 feet to 3,500 feet, while it rapidly varied its speed from 80 mph to 600 mph. This up-and-down chase continued for about fifteen minutes until the pilots maneuvered their T-6 to within 300–400 feet of the object's underside. They turned their landing lights on to illuminate the object. They could see a very dull, gray glow from the oblong-shaped intruder. The object did not allow the plane to remain close as it performed a very tight curve and headed away at 500–600 mph. This incident was also witnessed and confirmed by a staff sergeant on the ground.

Project SIGN was renamed Project Grudge on February 11, 1949. New people took over with the understanding that these strange objects do not exist, and reports needed to be explained away.[6] When they received a perplexing report, they consulted with their scientific advisor, astrophysicist Dr. J. Allen Hynek of Ohio State University. A change in attitude had begun.

Project Grudge stayed busy as over 300 reports of unknown aerial objects came in during 1949. Many reports were from military bases, with some bases reporting many repeat sightings over the year: Ft. Hood Army Base (18); Kirtland AFB (6); Los Alamos (11); and Sandia Army Base (30).[7] All of those military sites hosted nuclear weaponry. If Project Grudge noticed this, it was not to be found in their reports. Their goal was just to close out reports. The Air Force closed Project Grudge on December 30, 1949, with a final evaluation that concluded:

1. Evaluation of reports of unidentified flying objects constitute no direct threat to the national security of the United States.
2. Reports of unidentified flying objects are the result of:
    a. A mild form of mass hysteria or "war nerves."
    b. Individuals who fabricate such reports to perpetrate a hoax or seek publicity.

c. Psycho pathological persons.

d. Misidentification of various conventional objects.[8]

Project Grudge was short-lived, but the sightings of unidentified flying objects continued the following year, especially at U.S. nuclear weapons facilities. Multiple sighting reports were made by Kirtland AFB (2), Los Alamos (6), and Sandia Army Base (3). Most interestingly, Oak Ridge National Labs had nine different sighting reports and Holloman AFB, next to the world's first nuclear explosion at White Sands, reported seven sightings.[9] Reports from non-nuclear military bases numbered either zero or one report, with a couple of bases with two reports. These incidents at our nuclear facilities must have alarmed the military. How could the Grudge report have concluded that there was no direct threat to our national security? And surely reports from our closely guarded nuclear military facilities were not the results of items 2a through 2d, as previously noted by the Grudge report. Those items were the beginning of the stigmatization of the subject of UFOs. When digested, those four items indicate either a witness is lacking in knowledge or has some type of psychological problem. An option that the witness has made a correct determination is not listed as a possibility.

The year 1952 brought over a thousand sighting reports. It was also about the time that the Air Force stopped using the term *flying saucers* in favor of *UFOs* (unidentified flying objects). UFO reports came in from all over the United States as well as from U.S. military bases in Korea and Japan. Dozens of reports came in from the Washington, D.C., area that summer.[10] These were the reports that caused the Air Force the most grief because of the high interest from the media and the public. They wanted an explanation for this sudden rash of sightings. Fortunately, Project Blue Book went into operation in June of 1952.[11]

The public did not know everything that went on that summer. A very interesting incident was unearthed in 2008 during a research trip the author made with Dr. Michael Swords to Texas A&M's Cushing Archival Library. The library possessed an audio file of an interview made by Dr. Roy Craig of Boeing engineer Jay Nogle in 1967. The engineer recalls the event that led to a military order to fire on UFOs in the summer of 1952.

UFOs were detected on radar almost every night that summer, recalled Nogle. He described one of the more unusual nights when he was monitoring his M33 radar. The UFO showed up on his screen and was detected by two to three additional Army radar units. The signal was strong as the unknown object hovered at 18,000 feet. The UFO began to move on Nogle's screen after thirty minutes. It was traveling at over 1,000 mph by the time it reached the edge of his radar screen. Nogle's own words best describe the military's reaction:

We didn't think too much of it ourselves that night. But the next morning the Battalion commander, a light colonel, came into our radar area and wanted to know what happened and all the background. Apparently this report went all the way to the Pentagon that night, and the order came back that if another one came in then we were to fire on it. . . . After that first night, we had orders to fire on them, and we loaded our guns [90mm anti-aircraft rounds], which was an unusual thing to do in a populated area. We also scrambled fighters off McGuire AFB. About the time the F-94 fighters would take off, these objects would leave.[12]

Nogle recalled the last time that the UFOs showed up on his radar. Twelve F-94 Star Fighter jets were scrambled from McGuire AFB. The lead F-94 fighter locked onto a UFO with his fire control radar and indicated over the radio that he was closing in for the kill. Before he could fire, the UFO moved rapidly out of range.

The public and the media were not aware of how the military reacted to UFOs, but they were aware of the many reported UFO sightings in July. Capt. Ruppelt went in front of the press on July 18 to answer questions. Here are some of his remarks:

ground radar had tracked some aerial objects at speeds ranging between 1500 and 2000 miles per hour.

jet fighters equipped with the very latest radar have been sent aloft to "make contact" with the phantom objects, but all efforts to catch up with them have failed.

we are convinced that persons making these reports actually see something in the sky, but what they are is another question.[13]

Dr. Lincoln LaPaz, a meteor expert of his time, was interviewed by the press the next day. LaPaz listed the characteristics of UFOs: "They can reverse directions and cruise back and forth; they travel at high speeds in wide sweeping circles. They are spherical or disk-shaped and for the most part give off a steady yellow light; they travel at high altitudes and can be followed as long as 3½ minutes."[14] These comments by a top scientist only fueled the interest of the media and the public. The UFO phenomenon itself would soon pour gas on the fire.

On July 26 at 10:30 p.m. radar operators at Washington National Airport detected an arc of UFOs spread around Washington from Herndon, Virginia, to Andrews AFB. They called Andrews AFB; their radar had detected the same unknowns. Two F-94 jet interceptors were airborne at 11:30 p.m. The UFOs disappeared from radar just as the two F-94s arrived in the area. The jets searched the area for a few minutes before returning to their base. Radar detected the UFOs return within minutes of the jet's departure. The radar operators again called

Defense Command, and once again two F-94s were dispatched. This time the UFOs hung around. The jets were vectored to one of the targets by radar. Just as they got close enough to see more than just a light, the target sped away.[15]

The next day, the newspaper headlines were all about UFOs:

"FIERY OBJECT OUTRUN JETS OVER CAPITAL"
"JETS ALERTED FOR SAUCER"
"INTERCEPTORS CHASE LIGHTS IN D.C. SKIES"[16]

The Air Force did not want this type of publicity, especially on the doorsteps of the White House.

Air Force Intelligence received a call from the president's aide, Brig. Gen. Landry. President Truman wanted to know what was going on. Capt. Ruppelt told him that the radar target could have been caused by weather but that there was no proof for that theory.[17] This reply was insufficient.

Maj. Gen. John Samford, the director of Air Force Intelligence, gathered his team, and held a Washington, D.C., press conference at 4 p.m. on July 29. He assured everyone that the Air Force was working responsibly to re-solve the issues and that everything was under control. He discussed various possibilities that might explain the sightings, and he made a statement that gave a certain credence to some of the sighting reports: "However, there have remained a percentage of this total, in the order of twenty per cent of the reports, that have come from credible observers of relatively incredible things."[18] Gen. Samford's press conference calmed the furor, but the Air Force would need more than a press conference to keep the UFO phenom-enon from causing them more grief in the future.

Enter the Central Intelligence Agency (CIA). The CIA had two major con-cerns with the UFO phenomenon: (1) Could UFOs be used by our enemies as a psychological warfare tool to panic the public? Widespread panic could clog the phone lines and roads prior to an enemy attack; and (2) How would our military distinguish between real enemy craft and UFOs?[19] The CIA pro-posed a scientific committee to address the question of UFOs. They appointed their former chief science consultant, physicist Dr. Howard P. Robertson of Cal Tech, to chair a panel to investigate UFOs—to be known as the Robertson Panel. Robertson recruited astrophysicist Dr. Thornton Page early on. Atomic physicist Dr. Samuel Goudsmit and radiation physicist Dr. Luis Alvarez were brought in two weeks prior to their first working meeting on January 14, 1953. Atmospheric physicist Lloyd Berkner was also added, but he never attended a working meeting. None of these physicists had any background knowledge regarding UFOs. Also present at the meetings was a six-man CIA project team and three Air Force representatives, which included the Air Force consultant Dr. J. Allen Hynek. The Air Force had 300 UFO cases that they could not explain, but the panel only looked at a handful. The Robertson Panel concluded their meeting after two and a half days. Robertson was tasked to write the final report after dinnertime on the last day.[20]

The CIA and the Air Force obtained the results that they wanted. The Robertson Panel concluded that UFOs were not a threat to our national security, and "that the continued emphasis on the reporting of these phenomena does, in these parlous times, result in a threat to the orderly functioning of the protective organs of the body politic." Lastly, the Robertson Panel recommended that there be a broad educational program across all concerned agencies and a debunking program for the public. The Robertson Panel's actual words were Orwellian:

> The "debunking" aim would result in reduction in public interest in "flying saucers" which today evokes a strong psychological reaction. This education could be accomplished by mass media such as television, motion pictures, and popular articles. Basis of such education would be actual case histories which had been puzzling at first but later explained.

Lastly, the panel recommended that citizen UFO groups should be kept under surveillance by the government.[21]

Historians have wielded many complaints against the Robertson Panel: it was a shill game sponsored by the CIA and Air Force; it lacked scientific rigor; it was composed of sarcastic remarks and ridicule of UFOs; only a small percentage of cases were examined; and its conclusions were determined ahead of time. One of the panel's key members, Dr. Thornton Page, stated many years later, "H. P. Robertson told us in the first private session that our job was to reduce public concern, and show that UFO reports could be explained by conventional reasoning."[22] Perhaps it was Dr. Hynek's observations of the way the panel operated that caused him to write three months later in the *Journal of the Optical Society of America*:

> Ridicule is not part of the scientific method, and people should not be taught that it is. The steady flow of reports, often made in concert by reliable observers, raises questions of scientific obligation and responsibility. Is there . . . any residue that is worthy of scientific attention? Or, if there isn't, does not an obligation exist to say so to the public—not in words of open ridicule but seriously, to keep faith with the trust the public places in science and scientists?[23]

The Air Force followed the path laid out by the Robertson Panel. The immediate years after the panel's meeting remained calm. There were no major media stories about UFOs, and the Blue Book crew was able to slosh through the 400–600 reports they received each year without interference. This soon changed, as UFOs reared their head again in 1957. Nearly 1,100 UFO sighting reports came into Blue Book. Some of the most interesting UFO sighting reports to date were among those reports.

The B-47 was the Air Force's state-of-the-art bomber of the time. The RB-47 was a research version filled with radar and electronic gear: the precursor to the modern AWAC (Airborne Early Warning and Control). In the early morning hours of July 17, 1957, a UFO followed an RB-47 for over an hour as it flew from Mississippi, through Louisiana, Texas, and into Oklahoma. The RB-47's six-man crew tracked the UFO in three observation channels: visually, by radar, and using classified electronic intelligence equipment. Amazingly, the UFO emitted a radar signal at 2.8 GHz that was detected by the RB-47. This was the first recorded instance of a UFO emitting an EM signal at a specific frequency. This incident also involved several instances of simultaneous appearances and disappearances of the UFO on all three of those observation channels, and rapidity of maneuvers beyond aircraft possibilities. It is one of the top cases investigated by physicist Dr. James E. McDonald and presented to the American Association for the Advance of Science (AAAS) in December 1969.[24] UFO researcher Brad Sparks also has a very detailed analysis of this case in the book *The UFO Encyclopedia*.[25]

During the late evening hours of November 2 and the early morning hours of November 3, seven independent witnesses near Levelland, Texas, saw an oval-shaped ball of light approach their vehicles, causing their engines to stop and headlights to shut off. The sightings lasted from a few seconds to no more than five minutes. Once the ball of light left the scene, all witnesses were able to start their automobile engines and their headlights went back to normal operation.[26] Within twenty-four hours there were three similar sightings in southeastern New Mexico. By November 5 the reports were splashed across newspapers throughout the country, and forty more reports were sent to Blue Book. Another seventy-eight reports came in the next day before dropping to twenty-two reports on November 6.[27] The initial reports on November 2 and 3 were not driven by media coverage, but the follow-up reports almost certainly were.

These high-profile reports and the many other reports of 1957 reignited interest from the public and the media. This attention brought the U.S. Congress into the drama of UFOs for the first time. It wasn't what the Air Force wanted. Arizona senator Barry Goldwater expressed his interest in the UFO reports. Ohio congressman John Henderson asked the Air Force for their ten best cases. The Levelland, Texas, reports then made their full impact known. Complaints were made as to how the Air Force had investigated the incident. Powerful Texas congressman Lyndon Baines Johnson requested information from the Air Force. Less than a year after the Levelland UFO sightings, the misery culminated when John W. McCormack requested a congressional hearing. He was the chair of the House Select Committee on Astronautics and Space Exploration and one of the strongest and most irascible personalities in Congress. The briefing was to be given to the Subcommittee on Atmospheric Phenomena, chaired by another prominent politician, William H. Natcher of Kentucky. Mc-Cormack and Natcher informed the Secretary of the Air Force that they were going to hold hearings about UFOs with just two or three days' lead time.[28]

The Air Force assembled their Project Blue Book officers as well as their other intelligence and science representatives. They briefed the subcommittee behind closed doors. The subcommittee also wanted to hear from civilians and the former head of Project Blue Book, Edward Ruppelt, and without Air Force attendance. This never happened, as the subcommittee hearings were unexpectedly closed. Someone outside of the subcommittee had intervened.

The Air Force received a temporary reprieve, both in terms of a congressional investigation as well as from the phenomenon itself. The years 1959–1964 were quiet in terms of UFO activity. But UFO reports came roaring back in 1965 with almost 1,000 reports and a similar number in 1966.[29] It seemed like déjà vu. This time the Air Force's headache came from Michigan. Their policy of rapidly debunking public reports of UFOs would backfire.

There were several excellent cases during these two years, but it was one specific group of reports that would rock the Air Force. Over forty witnesses, including a dozen police, witnessed bright disk-shaped objects in the areas of Dexter and Hillsdale, Michigan, in mid-March 1966. The reports were in all the local newspapers and soon would be on the national news. The head of Blue Book, Major Hector Quintanilla, wanted to snuff this out quickly. Dr. Allen Hynek was sent to investigate. Witnesses described objects in the shapes of either disks or pyramids. One of the policemen said the object had zipped downward and had come within ten feet of a patrol car before a second object joined it.[30] Hynek was pressured by Blue Book to quickly debunk the reports before people got too excited. Someone suggested to him that it could be swamp gas, which is methane gas that rises from decaying material in swampy areas and can spontaneously ignite. Such a theory does not explain objects with geometric shapes or objects that moved downward, since methane rises. Nonetheless, Hynek called a press conference and debunked the witness reports as swamp gas.

The citizenry was outraged. Hynek had insulted their intelligence. Citizens called their congressional representatives. Unfortunately for the Air Force, a future president, House Republican leader Gerald Ford of Michigan, was involved. Ford called for an apology to his constituents, and a congressional investigation of Air Force UFO procedures.[31] Hynek became a laughingstock. Hynek would later comment as to his regret at offering the swamp-gas explanation: "This is the last time that I try to pull a chestnut out of the fire for the Air Force."[32]

Within a week of the public furor over the swamp-gas explanation, Allen
Hynek, Major Hector Quintanilla, and the Secretary of the Air Force, Harold
Brown, were called to testify on these matters by the House Armed Services
Committee. This was a serious situation, as the Secretary of the Air Force
was now involved. Hynek and Quintanilla were severely grilled, but Secretary Brown provided a way out. He suggested a study of UFOs at a major
university. The committee accepted his suggestion and stated they would look
forward to Brown implementing those solutions to this problem-filled situation Blue Book had created. Secretary Brown immediately informed the Air
Force chief of staff to search for a university.[33]

The Air Force averted a congressional investigation for the second time
in less than ten years. UFOs had become a monkey on their backs, and they
wanted it off. They needed a university that would perform a study of UFOs
and ideally would conclude that there was nothing of interest. MIT, Harvard,
and other prestigious universities were contacted, but each institution refused
to be associated with an investigation of UFOs. Academia considered the
subject taboo. But the Air Force found hope in the University of Colorado
through the help of an administrator at the university, Robert Low. He wrote
a secret memo where he pitched a way for the university to be comfortable
in accepting the project. His action was regrettable. It besmirched the committee's reputation and would later cost Low his position. The key portion of
Low's memo, written on August 9, 1966, stated:

> Our study would be conducted almost exclusively by nonbelievers who, al-
> though they couldn't possibly prove a negative result, could and probably would
> add an impressive body of evidence that there is no reality to the observations.
> The trick would be, I think, to describe the project so that, to the public, it would
> appear a totally objective study but, to the scientific community, would present
> the image of a group of nonbelievers trying their best to be objective, but having
> an almost zero expectation of finding a saucer. One way to do this would be to
> stress investigation, not of the physical phenomena, but rather of the people who
> do the observing—the psychology and sociology of persons and groups who
> report seeing UFO's. If the emphasis were put here, rather than on examination
> of the old question of the physical reality of the saucer, I think the scientific
> community would quickly get the message.[34]

Low was successful, and by mid-August the University of Colorado was
ready to take the chance. The contract was signed, and the project suggested
by Secretary Harold Brown began in October.[35]

The project was headed up by Dr. Edward Condon, a physicist at the University of Colorado. Robert Low was the administrator. There were many who
contributed in different fashions, but the other major members of the project
were: Dr. Roy Craig, a physical chemist from Colorado; Dr. William Hart-

mann, an astronomer; Dr. Norman Levine, a University of Arizona electrical engineer; psychologist Dr. David Saunders; physicist Dr. Franklin Roach; and psychology graduate assistants James Wadsworth and Dan Culberson. The public and the media believed this scientific investigation would provide the determinate answer as to the reality of UFOs; the Air Force was counting on the investigation as a way to end the public's interest in the subject.

The reality was that the project would be mired in controversy. Outside influences crept into the project. The anti-UFO groups such as the Air Force and CIA influenced some of the scientists to see the issue their way, while pro-UFO groups attacked from the other direction. Even various members of Congress became involved, as well as a General Accounting Office investigation. Internal issues within the scientific group were even worse. Previous statements made by Dr. Condon indicated he thought the subject of UFOs to be ridiculous and that they should be banned from discourse in the schools. Robert Low's prejudicial memo became public knowledge, so Condon fired him. Other members resigned or dropped out. Condon made charges against some of the scientists on his own team and then retracted his charges. Finally, he fired Drs. Saunders and Levine. Internally, the group was falling apart.[36]

A 966-page report was released two years after the project started and became known as the Condon Report. A unilateral, forty-three-page summary was written by Condon. Reading the summary provides a much different conclusion than when reading the entire report. Condon recommended that no funding or ongoing research be provided to the study of UFOs. Yet other authors of the report indicated that further research was warranted.[37] Various scientists supported the report while others disagreed. But perhaps one of the more interesting comments was made Dr. Thornton Page of the original Robertson Panel:

> Intelligent laymen can (and do) point out the logical flaw in Condon's conclusion based on a statistically small (and selected) sample, Even in this sample a consistent pattern can be recognized; it is ignored by the "authorities," who then compound their "felony" by recommending that no further observational data be collected.[38]

Whether one agrees or disagrees with the Condon Report, it provided the Air Force with the justification they needed to get the monkey off their back. The Air Force closed Project Blue Book on December 17, 1969.[39]

CIVILIAN UFO AGENCIES (POST 1970)

There would be no more military or government groups officially chartered to investigate UFOs for the next fifty years. This vacuum would be filled by large civilian UFO groups that had been created: National Investigations Committee On Aerial Phenomena (NICAP) 1956–1980; The Center for UFO Studies (CUFOS) 1973–present; The Mutual UFO Network (MUFON) 1969–present; National Aviation Reporting Center on Anomalous Phenomena (NARCAP) 1999–present; the National UFO Reporting Center (NUFORC) 1974–present; and more recently, the Scientific Coalition for UAP Studies (SCU) 2017–present. Membership in these groups ranged from dozens of members to thousands. The quality of the membership varied. The groups included individuals with no scientific background, seasoned police and military investigators, and scientists from all the various disciplines. These organizations collected UFO reports from citizens and completed a significant number of investigations. Most civilian investigations were not as thorough as those of Project Blue Book, but many of their investigations exceeded what was done by the Air Force due to scientists, technicians, and seasoned investigators being involved in the reports. They effectively used the Freedom of Information Act (FOIA) to get information from the government such as radar data and government reports. Our current knowledge of the UFO phenomenon would be very lacking if these organizations had not stepped in to fill the vacuum and handle the 3,000 to 6,000 reports that come in every year. It would be appropriate to list some of the best investigated cases of the last fifty years. More additional information on each of these cases can be found by obtaining a copy of the documents identified in the endnotes.

November 2, 1971; Delphos, Kansas. A mushroom-shaped UFO hovered just two feet above the ground of a Kansas farm. A sixteen-year-old boy saw the object at a distance of seventy-five feet and estimated its size at ten feet. It emitted a sound like a vibrating washing machine. After several minutes the object's base began to brighten, and it began to rise. The sound changed to a high-pitched sound as it began to depart into the sky. The boy ran into his home and told his parents. They all went outside and saw a very bright light about half the size of the moon as it departed. The son then took his parents to where the object had been hovering. A glowing ring could be seen on the ground. The parents took photos of the ring and the next day they contacted the local sheriff. He came out and took soil samples.

Chemical analysis was done by a chemist from CUFOS, Phyllis Budinger, as well as by chemist Dr. Erol Faruk. Samples were also sent to multiple universities as well as Oak Ridge National Labs for any soil radioactivity. Calcium oxalate was the contaminate and whether it was deposited by the object, created by a chemical reaction from an electromagnetic field and the soil, or was some natural byproduct of a fungal growth are open for debate. The amount of analysis done on these samples by CUFOS and others likely exceeded the amount of work that would have been done if Project Blue Book had still been active; and for certain the information was made immediately open to the public, rather than undergo military classification.[40, 41]

October 18, 1973; Mansfield, Ohio.   The four-man crew of an Army Reserve helicopter encountered a UFO while flying at an altitude of 1,400 feet above the terrain in north central Ohio. Five individuals also witnessed this even from the ground. Initially a distant light, a cigar-shaped object quickly approached, causing the pilot to dive down to 700 feet. The object stopped in front of the helicopter and filled the windshield, as it bathed them in green light. Their radio was filled with static, and their instrument controls were erratic. Inexplicably, the helicopter was at an altitude of 2,400 feet above the terrain at the time the object departed a few minutes later. This unusual incident is documented in a 134-page report put together by Jennie Zeidman of CUFOS.[42]

October–November 1975; multiple air bases along the U.S.–Canadian border.   UFOs violated the airspace of several U.S. and Canadian air bases during a two-month period. It was the use of FOIA requests to the U.S. Air Force that allowed these events to be known to civilian investigators. The Office of the Joint Chiefs of Staff released twenty-four documents regarding these intrusions. A summary of these reports is contained in a book written by two of the CUFOS investigators: *Clear Intent*.[43]

September 18, 1976; Tehran, Iran.   Iranian news reports alerted U.S. civilian researchers to a UFO encounter, which was further unearthed using FOIA requests to the Defense Intelligence Agency (DIA). The DIA document confirmed that two Iranian F-4 fighters had encountered a cylinder-shaped UFO near Tehran. One of the jets attempted to fire a missile. All the plane's weapons systems, communications, and instrumentation systems ceased to work until the jet departed the area of the UFO.[44] Despite the Air Force claim of exiting the investigation of UFOs, the following comment regarding this case was found in a journal at the Air Force Electronic Warfare Center:

> Sometime in his career, each pilot can expect to encounter strange, unusual happenings which will never be adequately or entirely explained by logic or subsequent investigation. The following article recounts just such an episode as reported by two F-4 Phantom crews of the Imperial Iranian Air Force during late 1976. No additional information or explanation of the strange events has been forthcoming; the story will be filed away and probably forgotten, but it makes interesting. and possibly disturbing, reading.[45]

Did the Air Force truly stop its investigations of UFOs? These types of incidents make one wonder.

November 17, 1986; Alaska.   Sometimes a thorough UFO investigation was taken up by an individual UFO researcher, rather than an organization.

This happened when a former Navy physicist, Dr. Bruce Maccabee, investigated Japanese Airlines (JAL) flight 1629's encounter with two acorn-shaped UFOs the size of aircraft carriers over Alaska. The incident had multiple types of evidence. There were the witness statements from the pilot and co-pilot; there was the voice transcript of the pilots, the Federal Aviation Administration (FAA) traffic controllers, and the North American Aerospace Defense Command (NORAD) radar operator; there was the FAA radar data; and the NORAD radar data, which have never been released to this day. The JAL encounter is one of the most interesting and well-documented cases of a UFO encounter. It is well worth reading Dr. Maccabee's extensive analysis, and his thoughts regarding the incident.[46]

November 7, 2006; Chicago O'Hare International Airport. The most famous case investigated by the NARCAP organization is the sighting of a disk-shaped UFO hovering at about 1,700 feet over Chicago O'Hare International Airport during broad daylight. There were eight witnesses on the ground that testified to viewing the object for several minutes before it rapidly departed, leaving a hole through the lower cloud layer through which it passed. Dr. Richard Haines and several other researchers at NARCAP completed a 155-page report on the events of that day.[47]

January 8, 2008; Stephenville, Texas. The UFO sightings near Stephenville, Texas, involved almost two dozen witnesses over a four-hour period of time. The witnesses included police, a constable, a pilot, and an air traffic controller. They reported lights moving at extreme speeds and with sudden changes in movement. Were these real objects or just lights? Civilian researchers Glen Schulze and Robert Powell investigated the incident using FOIA requests for radar data to the FAA. The FAA provided radar data from five different radar sites in the area. The investigators produced a seventy-six-page report that included statements that they obtained from witness interviews as well as analysis of the radar data. The data corroborated the witness statements. Unknown objects were detected by radar at the exact time, location, and direction where UFOs were sighted by some of the witnesses.[48]

April 25, 2013; Aguadilla, Puerto Rico. An infra-red video made by Homeland Security off the coast of Puerto Rico came to light in late 2013. The SCU put together a team to analyze the video. They spent two years analyzing the video before releasing a report. The IR video showed an object moving at treetop height over the town of Aguadilla at 9:30 p.m. The first striking part of the three-minute video shows the unknown object impact the ocean, remain submerged for a few seconds, and come back out with very little disturbance to the water. Even more striking is when the object splits into two equal parts after coming out of the ocean, with one part going back into the water and its sister-half submerging not long afterward.[49]

November 14, 2004; eighty miles southwest of San Diego, California. Two F-18 Super-Hornet fighter aircraft encounter an object shaped like a Tic Tac candy off the southwest coast of the United States. They watch from 20,000 feet altitude as this object moves near the ocean surface with sudden stops, starts, and changes in the directions of its movement that defy explanation. The commander of the squadron decides to engage the unknown craft. He dives his F-18 toward the ocean in pursuit of the Tic Tac–shaped object. This incident was first made known to a large public audience on December 17, 2017, on the front page of the *New York Times* Sunday edition.[50] History is still being written on the implication of this story, but it has already brought the military and the U.S. government back into a publicly acknowledged investigation of unknown craft in our skies. This particular incident will be examined more thoroughly later in this book.

A WORLDWIDE PHENOMENON

It is incorrect to think that the UFO phenomenon was mostly driven by events in the United States. The encounters with Foo Fighters began in Europe during the Second World War. Sweden and Norway were plagued with reports of fast-flying, missile-like objects in the late 1940s that they called Ghost Rockets.[51] France and Italy were plagued with hundreds of UFO reports in 1954,[52] while that was a relatively quiet year in the United States. UFO sightings have occurred throughout the world. It is important to understand the similarity of reports, as well as the different manners in which other nations reacted to the phenomenon.

France's approach to the UFO phenomenon was somewhat unique among the major nations. Like the United States, the French Air Force investigated UFOs after the Second World War from a national security perspective. After their initial investigations, the French were much more direct than the Americans, and their military did not require any university studies to "get out" of the UFO investigation business. The French view was summed up by Lt. Col. Alexis of the Office of Prospective Studies when he stated in 1976:

> One could say that since 1951, no evidence calls into question the French Defense or the French Air Space. As you can see be a number of statistics, we have not seen any aggressive cases, nor any particular location of OVNI [UFO], be it on military sites, industrial zones, cities, etc. In short, these observations remain very random. As it is clear, through this evidence, that the National Defense is not involved, you can imagine that it would not be easy for the military to judge the nature of the phenomenon . . . this phenomenon is absolutely harmless to the

French people, send it to the scientists so that they may do their work, that is to say, search for and reveal the origin of these phenomena.[53]

"Send it to the scientists" was exactly what the French government did. France's UFO investigative group, GEPAN (Groupe d'Études des Phénomènes Aérospatiaux Non-Identifiés), was placed beneath their space program, CNES (Centre National d'Études Spatials), in 1977 and was directed by physicist Dr. Claude Poher. Although the name was changed to GEIPAN in 2005, the organization's mission and its connection to France's space program remain the same.[54] GEIPAN receives about 500 UFO reports every year. Although one could argue whether the French program is adequately staffed and funded, France is clear in its desire to run their UFO program in a scientific manner. Their desire was converted into action in UFO reports investigated in Trans-en-Provence in January 1981 and the city of Nancy in October 1982. The French used their state-of-the-art national laboratories to analyze soil and plant samples. Neither of these incidents was solved, but both cases demonstrate the need to use all available scientific facilities in the study of the UFO phenomenon.[55, 56]

Great Britain, Australia, Canada, and New Zealand have all investigated UFO reports for much of the last seventy years. This group of nations, along with the United States, share signal intelligence and are sometimes known as the Five Eyes. Various documents that have come to light indicate that they also shared UFO reports, with the United States seeming to be the primary depository for information. All of these nations have released their UFO reports to the public, which consist of thousands of cases. One of the most famous involved two airbases in Great Britain: RAF Woodbridge and RAF Bentwaters. Also known as Rendlesham Forest, this UFO case supposedly involved a craft that landed near RAF Woodbridge on December 27, 1980, with two patrolmen coming into proximity of the object before it departed. Witnesses to various parts of the story included three USAF patrolmen as well as a U.S. lieutenant colonel. The British Ministry of Defense released a 191-page file on the incident in 2009.[57]

Belgium had a massive sighting of triangles during much of November 1989. This wave of sightings piqued on November 29, when a total of 143 sightings were reported by approximately 250 people. Several policemen saw a large triangular platform with a bright white light at each corner of the triangle. They estimated the object was at 500 feet with a wingspan of 100 feet. The policemen followed the slow-moving craft for thirty minutes. During that time, they witnessed the craft repeatedly emitting two beams of red light with a red ball at the end of each beam. The red balls would return to the center of the vehicle, after which another cycle would begin.[58]

The citizenry began calling the Belgian Air Force. There was no government UFO investigative organization, so the Air Force Chief of Operations, Colonel de Brouwer, took charge. Reports of UFOs were sporadic until March 30 and 31 of 1990. Radar returns resulted in the Air Force scrambling two F-16 jet planes. One pilot took photographic records of the radar responses from his instruments. The Belgian Air Force verified these were not U.S. triangular aircraft, nor did they have any other explanation. De Brouwer's public statement was that the Air Force "was unable to identify the nature or the origin of the phenomena."[59] Within a few days of this event, Mr. Petit-Rechain claimed to have taken a photo of a triangular object in the sky. He later admitted that he had faked the photo. Unfortunately, his theatrics took away from the importance of the overall Belgium UFO Wave.

The South American nations have also had thousands of UFO reports during the last seventy years: Brazil, Chile, Argentina, Peru, and Uruguay. The Peruvian Air Force even fired on a UFO with the supposed result being that the 30mm shells passed through the object.[60] The South Americans have been much more open about the subject than most European and English-speaking countries. Russia and China have also had many UFO reports, but their level of secrecy is much higher than other countries, so it is difficult to quantify UFO activity.

There have been hundreds of thousands of UFO sightings over the last eighty years across the entire planet. This is a drastic change compared to what people saw in the late nineteenth and early twentieth centuries. Why the sudden increase in sightings beginning in the 1940s? Some believe that the UFO phenomenon is not real but has self-perpetuated itself through the media; that it has become an urban legend similar to fairies and leprechauns of the eighteenth and nineteenth centuries. Is there any reasonable explanation for the ongoing sightings of UFOs? They have been sighted and reported by presidents, scientists, engineers, pilots, and astronauts. UFOs have been detected by radar, engaged by military aircraft, and even fired upon. Governments have devoted mostly military agencies to studying the phenomenon, and to seemingly no avail. What do we really know about UFOs after eighty years of sightings and studying this enigma?

Chapter Two

More Than Our Collective Imaginations

Military and civilian organizations from many different nations have been investigating the UFO phenomenon for eighty years. There are now several hundred thousand cataloged reports—roughly 3,000 reports every year. Yet the solution to this phenomenon still eludes us, and there isn't even a consistent belief that the phenomenon is real. Why is that? The "why" will be discussed in later chapters. First, we will discuss the type of information that has been collected, how it is collected, and what we can conclude from that data.

UFO INVESTIGATIONS

The follow-up investigation of a UFO sighting is as important as the sighting itself. Assume for a moment that a UFO is sighted over a rural community by a dozen townspeople. The UFO then lands in a distant farmer's wheat field and is witnessed by the farmer, his wife, and two neighbors. The sighting is reported by two of the townspeople to the local newspaper, while the farmer contacts a civilian UFO organization. After a few days the farmer receives a call from the UFO group and discusses the event on the phone. A member of the UFO group comes out to investigate after a few more days go by. The investigator is not a scientist but is enthralled to be able to investigate such an unusual case—an actual landing! The investigator talks to the farmer and asks the farmer to draw a picture of what he saw. He then tramps out into the wheat field to get some samples. Dirt is scooped up and the investigator heads home to file a report. The report says that the farmer's family all saw a disk-shaped object land in the wheat field and that what the farmer told the investigators is pretty much what the farmer said when he first called to make a report. The report concludes with the farmer's drawing of the UFO and a statement stating that a sample of the dirt has been sent to his UFO headquarters to be analyzed. Unfortunately, the quality of the investigation did not match the magnitude of the event that had just transpired. Although this is a hypothetical example, this is unfortunately what often happens in most UFO investigations. When the collection of evidence is poor, the UFO might as well have never existed.

What should have happened in the UFO investigation that was just mentioned? Ideally, there should have been an investigative team at the site within twenty-four hours of the farmer's report. The team would consist of a seasoned investigator familiar with open-ended and closed-ended questioning techniques used by detectives; a geologist familiar with sampling techniques for soil; a biologist who could sample the wheat; and a physicist who could examine the area for any radioactive, magnetic, or EM anomalies in the area. Each of the witnesses at the farm would be interviewed independently, and all the towns' people involved would be interviewed. A Freedom of Information Request (FOIA) would be sent to the FAA for a copy of radar data for the appropriate time and location. The scientists on the team would discuss with each other the best sampling plan, how to avoid contaminating the area, types of control samples, whether they should video their sampling operation, the types of tests that they should run, and so forth. It would take the team many months to complete their analysis and their report, which would likely be a document of well over a hundred pages. This is what should happen. But the type of analysis described is a rarity in the investigation of UFOs. Historically, neither civilian nor military UFO investigative organizations have conducted effective investigations. Why? They have not had the necessary scientifically trained manpower.

The large variation in how cases are investigated can be seen in some of the Project Blue Book files. What follows is an example of a poorly investigated UFO incident that occurred over a military base in N. Luffenham, England, on October 21, 1957. There was only one page in the report besides the summary page card shown in figure 2.1, and that one page was simply the pilot's report.[11] There was no investigation. There was no interview statement taken from the pilot. The pilot saw the object as he was flying over an atomic-bomb training base. One would think that would generate some scrutiny, yet there was no attempt to determine if there were witnesses on the ground or the status of any atomic training exercises that might have been ongoing. The object was confirmed on radar, but there is no information in the report to indicate the object's speed or its direction of flight. The conclusion on the report was that there was "Insufficient Data for Evaluation." A potentially very good incident was worthless because there was not a proper investigation. Project Blue Book is littered with examples like this.

1. DATE - TIME GROUP	2. LOCATION
21 October 57 21/2118Z	N. Luffenham, England
3. SOURCE Air Attache (USAF)	**10. CONCLUSION** INSUFFICIENT DATA FOR EVALUATION
4. NUMBER OF OBJECTS One	Visual object resembles a/c observation of balloon with package. Additional investigative data not received. Case regarded as insufficient data in view of lack of additional report.
5. LENGTH OF OBSERVATION Not Reported	**11. BRIEF SUMMARY AND ANALYSIS**
6. TYPE OF OBSERVATION Air-Visual - Ground-Radar	Pilot flying 28,000 ft at night suddenly came upon an object having 6 lights, taking evasive action he approached object from the side. When his aircraft drew near lights went out and object vanished. This took place over an atom-bomber
7. COURSE Unknown	training base. Object was confirmed by ground radar. Attempt is being made by Air Ministry to resolve sighting.
8. PHOTOS ☐ Yes ☒ No	
9. PHYSICAL EVIDENCE ☐ Yes ☒ No	

FORM
FTD SEP 63 0-329 (TDE) Previous editions of this form may be used.

Figure 2.1.   Summary card from Project Blue Book, N. Luffenham, England, October 21, 1957. *Source:* **USAF, Project Blue Book**

But sometimes there were good investigations that were completed. Here is an example that occurred near Misawa Air Base in Japan on December 12, 1957. In addition to the summary page card shown in figure 2.2, there were forty-nine pages in the report.[2] There were statements from four officers, three sergeants, and six other servicemen within the report. Photos were included and angular size measurements were made of the object based on the camera used. Radar data was detailed so as to provide the object's altitude, direction, and speed. The speeds were highly variable and ranged from 95 mph to 1,686 mph over the course of thirty-five minutes. This variation led to the conclusion that the radar reading might be anomalous propagation. Whether the radar returns were false or not is open to debate. But what is important is that the investigation was well carried out and provided a lot of information.

This same type of variation in the quality of UFO investigations can be seen in civilian reports as well. Unfortunately, the majority of cases are not properly investigated. Does this mean that all UFO reports should be thrown out? Not at all. But it is important that anyone who studies this subject in depth understands the potential weaknesses in the data. It is also important that anyone interested in investigating the phenomenon have some guidelines that can be used when questioning a witness to a UFO sighting. An investigative guideline used by the author is provided for those readers interested in doing UFO investigations. Located in the appendix is a form that can be used for generic UFO sightings as well as a form for UFO sightings that include electromagnetic (EM) effects. These tools are helpful, but they cannot replace a trained investigator's knowledge of how to ask open-ended and closed-ended questions without prejudicing the witness.[33] Nor can they replace the value of a team working together to determine the best approach to investigate a particular incident.

PROJECT 10073 RECORD CARD

1. DATE	2. LOCATION	12. CONCLUSIONS
12-15 December 1957	Chitose-Hokkaido, Japan Misawa AB, Japan	☐ Was Balloon ☐ Probably Balloon ☐ Possibly Balloon
3. DATE-TIME GROUP Local _____ GMT 12/0845Z to 0950Z	4. TYPE OF OBSERVATION x☒ Ground-Visual☒X　x☒xGround-Radar ☐ Air-Visual　　☐ Air-Intercept Radar	☐ Was Aircraft ☐ Probably Aircraft ☐ Possibly Aircraft
5. PHOTOS X☒ Yes ☐ No	6. SOURCE Visual☒x USAF Personnel (13)	☒x Was Astronomical Venus ☐ Probably Astronomical ☐ Possibly Astronomical
7. LENGTH OF OBSERVATION 1 hour 5 minutes	8. NUMBER OF OBJECTS one	9. COURSE Photox☒ SSW Radar=	☐ Other_____ ☒ Insufficient Data for Evaluation ☐ Unknown Anamalous Propogation
10. BRIEF SUMMARY OF SIGHTING Approximately 13 persons observed a very bright light in the SSW sky. Many viewed it with binoculars. Two a/c were scrambled. Aircrew claimed they picked some object up on radar - but could not close in on it. 2-3 days later a photograph of a fuzzy white li light was taken purporting to be the same object.	11. COMMENTS A plot of all the directions and azimuths of the object giving definitely shows the obj was Venus, now so bright that newspapers have commented on it & pilots have tried to chase it (see clippings im UFO file)Attempt to relate some return on radar w/Venus not valid. Photo analysis: doubtful that obj in photo same as obj claimed seen 2-3 days before.	

ATIC FORM 329 (REV 26 SEP 52)

Figure 2.2. Summary card from Project Blue Book, Misawa Air Base, December 12, 1957. *Source*: USAF, Project Blue Book

MEMORY AND ANECDOTAL EVIDENCE

Let's assume a case is properly investigated and the witness is not influenced by leading questions. How dependable is the witness's testimony? Naysayers will often claim a hoax. But hoaxes are not common, especially if you talk to the witness in person. Data that I compiled from the MUFON database, when I was their director of research, indicated hoaxes amounted to about 5 percent of case reports. Battelle Memorial Institute's analysis of the Project Blue Book data did not even list hoaxes as a category.[4] Hoaxes are not a significant problem. The most common causes of unreliable witness testimony are changes in memory and the inability of the witness to recognize known objects.

Let's begin with the reliability of a witness's memory when recounting a UFO sighting. Some believe that memory cannot be relied upon. There is both truth and falseness in that view. The dependability of our memories is core to our very own sense of self. Who are we, if we cannot depend on our memories? Our shared belief in the accuracy of each other's memories grounds our collective social fabric and affects the outcomes of our justice system. Our memory shapes who we are. On the other hand, we all know that memory is not a perfect record of the past. Memories fade or disappear altogether. And more dramatically, we sometimes remember incorrectly, warping or augmenting the details of past events. A close-up UFO sighting is a significant life event. Like a car wreck, we may not remember the date it happened, the color of the car, or exactly who was at fault. But we can trust in our memory, that the car wreck happened. And if there were multiple witnesses to a UFO sighting—witnesses who did not know each other—it's difficult to explain how their similar memories of an event could all be wrong.

The inability of the witness to recognize known objects is the most common cause of erroneous UFO sightings. In a perfect world a UFO sighting is accompanied by multiple sensory modalities. Most of the sightings noted in chapter 1 are UFO reports involving detection by multiple methods such as radar, trace evidence, video, and multiple human witnesses. And yes, a human witness is a form of sensory detection that involves multiple sensory components. Our eyes can detect the electromagnetic spectrum between 380 to 700 nanometers and a certain amount of depth perception is also provided in our vision. Our ears are auditory sensors that can hear sound from 20 to 20,000 hertz, and we have a computer (brain) to analyze the event. This type of sensory data is sometimes referred to as anecdotal evidence. Anecdotal evidence is not considered as strong as other sensory evidence because the latter is unchanging and is collected in a non-prejudicial manner. The human brain constantly refreshes its thoughts, its memories change, and the observer can be influenced by their own beliefs. Most UFO reports are comprised of only anecdotal evidence. This has led some critics to argue for the wholesale dismissal of many UFO reports because they only consist of anecdotal evidence. It is appropriate at this time to delve a little more deeply into anecdotal evidence and its scientific application.

Can anecdotal data be used in a scientific manner? The validity of the information is open to question when anecdotal evidence consists of only one or two witnesses. When anecdotal evidence consists of many witnesses, at multiple points in time, and some of those witnesses are trained observers, then it should not be summarily dismissed. Good examples of this are the multiple witness UFO reports mentioned in chapter 1 from Michigan in 1966, the Army Reserve helicopter incident of October 1973, and the November 2006 incident over O'Hare International Airport. Should a scientist dismiss these reports because they are anecdotal? You might be surprised to know that science uses anecdotal reports, especially if large numbers of anecdotal reports can be assessed. Consider the fields of psychology and sociology; they depend on a human's subjective view of what they feel. Scientific studies in medicine also use anecdotal reports. The FDA determines the efficacy of pain medication based on anecdotal reports from large numbers of people. The release of pain killers such as Vioxx are based on how patients felt after taking the drug. As stated in the FDA report on Vioxx,[5] "The primary assessment of efficacy was based on patients' self-rating of headache severity on a 4-grade scale (0 = no pain, 1 = mild pain, 2 = moderate pain, 3 = severe pain)." There are other areas where science uses anecdotal evidence, even in a life-and-death situation. We trust our health to exploratory surgery when a surgeon makes an anecdotal observation of how much of our tissue is cancerous and whether he should remove that tissue. There is no medical instrument that tells him the tissue is cancerous during the middle of surgery. He may test our tissue later to verify that his judgment was correct, but we trust him to make the right decision for us based on the anecdotal evidence that his eyes perceive. Yet if that same surgeon were to tell us that he saw a disk-shaped object hover 200 feet from his home, we would likely not trust his observational skills. Why is that? We will discuss this perplexing inconsistency later in this book. But we can state that we trust decisions based on anecdotal information in our daily lives and that science does utilize anecdotal data.

SEPARATING THE WHEAT FROM THE CHAFF

One way to analyze anecdotal reports of UFOs is in a manner utilized by science: statistical analysis of large amounts of data. The first step that must be taken is to "clean up the data." There is a large variation in the quality of UFO reports because we are dealing with anecdotal reports by witnesses whose observational abilities vary. We know that more than 90 percent of UFO sightings are incidents where individuals thought they had seen an un-identified object that turned out to be a balloon, bird, plane, star, satellite, or other ordinary object.[6, 7] There exist several hundred thousand UFO reports from various databases that have been made from all over the world in the last eighty years. So how do we analyze such a large volume of information?

Let's introduce an analogy that will help in the understanding of the prob-lem at hand. Assume for a moment that we are searching for a bird that we're not sure exists, called an eagle. People have seen turkey vultures, hawks, crows, and many other types of birds; we know they exist. We have thousands of reports from people who claim to have seen an eagle. We know that in 95 percent of these reports people saw some other type of bird and in 5 percent of the reports we think that it is possible these could be true reports of eagles. We want to know if all our thousands of reports will give us some information that says whether eagles really exist. We have heard that eagles prefer to nest in mountainous areas, so let's see if we can glean that information from our thousands of reported sightings of eagles. So, we make a graph that plots the type of terrain versus the number of reports of eagles. Our graph tells us that most of our reports indicate that eagles live in cities. Why? Because that's where most of our witnesses live, and they're actually reporting when they see common birds, not eagles.

Any attempts to draw correlations using data that is more than 90 percent invalid will lead to false conclusions. As the old axiom says, "Garbage in, garbage out." So how do we eliminate all these false cases so that we are mostly examining valid UFO reports? Or, in the case of our analogy, how do we find the actual reports of eagles and not reports of birds that people think are eagles? There are two ways this can be done.

One method is to eliminate all cases that do not involve a well-lit object within 500 feet of a witness. At such a close distance there is very little likelihood that a witness will not recognize a noisy aircraft, a bird's flight, or a hovering drone. It is difficult to improperly identify an object at close distance unless the witness is either fabricating the story or is hallucinating. This group of cases can then be further screened by only using reports with multiple witnesses. And to do this, all these cases need to be read and a determination made as to whether the case meets the criteria of closeness, being well lit, and having multiple witnesses. This method is effective, but it is also very time-consuming.

The other method is to screen the reports using a technique known as Natural Language Processing (NLP). Have you wondered how the FBI or police identify potential terrorists or mass killers on social media sites? They don't do it by having hundreds of agents scrolling through everyone's Facebook, Instagram, and Twitter pages or feeds. NLP is used by the FBI and other investigatory bodies to search social media sites for key words that have been correlated to a tendency toward violence.[88] NLP is used by marketing firms to track your online searching habits and determine what type of product you are most likely going to purchase. Do the key words that you search indicate that you are most likely to buy a Brand X dishwasher? NLP does this by utilizing artificial intelligence (AI) that is trained against patterns detected when other individuals searched for similar keywords and then using that knowledge to predict your behavior.

Let's examine how NLP can be utilized with UFO reports. Here are four examples of portions of actual UFO reports:

1. I pulled my patrol car onto the shoulder to meet another deputy. . . . When the disc stopped moving forward it was about 50 yards from our position.
2. I was traveling west on Highway Loop 1604 south of Camp Bullis Military Reservation. My 20-year-old son and two other adult friends all witnessed the event. . . . My vehicle was within a few hundred yards of the craft as it passed slowly over the highway.
3. I saw a bright white flashing light on the horizon and my first thought was UFO because that's how I am. . . . I frequently have reoccurring dreams of UFOs flying over me being terrified and the UFO would fly back over me hover and my dream would end.
4. My husband and I have been abused by these aliens and I know some of them by names. . . . I saw so many people held hostage in that underground lab.

It is easy in these examples to determine which reports are more likely to be actual events versus which reports are not.

Training an NLP program requires a lot of testing and verification to create the most effective AI program possible. One starts this process by having a group of skilled investigators and scientists identify twenty to thirty of the strongest historical UFO reports that cannot be explained. This same group also identified twenty to thirty UFO reports that have been explained. The AI program provided these reports as examples of good and bad reports. The AI program looks for commonalities in word usage between the two data sets. This is called training the AI system. The same group reviews how the AI program differentiated between good and bad reports. Based on that output, the program is tweaked further until the AI program has successfully separated the two groups of good and bad reports. This process is repeated until the AI program is segregating good from bad reports in the same manner that a trained human investigator would do.

Once a database of UFO reports is filtered through an AI-based NLP program, then the effectiveness of the algorithm can be determined by statistically comparing the groups of cases using their NLP rating. Think back to the example of marketing companies that use NLP to predict your buying habits. If their NLP program is working effectively, then they should be able to compare the lower scored data set (buyers in the marketplace with low scores) against the higher scored data set (buyers in the marketplace with high scores) and find that the buyers in the marketplace with higher scores actually bought more Brand X dishwashers. The same can be done with UFO reports. The group of UFO reports identified by the NLP program as more likely to be real should have different characteristics than the group of UFO reports identified as less likely to be real.

This is the same technique that I used when I trained an NLP program to evaluate 28,000 UFO reports from the MUFON database and compare the top 4,500 cases rated by the NLP program against the bottom 4,500 cases. What I found was that a witness's use of descriptive and nonemotional words was an indicator of a higher likelihood of a true unknown than a witness who used prejudicial and emotional words. The NLP program gave higher values in its algorithm for the use of words such as *azimuth, elevation, engineer,* or *perfect.* The program gave lower values in its algorithm for the use of words such as *alien, attack, bedroom, starship,* or *trance.* These were words that the NLP's AI system noticed as a differentiation between the cases that experts had identified as good and bad reports. Remember the four example UFO reports that were mentioned previously? The NLP program rated those four cases using a scale of +10 (high veracity) to –10 (low veracity). The first case received a +10 rating, the next a +7, the next a –4, and the last case a –7.

Next, I looked for parameters that differed based on the NLP rating. The year of occurrence, shape of the UFO, time of day, and location of sightings indicated that the NLP program had successfully segregated the population of UFO reports. This difference was statistically evaluated using what is called a P value. The P stands for probability and measures how likely it is that any observed difference between two groups is due to chance. A value of 0.05 means that there is a less than 5 percent chance that two populations are not different. The year of occurrence indicated a less than 1 percent chance the NLP program had not created two different population sets and the other three parameters (shape, time of day, location) indicated a less than 0.1 percent chance that the two populations were not different. The P value indicated that the NLP program had successfully separated the UFO reports into two groups.

Figure 2.3 compares numbers of UFO reports based on whether the NLP program defined a report as a "low" likelihood of being real (light bars) versus those with a high likelihood (dark bars). The stronger reports show that the year 2012 was a very unusual year, with many more reports than in other years. The weaker reports show 2015 as the highest year, with 2012 as the second highest. This graph illustrates that we would draw the wrong conclusion unless we segregate out the stronger UFO reports.

Figure 2.4 compares UFO shapes based on whether the NLP program defined a report as a "low" likelihood of being real (light bars) versus those with

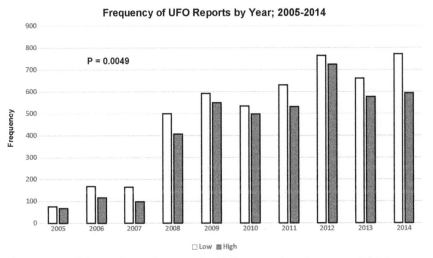

Figure 2.3. High-veracity vs. low-veracity UFO reports based on year of sighting. *Source*: From the author

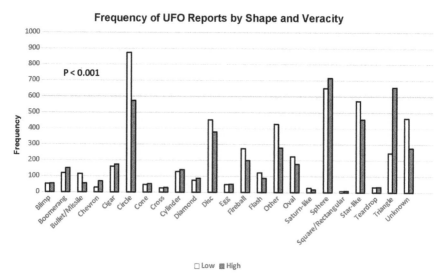

Figure 2.4. High-veracity vs. low-veracity UFO reports based on shape of object. *Source:* From the author

a high likelihood (dark bars). The most striking difference seen in this graph is the difference in triangle reports. Reports of triangles are the second highest category in the higher quality reports (dark bars), and the number of triangle reports is more than twice that of the lower quality reports. Triangle sightings are tied for fourth place in the lower quality reports. This tells us that if we eliminate the lower quality reports, then we will find that triangle reports are more numerous than we would have realized and are more common than reports of disk-shaped objects. This leads us to a very different conclusion simply because we are now examining the UFO reports that are more reliable and that are less likely to have a prosaic explanation.

Figure 2.5 compares the hour of the day when UFO reports are sighted based on whether the NLP program defined a report as a "low" likelihood of being real (light bars) versus those with a high likelihood (dark bars). Both groups show that people see more UFOs between 7 p.m. and 10 p.m. (20–22 hundred hours). This is because that is the time of day when people have returned from work and are more likely to be outside and looking at the sky. Whether a UFO sighting is real or not, there will be more reports during the time of day when people are examining the sky. What is different is the early morning hours from 5 a.m. to 6 a.m. The low-quality reports show a decline in reports from 9 p.m. until 8 a.m. the following day. The high-quality reports show something different. The number of sightings drops at 3 a.m. when they level off and then

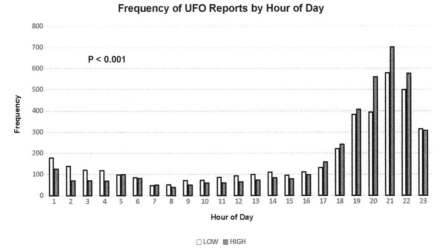

Figure 2.5. High-veracity vs. low-veracity UFO reports based on hour of the day.
Source: From the author

actually increases from 5 a.m. to 6 a.m. Why is there this mini-upward move in reports just before sunrise hours? I have no idea, but it exists.

Figure 2.6 compares the U.S. state where UFO reports are sighted based on whether the NLP program defined a report as a "low" likelihood of being real (light bars) versus those with a high likelihood (dark bars). This graph is a way to display reports based on population. Recall the analogy of searching for eagles and how more eagles would be seen in the cities because most of the reports were common birds and since most people live in cities there will be more "false" sightings of eagles in the cities. The same is happening in figure 2.6. Since we know that greater than 90 percent of the UFO reports are false, those false reports are going to be more prevalent where the most people live. Notice how the reports that the NLP program indicate are less likely to be real occur more frequently in the populous states than the reports that are more likely to be real. Look at the higher population states of California, New York, Pennsylvania, Florida, and Texas. On the other hand, the higher veracity reports dominate the lower veracity reports in the less populated states of Wyoming, Utah, Colorado, Vermont, and New Hampshire.

NLP is a powerful tool that can be used to segregate large numbers of UFO reports into meaningful information. What has been demonstrated here just scratches the surface of what can be done using this tool. More interesting information will arise regarding UFOs as more researchers use this technique to analyze the last eighty years of reports.

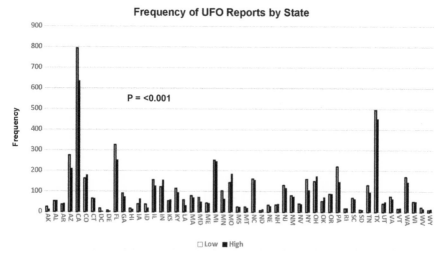

Frequency of UFO Reports by State

Figure 2.6.   High-veracity vs. low-veracity UFO reports based on U.S. state.
Source: From the author

UFO FLAPS

Recurrent UFO flaps have been one of the arguments made to establish the reality of UFO sightings that have continued over the last eighty years. The term *flaps* in this context means a non-periodic wave of UFO reports that suddenly occurs. There have been two major arguments made in this area. The first argument is related to the sudden onset of modern UFO reports which began during the Second World War. The second argument relates to the sudden increase in UFO reports that may occur in a given year, during a few months, or even during a period of just a few days or weeks. Both arguments are based on the view that if these objects are not real, then there should only be a constant background level of sightings but not sudden increases in sighting reports. A sudden increase in reports indicates that something occurred to suddenly garner the attention of a large number of people. There are also counterarguments as to why this might happen. These arguments and counterarguments will be examined.

When did the modern UFO phenomenon begin? You may have heard that the modern UFO era began with Kenneth Arnold when he reported disk-like objects flying near Mt. Rainier on June 24, 1947.[9] It would be more accurate to state that 1947 is when the U.S. public first became aware of UFOs, and not when the modern UFO phenomenon actually began. I have examined all the major UFO databases that include an investigative component (MUFON, NICAP, CUFOS, GEIPAN, Project Blue Book, Project 1947) as well as a database that concentrated on newspaper reports going back into the nineteenth century, the International Catalogue of UFO Reports. Prior to the year 1942, UFO reports were few and far between. An exception was the year 1897, when there was a myriad of reports of gondola-type objects seen. But they don't sound like the modern UFO. They were an impossible combination of gas bag, propeller, and bat wings, said to be powered by steam or electricity. Figure 2.7 displays the number of UFOs from the previously mentioned databases for the years 1890 through 2000.

This graph makes it very clear that the first significant rise in UFO reports began during the Second World War. There are very few reports prior to that time period. These reports from the Second World War came from U.S. and British pilots as well as aviators from Germany and Japan. None of these sightings were known to the public until 1992, when researchers found the reports in some of the nighttime fighter squadron logs. The reports of those squadrons are housed in the U.S. National Archives.[10] UFO sightings have never abated since that time. Look at figure 2.7 again. The graph itself beckons to us—come investigate; find out the why behind the modern UFO era.

Naysayers argue that the modern UFO phenomenon is driven by the imaginations and hopes of people. When asked why UFO reports did not exist in great numbers until recent times, they argue that it was the press coverage of Kenneth Arnold's sighting that put the idea of UFOs into the public's imagination. Once that idea sprouted it became akin to a human cultural desire to believe in things such as fairies, elves, and other magical beings. The desire to

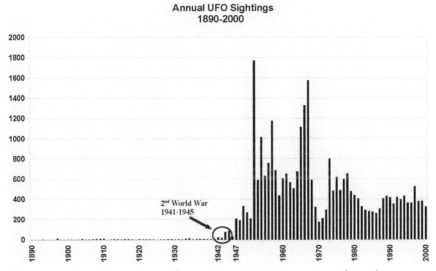

Figure 2.7. Annual UFO Reports from 1890 to 2000. *Source*: From the author

believe in UFOs caused UFO reports, which created media coverage, which caused more UFO reports, and it became ingrained in our culture. No study has been done to support these contentions; it is an assertion to explain why the modern phenomenon began and has continued to persist. Some even saw UFOs as a way for the public to escape from the reality of the world. William Hartmann, an assistant professor of astronomy, asserted in 1972, "In this way, the sociological reaction to Arnold's report in 1947 can be explained by the fact that postwar society was primed for the acceptance of alien spaceships."[11]

Hartmann had no evidence for his assertion. Furthermore, he was an astronomer and not a sociologist. These types of statements are heard often and are still made to this day. Astrophysicist Neil deGrasse Tyson will often lampoon UFOs yet he has probably never studied the subject beyond what he has heard on the evening news. These types of statements are no different than someone with a PhD in sociology commenting on whether dark matter exists. Hartmann never tells us why the postwar society was primed for acceptance of alien spaceships. Furthermore, Hartmann was not even aware that the UFO phenomenon did not begin with Arnold's report of 1947; it began five years earlier during the Second World War. Hartmann had not studied the subject sufficiently to make conjectures on a topic outside his field of study.

Let's delve into this subject a little deeper than Hartmann's assertion. Let's make an assumption that UFO reports are due to the overactive imagination of people. If that is true, then their imagination must be very overactive because those UFO reports continue to this day. Look back at the graph in figure 2.7. The UFO reports started in 1942 and those people with overactive imaginations passed it on to their children, their grandchildren, and now their great-grand-children. If we are to accept the view that UFO sightings are due to overactive imaginations and the desire to "believe," then it is only logical that we ask the question, "Where were those overactive imaginations before 1942?" Didn't people have overactive imaginations in 1900 and 1920? Surely Orson Welles's famous hysteria-generating radio broadcast of 1938, "War of the Worlds," should have caused a multitude of UFO reports. It did not. The graph in figure 2.7 doesn't even show a blip for the year 1938. Something began in 1942 and it has continued to this day, and unproven assertions will not make it go away.

We've discussed the arguments around the sudden beginning of the modern UFO phenomenon. Let's turn our attention to the various UFO flaps that have occurred since the phenomenon began. The three dominant flaps were in 1952, 1957, and 1965–1967. These can be seen in figure 2.7 and are labeled at the top of their peaks. The argument made by naysayers is that these jumps are caused by media reports that result in more people looking at the sky in hopes of seeing UFOs and then sending in false reports. There is a certain truth to this argument. Whenever media reports on UFOs, it is only natural for people to go outside and look at the sky and observe the stars, aircraft lights, a drone, or the planet Venus. Most people will recognize what they're seeing, but a small number will assume they're observing a UFO. Should someone release a few Chinese lanterns during this period, then a lot more people will think they've witnessed a UFO. So, it is natural that media reports might result in more UFO reports. I've seen this firsthand in UFO sightings that I have personally investigated. But just because media coverage can induce UFO sightings, we cannot wave our arms and draw the blanket conclusion that spikes in UFO reports are due to the media. There is a big difference from logically inferring that media could affect UFO reporting, to jumping to the conclusion that media is the major cause of any sudden increase in UFO reports. This logic is like arguing that media broadcasts of mass shootings can lead others to glorify themselves through a mass shooting, and therefore the media is the cause of mass shootings. We must look for the cause of the initial UFO reports that caused the media coverage. Was it due to an unusual military exercise, or was it due to some other unidentified aerial object?

Before we look at some of these annual flaps, let's get a better understanding of UFO flaps by looking at a flap that occurred during a short period of time. The Stephenville UFO sighting of 2008 that was mentioned in chapter 1 is a good example. I personally met with the witnesses to this incident and spent weeks investigating the case. Before looking at the flap itself, a brief overview of the event is needed. The UFO sightings that unfolded in Stephenville, Texas, on January 8, 2008, caught the attention of the media worldwide. It was splattered across newspapers in the state of Texas and made all the national TV outlets.[1212] Over twenty different witnesses at a dozen different locations and at different times saw lights perform maneuvers that the witnesses did not believe could be explained by conventional aircraft. Witnesses included the police and a chief of police, a pilot, a constable, a former air traffic controller, and businesspeople. Additionally, radar data that was obtained supported their claims.[1313]

The Stephenville incident is a very good example that allows an examination of the media impact on UFO reporting as well as whether there is more to UFO reports than just the media. The city of Stephenville and the outlying area had a population of about 52,000 people in 2008. Based on the number of reports made to MUFON that year, one or two UFO reports would be expected each year for that population size. The actual number of reports was much larger. This information as well as the actual and expected number of reports for years before and after 2008 are shown in figure 2.8. The dark bars in the graph represent what would be expected as the normal background noise of UFO reports. The lighter bars represent the actual reports made to MUFON during the period 2005–2012.

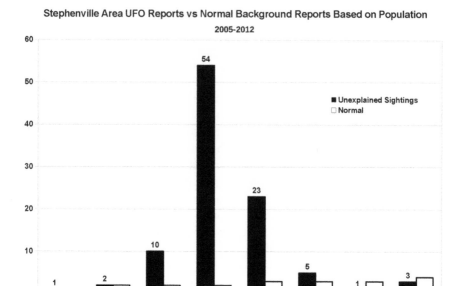

Figure 2.8.   Annual UFO reports from Stephenville, Texas, area (2005–2012).
Source: From the author

Look at the years 2005 and 2006. The actual number of reports matches the number of reports expected for the Stephenville area. This indicates that everything was normal in terms of UFO reports.

The year 2007 is different. Eight of the ten reports occurred in December of 2007. Those reports were made after the January 8, 2008, Stephenville incident for the year 2007, so these were due to media attention. My experience is that these types of reports are made by people who saw an object in the sky during 2007 but were either not comfortable reporting on it initially, had just not gotten around to reporting until they were spurred on by the media reports of 2008, or were people who just wanted to join the exciting fray. These 2007 reports were caused by the media attention in early 2008, although we can't conclude anything about the validity of the reports.

The year 2008 tells us that something unusual happened on January 8 and it was not related to any media reports. There was a total of eight sightings from thirteen different witnesses that were made before there was any media attention on the Stephenville incident. Those reports came in within forty-eight hours of each other and they were the cause of the media attention. Already there were enough reports that 2008 would have been a UFO flap year even if no more reports had come in. These reports can only be explained by agreeing that something unusual spurred these sightings. We can debate what caused these sightings, but we cannot toss out the sudden increase in

UFO reports by blaming it on the media. The media did not cause the flap; the UFO sightings caused the flap. Another fourteen cases came in during the remainder of the year related to the January 8 incident. The remainder of the cases reported in the latter parts of 2008 as well the higher-than-normal number of reports in 2009, whether real or not, can be potentially linked to the media. By 2010 and beyond, figure 2.8 shows that the number of UFO reports from the Stephenville area was back to background levels. The media can cause more people to come out and give their reports, but the media is not the initial cause of the sightings nor the cause of the flap. Anyone who tries to write off UFO flaps as due to the media has either not taken the time to study the details or is trying to brush the subject off without due consideration. Let's examine the 1952 UFO flap.

The beginning of the UFO flap of 1952 can be determined by looking at the monthly report rate as well as reports day by day. Records from Project Blue Book were used to create the graph seen in figure 2.9. A time period from April 1951 to April 1953 was used so that it is easy to see the month when the flap began. The individual daily reports were then examined to determine when in the month the flap began. The 1952 UFO flap began in April. This can be clearly seen in figure 2.9. Twenty reports, mostly military, were made in the first seven days of April. Those are more reports in seven days than were made in any given month from November 1951 to February 1952. It can also be seen that by March 1953, the flap of 1952 had begun to die down.[14]

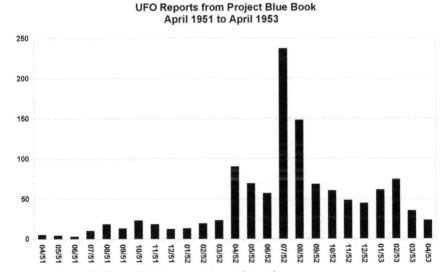

UFO Reports from Project Blue Book
April 1951 to April 1953

Figure 2.9.   UFO flap of 1952. *Source*: From the author

Although there is no "smoking gun" that establishes from where UFOs originate or that they're intelligently controlled, these flaps leave us with the impression that something is going on and that we should take these witness reports seriously. There were many interesting reports during those first seven days of April 1952, reports that beckon to the curious and open-minded:

1. **April 2, 9 a.m. Lake Meade, Nevada.** An Air Force sergeant, his wife, and friend see a silver cylindrical object moving at a very high altitude.
2. **April 3, 8:23 a.m. Benson, Arizona.** Three civilian instructors for the Air Force site a bright silver sphere and view it for an hour. They take actions to verify it was perfectly stationary and at very high altitude before it disappeared.
3. **April 5, 10:40 a.m. Phoenix, Arizona.** Four civilians witness a flight of three circular objects in a V-formation. They appeared like dull aluminum and were moving at high altitude and high velocity.
4. **April 5, 9:15 p.m. Miami, Florida.** An amateur astronomer and his son see four circular objects pass in front of the full moon. Each object's angular size was about half that of the moon. The objects were dark and unlit.
5. **April 5, nearing midnight. Kadena AFB, Okinawa, Japan.** A bomber crew of four airmen spot a formation of five elliptical objects, each with a brilliant white light that blinked every 1–2 seconds. Objects are estimated to be 2–3 feet long and at 20,000 feet with no means of propulsion. Speed estimated to be 1,000 knots.
6. **April 6, 2:59 p.m. Ft. Hood, Texas.** Single witness of a circular formation of grayish metallic objects that are disk-like in shape. The objects constantly change position in formation and every 12–15 seconds they tilt in unison similar to a Venetian blind being opened.[15]

The flap of 1952 culminated in the month of July with sighting reports up and down the East Coast of the United States and supported by unknown target showing up on military and civilian radar with speeds approaching 2,000 mph. The most famous incident involved the nation's capital with radar targets detected at Washington National Airport and Andrews Air Force Base. The Washington, D.C., sightings made the front page of the *Washington Post*.[16] The Air Force only compounded the excitement when an Air Force public information officer told the press, "The jet pilots are and have been under orders to investigate unidentified objects and to shoot them down, if they can't talk them down."[17] The Air Force brass came to D.C. under the orders of the Assistant Chief of Staff of the Air Force, Lt. Gen. Nathan Twining. Maj. Gen. John Samford led the Air Force delegation to D.C. Samford talked before the national press corps to explain how the Air Force was handling the

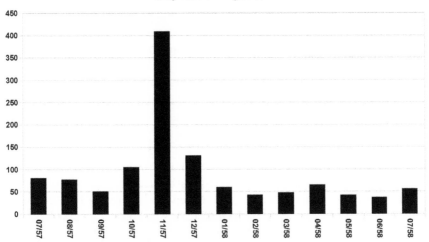

Figure 2.10.   UFO flap of 1957. *Source*: From the author.

situation. It was during this press conference that he made his famous admission that there have been "credible observers of relatively incredible things." A video of his talk is available in the national archives.[18] An appropriate way to close out the peak of the 1952 UFO flap.

The UFO flap of 1957 is the most spectacular of all flaps. It was very sudden. Sighting reports during the month of November increased six- to sevenfold from the typical month in 1957. The month of November drove the flap of 1957. On November 6 there were eighty-eight reports in a single day. Figure 2.7, displayed earlier in this chapter, shows the sudden increase in reports for the year 1957. Figure 2.10 breaks out the time from mid-1957 to mid-1958 into monthly reports.

Critics argue that these sightings were not real but were caused by national press coverage of UFO sightings in Levelland, Texas, on November 2. Of course, press coverage will occur when major UFO events take place. That correlation will always be there, but as we know, "correlation does not equal causation." Nonetheless, let's examine the assertion that the Levelland sightings caused the hundreds of reports that happened in November. But first a brief synopsis of the report that garnered the media attention in early November.

It was just before 11 p.m. on November 2. Two truck drivers about four miles northwest of Levelland reported to the sheriff's office that a 200-foot-long egg-shaped object flew over their truck and caused their lights and engine to fail. An hour later the sheriff received another call from a driver four miles east of town who described the same object and his car also failed. A few minutes later the sheriff took another report from a motorist who was ten miles north northeast of town. It was egg-shaped and his motor and lights also went out. Soon, a fourth call came in. You can guess the description and resultant automotive difficulties. Before the night ended, there would be a total of ten such reports.[19]

An hour after the last Levelland sighting report was made, 230 miles to the southwest, a two-man Army patrol in White Sands, New Mexico, reported an unknown object near their base.[20] Two days later, on November 4, a twenty-year Navy veteran and electronics technician was just south of White Sands when his radio began to fade out and then his engine died. There were other cars stopped along the road as they observed a large egg-shaped object.[21] By November 4 the Levelland sighting was an Associated Press story on the wires and by November 5 the number of UFO reports had begun to mushroom. Within the next two days most of the newspapers had picked up the story.

No one has proven that the 400+ reports in November 1957 or the 130 reports in December were due to media coverage of the Levelland UFO incident. There are several pieces of information that argue the reports were a true flap and not the result of media coverage. First, it is not a given that everyone who reported a UFO even knew about the Levelland sightings. Most news reports beyond the local papers did not place the story on the front page. Furthermore, before the media story had really broken out there were already fifteen reports on November 2, eight on November 3, and sixteen on November 4. Already, thirty-nine reports from those three days would constitute a flap if projected across the rest of the month. Secondly, there were twenty military reports across November 5–6. Seven of those reports were outside of the United States. It doesn't seem likely that those would be driven by the media. Lastly, there were four radar sightings of unknowns during those two days. Whitman AFB in Missouri reported visual sightings at distance and detection on radar of at least seven unknown objects the size of aircraft with speeds up to 350 knots. Cannon AFB in New Mexico detected seventeen aircraft-size objects on radar. Laredo AFB in Texas had seven unknown targets move across their radar screen over an eleven-minute time period with speeds reaching 2,600 mph. Last was a visual and radar sighting from the Coast Guard cutter *Sebago* in the Gulf of Mexico.[22] It is unusual to have four radar sightings of unknowns within a two-day period of time and across different geographic areas. We can wave our hands and chalk all of this up to coincidences and the media, or we can make a concerted effort to try and understand what is going on.

The database for the UFO flap of 1965 to 1967 is different than the previous flaps, which were based solely on Project Blue Book data. This was the

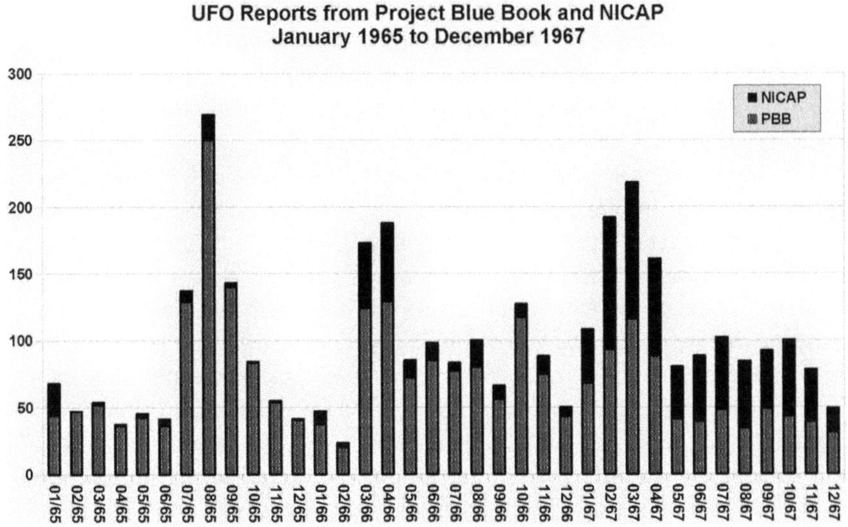

UFO Reports from Project Blue Book and NICAP
January 1965 to December 1967

Figure 2.11. UFO flap of 1965 to 1967. *Source:* From the author.

dominant database of the 1950s. However, the Air Force's collection of cases began to drop off in 1967 through 1969 due to the Colorado Project (aka Condon Committee), which was the Air Force's planned demise of Project Blue Book. The other major database during that time frame was that of the NICAP.[23] Both databases were brought together to examine this flap. NICAP has some Blue Book reports in its files; those were eliminated so as to avoid duplication. The resultant history of those reports is shown in figure 2.11.

The number of UFO reports jumped from 41 in June of 1965 to 137 reports in July before peaking at 259 reports in August. Reports reached a crescendo from July 30 to August 4, with 78 sighting reports. The location of those reports is interesting. One-third of all the reports came out of the central United States, specifically the states of Kansas, Oklahoma, and Texas. Those states only made up 7.8 percent of the U.S. population in the 1960 census.[24, 24] This argues against reports being caused by the media since that should have been a function of the population. International reports comprised the second highest number with 12.5 percent of reports—another argument against media inducement since American media did not quickly reach foreign papers in the year 1965.

Late March and early April 1966 saw a large influx of reports into the Air Force. These reports were on the heels of the historically well-known Michigan UFO reports that resulted in the infamous "swamp-gas" explanation by Dr. Hynek. This UFO incident was discussed in detail in chapter 1 and can arguably be described as the source of events that led to the beginning of the end for Project Blue Book.

Was the flap in 1966 due to the media coverage of the "swamp-gas" incident? If there was a flap that one was going to try and link to media coverage, it would be this one. But it is difficult to argue that the events in Dexter and Hillsdale, Michigan, were not valid sightings of some unknown object. Just ask Hynek and the Air Force.

It is hard to find a specific inflection point for the spike in UFO reports seen for the year 1967 in figure 2.7. Figure 2.11 shows that the year 1967 has more sighting reports in the months of February through April. But there are also more elevated reporting numbers for every month of that year except for December. An examination of the number of reports on individual days does not show a grouping of days either. The flap of 1967 appears to be a generic increase across the board. This type of flap does not support a media-induced explanation either.

After 1967 there were two other minor UFO flaps that raised annual sighting numbers. There was a small flap in 1973, which can be seen in figure 2.7, and another one in 2012 that is visible in figure 2.3. The time period from 1998 to 2008 is more difficult to ascertain because many of the civilian UFO databases were switching from paper reports to electronic reports using the internet. This resulted in a large increase in case reports that did not level off until about 2008. Will there be another year in the near future with an increase in UFO reports? One would expect that there will be, based on history.

A lot has been covered in these first two chapters. Now you should have a good general understanding of the history of the UFO phenomenon. The importance of an investigation and the weaknesses in human memory and anecdotal evidence have also been discussed. You should now be familiar with ways that anecdotal data can be improved using NLP. The modern beginning of the UFO phenomenon and the UFO flaps that have constantly come and gone should pique your interest as to why. Why do people continue to report sightings of these objects? It is one thing when someone reports that they have seen lights in the sky; it is something very different when someone encounters an object at such a close distance that there is little possibility that they have incorrectly identified a common object. The next four chapters will cover some of the strange characteristics that have been reported regarding UFOs—characteristics that suggest we're dealing with an object that is technologically advanced.

Chapter Three

The Strangeness of the Phenomenon

There are now thousands of UFO reports made each month thanks to the ease of reporting created by the electronic age and the internet. Most of those reports either lack sufficient information or are misinterpretations of known objects. Many are lights seen in the night sky, which could be anything. But there is one type of report from the past that still exists today—reports that are so strange that there is an odd truth to them. It's a report that is so incongruous that it makes the investigator wonder why the witness would say such a thing if they were fabricating the story. Mark Twain said it well in his novel about Pudd'nhead Wilson, "Truth is stranger than fiction, but it is because fiction is obliged to stick to possibilities; truth isn't." Many longtime UFO investigators have experienced such stories. I've interviewed over 150 individuals and have heard two that would fit the definition of what is called "strangeness."

The oddity of these strange reports is rooted in the fact that they are heard multiple times. If someone told you that they saw rocks fall out of the sky, you wouldn't think much of it. But if you kept hearing reports of rocks falling out of the sky, then you might begin to wonder. This is how meteors were described until the early nineteenth century, which is when science realized that meteors originate from space. The same is true with UFO reports. What do you make of a strange UFO characteristic reported that keeps popping up in occasional reports?

J. Allen Hynek was the first scientist to notice these strange aspects of UFO stories, and to use this aspect to measure the veracity of a UFO sighting. Although Hynek was initially Project Blue Book's scientific assassin for UFO sightings, he later became one of the strongest proponents of the reality of the UFO phenomenon. Hynek created what he called a "Strangeness Rating" to UFO reports.[1] For example, a light in the night sky that seemed to move in a random manner unlike an airplane or balloon would have a low strangeness rating. The motion of the object was the only characteristic that was strange. A witness reports a large barbell-shaped craft that hovers 300 feet away without any sound, affects the operation of the witness's phone and camera, and then suddenly zips away at high speed would have a very high strangeness rating. Its lack of aerodynamics, the EM effects, the lack of sound at close range, and the ability of a large object to hover silently and fly at extreme speeds are all strange characteristics that defy common sense, especially when taken together. Hynek argued that when several independent UFO witnesses, at different times and places, reported something very strange such as "the disk was flipping end over end as it flew," then it justified giving those reports extra attention. Hynek's strangeness parameter was utilized by CUFOS, the organization he founded. But its use has slipped away over time and certainly is not used by the new government UAP investigative groups that have been in the news during the 2017 to 2022 time period. Its use should be reconsidered. The following several pages help illustrate some interesting and strange UFO characteristics that help demonstrate the value of the strangeness indicator.

FALLING LIKE A LEAF AND WOBBLING

Imagine a witness tells you that they saw a disk-shaped metallic object drop toward the Earth in a controlled fall similar to how a leaf sways back and forth as it drops toward the Earth or that they saw it wobble or teeter from the left to the right as if it was about to fall from the sky.[2] This was a description that was more common in the beginning of the modern UFO era in the 1950s.

March 29, 1952, 8:42 a.m.; Misawa AFB, Japan. The pilot of a T-6 was performing practice intercepts with two F-84s. The pilot's concentration was interrupted by a shiny, disk-shaped object. He described its strange movement as follows: "It had no apparent projections and left no exhaust or vapor trails. An unusual flight characteristic was a slow, fluttering motion. It rocked back and forth in 40-degree banks at one-second intervals throughout its course."[3]

August 28, 1958, 4:20 p.m.; Georgetown, Ohio. Two Ohio highway patrolmen were traveling on patrol two miles east of Georgetown, Ohio. They spotted a large silver disk hovering over a field as they traveled down State Route 125. The patrolmen turned their car around and drove back toward the disk. They parked their car about 500 feet away and exited their vehicle. The object rose about fifty feet and then departed at an angle. It wobbled as it moved, according to their testimony.[4]

Wobbling and falling toward the ground like a feather is a strangeness aspect to UFOs that is not heard as often from witnesses after the mid 1960s. Consider this sighting by a witness who had never read UFO history, so he had no reason to have knowledge of UFO reports from the 1950s.

June 14, 2012, 10 p.m.; Yuba, California. A thirty-five-year-old security guard witnesses a strange object in the sky. The ex-Army witness was able to identify the distance to the object as 300–400 yards because he could see its light on the tree line. Using Google Earth to calculate, I found that the exact distance to the disk based on the tree line and the witness's location was 510 yards. His estimate was close. At that distance an object fifty feet in size would appear to the eye as three times the size of the full moon. Figure 3.1 illustrates the location of the witness and the UFO. Here are excerpts from the lengthy description he made of the object he saw that day:[5]

I first noticed a glowing white amongst the trees.

It was about 40 to 50 feet, a glowing white saucer shaped UFO, with 3 exterior lights that were blue, green, and red and these exterior lights flashed alternately.

I stepped out of my vehicle with my binoculars and the night vision. This duration was approximately 5 minutes.

My observation was the craft was a few feet above the trees gliding along following the tree line. It was moving slow and at that time it swayed from side to side then hovered, at a complete standstill. Even at a standstill it appeared to be swaying from side to side at times.

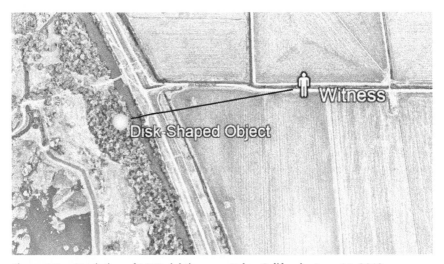

Figure 3.1. Depiction of UFO sighting near Yuba, California, June 14, 2012.
Source: Google Earth

This is not a normal movement for a man-made aerial object. We don't know why UFO reports of a tilting, falling disk became such a rarity after the 1950s. Yet here we have a modern report of a UFO attribute that is from the past. It is a flight characteristic that the witness did not harp upon, but a strange characteristic that adds credibility to his story. Why would a witness create a hoax story about an aerial craft that tilts from side to side as it moves? One wouldn't expect strange unbelievable details in a hoaxed story. One would expect believable details. The same is true of a witness who misinterprets what they are seeing. An observer might think an object is hovering when it is actually moving slowly at a distance or can think they are looking at a cylinder when it is actually an airplane at an angle such that the wings are aligned with the body and aren't readily apparent. But how does a witness who is close to an object imagine it is swaying from side to side?

TUMBLING

Most of us have seen balloons tumble through the air or objects caught up in a strong windstorm. However, if we see any type of aircraft tumble through the sky, then we usually would expect an impending calamity with the aircraft impacting the ground—not so with UFOs. The tumbling motion of a UFO can be listed as another strange aspect that is sometimes reported.

June 5, 1952; 8:42 a.m.; Kimpo Airfield, South Korea. This is one of the earliest cases of a disk-like object that tumbled through the air as it moved. Project Blue Book has eight pages on this incident. It was described by a sergeant on the ground as seven times as long as it was thick and about the size of an F-86 fighter jet. He was able to estimate its size as fifty to sixty feet as it was in his same line of sight as the F-86. The sergeant observed the object for four minutes, sufficient time to pick up several details. He describes its features and its odd tumbling and spinning characteristics:

> The color of the edges was dark blue (twice as dark as sky color), and the top and bottom was silver (dull enough not to reflect any considerable amount of light). On the large surface, which appeared to be the top, several evenly spaced concentric dark or black lines were observed.
> It then climbed straight up for six seconds decreasing one half in size, paused again, picked up a 60-degree heading and began to proceed on a straight course alternately spinning and tumbling in the same manner as before.[6]

The witness sounds credible due to his very descriptive report and his use of the object's angular size to measure the object's movement. If this was the only report of such unusual movements, then we could discount it. It only took a month for the second similar report to be received. This time in the United States.

July 14, 1952, 9:12 p.m.; Norfolk, Virginia. There are seventy-four pages in Project Blue Book describing this sighting just north of Norfolk. Two pilots of a DC-4 were approaching the city at 8,000 feet altitude when they saw six disks with a reddish-orange brilliance approaching in an echelon formation below their altitude at about 2,000 feet. They had a sharp outline to their appearance and the pilots estimated their length at six to seven times the width, very similar to the ratio of the object in Korea. As the objects continued to approach the DC-4, they did something very unexpected. All six disks flipped up on their edges for a moment: a very non-aerodynamic maneuver. This flip resulted in all the disks almost completely reversing their direction before they flattened out again prior to departing. The pilots described the departure of the disks the next day to Air Force Major John Sharpe: "This change of direction was made with the suddenness of a bullet ricocheting off a stone wall and was not a turn in the sense that conventional aircraft make a turn." They went on to state that their estimate was that the disks were moving at about 1,000 mph. The interviewing officer concluded in his report, "The observers are considered reliable, and evidently saw just what they described."[7]

What do we make of these two reports? We could ignore them and just write them off as overzealous witnesses. We could use circular reasoning to contend that they must have been poor observers because the movements that were described make no sense. With that logic, we could dismiss any UFO sighting that just seemed too odd to be true. Or we could just wave them off because these reports were from so long ago. We would be wrong.

July 15, 2013, 10 p.m.; Bellingham, Washington. A six-page civilian report of this incident has been summarized here. A postal worker and his wife, who served in the USAF in intelligence, witnessed a rectangular-shaped object maneuver through the sky and come within 100 feet of them. It tumbled along its center axis as it moved. The object executed perfect turns as it avoided electrical poles, wires, and streetlights. Both witnesses described the object's color as changing from a glowing red to a dull gray as it performed a banking turn and came to a standstill. The color change was not uniform as the color change began at the top of the object and moved downward toward its base. The object was described as about the size of a large SUV and at its closest approach about palm-width in size at arm's length.[8]

How do we argue against a sighting from two witnesses who were within 100 feet of the object? It is very difficult to say that they saw a balloon, bird, or helicopter and incorrectly identified it as an aerial craft tumbling through the sky. This is one of those cases where we either decide the witnesses were lying or we believe their story as something that happened. Witness reports of aerial craft that tumble through the sky as they move are not common, but they occur often enough that they must be given consideration as potentially valid events.

Wobbling motions in the air and acrobatic tumbling moves have a commonality. They are both motions that are non-aerodynamic and they suggest that there might be a lack of interaction with the atmosphere. These are not the only movements expressed by UFOs that lack a certain aerodynamic quality.

BARBELLS

It is difficult to imagine a less aerodynamic shape than a barbell—two large weights separated from each other and their only connection a bar that keeps the two sides together. This is not the type of structure that one would expect to see flying through our atmosphere. The mind rejects such a concept. The first inclination in seeing such an object in the air would be that it should immediately fall to the ground. It certainly is not something that we should expect to hear about a UFO sighting. Who would believe such a report? Yet people have reported exactly this type of shape. It is nowhere as common as a disk, cigar-shape, triangle, cylinder, sphere, boomerang, or delta shape. The mystery is that such a shape should be reported at all. If we believe that such a shape was accurately reported flying through our skies, then we have no choice but to accept that someone has come up with a manner of travel that is completely non-aerodynamic. I have collected every report on sightings of flying barbells that I've been able to find in the last fifteen years. I now have sixty-one reports of barbell-shaped UFOs that have spanned the time period from 1950 to the modern era. It is not surprising that these reports are almost entirely during the day when it is easier to discern an object's shape. A sampling of those reports across the decades is provided.

July 8, 1950, 2 p.m.; Peril Strait, Alaska.   The first record of a sighting of a barbell-shaped UFO comes from the Project Blue Book files. Three U.S. coast guardsmen were the witnesses, and their report was turned over to Project Blue Book.

It was a windless day. The object was first sighted overhead and viewed for two and a half minutes as it moved to the west. The barbell was an opaque white. They saw it clearly and in detail: "Object was distinctly observed below the highest cirrus clouds, and it appeared to be banking and climbing while maintaining course. While banking and climbing, end and side views were observed in addition to [an] oval bottom view." The guardsmen provided a drawing from three angles, as can be seen in figure 3.2. They estimated its size as 100 feet by 60 feet and its speed as 350 mph. The cirrus clouds defined the object's maximum altitude at 15,000.[9]

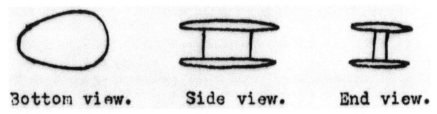

Bottom view.   **Side view.**   **End view.**

Figure 3.2.   Drawing from Project Blue Book, Peril Strait, Alaska, July 8, 1950.
Source: USAF, Project Blue Book

Project Blue Book never investigated the report they received. They filed it and wrote it off as a balloon. It would have required two balloons connected by some lightweight material to have appeared to look like a barbell. Balloons would also have needed to be close to the boat and would have required a wind, which was nonexistent that day, to mimic the movement the guardsmen saw. Unfortunately, this is another example of a typical Project Blue Book investigation.

September 4, 1960, 2 p.m.; China Lake Naval Air Facility, California. There were eleven sightings of barbell-shaped UFOs between 1950 and 1960. They came from Australia, Sweden, Great Britain, and the United States. The next barbell report that will be highlighted involved two Navy men and comes from the files of Dr. James McDonald.

J. H. Kirkpatrick and Warren Specht were monitoring a non-piloted Navy test flight when they noticed another object following their drone. The drone was at 8,000 feet altitude and the other unknown object was several feet above it and appeared to be monitoring the drone. They described the object as very bright and composed of a shiny, red metal that reflected the sun. They saw the object clearly, as described by Kirkpatrick:

> Its shape was very unique, I think. It looked like a dumbbell, that is two spheres connected by a tube or a tunnel. Its height made it impossible to see any parts, fins, or antennas, or determine any type of propulsion system. The sun was at our backs which made the target and the object stand out very distinct against the light blue sky.
>
> We continued to watch the object for approximately two minutes, then with a burst of speed it made about a forty-five degree turn sharply and climbed out of sight within a few seconds, leaving no trail of any kind.[10]

The object described by Kirkpatrick was the basic description of the barbell-shaped UFO that had been described in the previous decade and in decades to come. Reports of barbell-shaped objects came in from multiple European countries as well as Canada and Russia during the 1960s and 1970s. The descriptions mirrored those in the United States. The final report of those two decades comes from a mother driving with her young son near Sarnia, Ontario.

July 1979, daytime; Sarnia, Ontario, Canada. It was a beautiful day as a young mother was driving her four-year-old son to a nearby town. Her son was sitting directly behind her in the back seat. As she drove along a rural area of mostly fields, she kept hearing her son ask, "Mommy, what's that?" Without looking she just answered, "a bird," "a phone wire." Her son asked her again, "Mommy what's that?" This time the mother looked out of her window and looked up. She was amazed to see a chrome, silver-colored object in the sky hovering above her car. The mother's own words best describe the object:

> I can remember how beautiful the blue sky was against this object. It was barbell shaped (cylinder shaped body with round balls at each end of the cylinder). I watched it as I drove. We had to drive about a quarter mile before I could stop. It followed us around a bend and over a bridge. When I pulled the car over and got out it started rising straight up until it was out of sight. It made no noise.[11]

The undeterred and determined voice of a child awakens in us a part that we've lost along the way as we became adults.

We close out the twentieth century with a report off the northeastern U.S. coast.

June 1992, daytime; near Boston, Massachusetts. Four crew members and their captain spotted a silver/white reflective craft in the sky, while commercial fishing on Georges Bank. A crewman described it: "It was shaped liked old-fashioned barbells, like what strong men lifted in old circuses; two spheres connected by a bar or tube. The scale of spheres to bar was just like the old barbells as well." The men observed the barbell for two or three minutes. The captain attempted to obtain a photo of the barbell. He lifted a camera with a zoom lens and the moment he started to aim for a photo, the craft sped off upward at perhaps a seventy-degree angle so fast as to seem to vanish instantly. The five men did what often happens when the impossible is witnessed: they agreed to tell no one as they were afraid of being ridiculed. Thankfully, they changed their minds as time went by.[12]

Half of all the barbell-shaped UFO reports over the last seventy-five years have come in the first two decades of the twenty-first century. The most detailed barbell report came from a scientist while on a trip in the wilds of south-central Ontario, Canada, in 2013. Phil Leech, a former detective, and I investigated this incident. The witness and his two comrades wished to remain anonymous because of Department of Defense (DoD) contract work performed by the primary witness, who was also the scientist. I was so intrigued by this case that I flew to his place of business to verify the validity of his claims.

The scientist was who he said he was. Prior to flying out to meet him, I had already verified his personal information, the identity of his company, and the patents that he held. I arrived early in the morning. His place of business and home was that of someone who was well off. He gave me a tour of his R&D facility. There were several engineers who worked for him. He had multiple 3D printers in his facility and one that must have been fifteen to twenty feet across. He warned me up front that my cell phone would not receive a signal as that was part of his security protocols for handling DoD projects. He also gave me a tour of a nearby DoD facility that manufactured some of his products based on his patents. The facility covered over an acre of land under one roof. I provide these details to establish that he had no need or motivation to fabricate this story. His only objective was to understand more about the object he witnessed that August evening. And now the story. The names used in the story are fictitious for the protection of the witnesses' identities.

Gavin had taken time away from his research work and was on a black bear hunting trip in a remote wooded area of Ontario, Canada, with two of his friends, Kaleb and Wade. The area was only accessible by an old logging trail. It was so remote that their cell phones could not pick up any trace of a phone signal. They had spent much of the day hunting, and it was time to depart. The three men got into their truck and headed down the logging path. It was 9:40 p.m. and the skies were already quite dark with the stars shining. Kaleb was driving as he owned the land and was familiar with the logging path. Wade was in the passenger seat and Gavin was sitting in the back.

The truck slowly went around a bend in the road and up a hill. Kaleb was concentrated on the dark road ahead. He didn't notice what Gavin was watching from the back seat. Gavin could see some unusual distant lights flying low over the trees. He thought it might be a helicopter. But why would a helicopter be flying in the middle of nowhere during the dark of night? Gavin found this concerning, so he continued to watch the lights.

The distant lights began to directly approach the truck. Gavin's window was rolled down, but he could not hear a sound. He knew that he should be able to hear a helicopter. Why was there no noise?

Gavin asked Kaleb to stop the truck. He took out his Sony Cybershot camera once the truck came to a halt. He wanted to take a video of what was happening. He turned the camera on but as soon as it came on, it would immediately power off. He tried this several times with always the same result.

The lights continued to approach the men and soon they could see the shape of the object that was emitting the lights. There were two large disks on each end with a bar connecting the disks. The lights revolved around each saucer section and moved in opposite directions. It looked like an optical eggbeater, and it was huge. Gavin's outstretched hand would cover only half of the object. He used that information, the fir tree height that it passed over, and the width of the road to calculate its size. It was 170 feet long and as tall as a house. Its surface looked like shiny metal and there were very dark black bands around the disks. It was moving slowly over the treetops, and it was so close they could have hit it with a rock. But the crazy thing was that it made no sound.

The object's motion was as equally strange as its non-aerodynamic shape and its lack of sound. The barbell slowly rotated around the center of the bar as it moved at 15–20 mph. It also had a huge tail of sparkles or fire. This plume of plasma with tiny sparkles cascaded out the rear of the craft for more than 150 feet. This plasma was always opposite to the object's direction of motion. It wasn't affixed to an exhaust motor or structure. The plasma reminded Gavin of the aurora borealis.

The entire craft was covered 12–16 inches in a deep shade of indigo blue plasma reminding Gavin of high voltage and high frequency electricity. He pulled out his Motorola Droid phone to try and take a photo. He had no success as the phone acted as if it was going through a boot-up. He tried his Sony camera again and it still refused to stay powered up.

Wanting to get a closer look at the object, Gavin took out his hunting rifle and used its 9x scope for a closer view. Wade became excited and yelled at Gavin, "Shoot it! Shoot it!" Gavin replied, "I'm not going to shoot at something when I don't know what it is." Gavin spent the next minute or two closely observing the craft through his rifle scope. He wanted to see if there was any indication that this might be some new kind of military aircraft. He could find no indication of any rivets or hardware on its surface. None were found. The lines of the craft were as smooth as liquid mercury. It looked as if it was forged as a single solid object.

The craft moved slowly away from the men. As it got farther away, Gavin grabbed his Sony camera again to see if he could turn it on. This time it stayed on. He pushed the video record button. The camera was running but the screen was black. He recorded for several minutes. During this recording the men saw an extremely fast-moving object move across the night sky. They believed it was the barbell that had moved out of sight. Gavin would later find that audio was recorded by his camera, but the video portion was filled with noisy interference. Gavin also gave his cell phone another attempt, but it was hot to the touch and would not operate. He asked Kaleb to call another hunting party in the area using their Motorola radio. The radio was dead. Its electronics were apparently damaged, and it would never operate again.

Gavin began writing down notes as soon as they reached their hotel. He used those notes to write a twenty-four-page paper on the events of that evening. It is worth highlighting the major conclusions that this scientist drew from his experience observing the barbell-shaped UFO.

Facts based upon my observance:

1. This craft was not an airplane, helicopter, or lighter than air blimp.
2. This craft was huge with dimensions estimated at 170' × 60' × 20'.
3. This craft did not fly with typical propulsion jet engines/propellers/rotors etc.
4. This craft had an immense high frequency AC electrical field about it.
5. The lights around the disk portion of the craft were operating in synchronous form.
6. The craft had a very thick deep indigo blue plasma field close to the hull.
7. The craft emitted no noise. We were in a 30dba ambient environment yet it was dead silent even up close.
8. The craft produced no obvious heat signature for something with immense power.
9. Craft was constructed of a metal that looked like polished bismuth yet with silky smooth lines.
10. Craft had several locations on the hull beam with small, unusual markings almost a hieroglyph.
11. Craft traveled in a slight zigzag pattern with an approximate 10 sec interval.
12. Craft was very slow spinning on its center axis with approximate one-minute intervals.
13. Black center section of each disk was totally opaque with no reflections.
14. Metal of the craft on the topside was very reflective as I could see stars reflected from above.
15. Post processing of the video from the camera netted a white noise screen with a perfect pulsation function that is timed to the revolution of the lights from the disks at roughly 0.5 sec interval.
16. All light emitted from the craft was of diverged coherence in property, similar to a laser beam striking a divergence optic.
17. All light colors emitted from the craft were of pure color almost pristine in singular wavelengths. Similar to grating tuned laser optical resonators where color stability is incredible.
18. I noted 16–17 colors emitted from the positions on the hull however each light position emitted in synchronous all colors a light position that was previously red might be blue next then yellow then green etc.
19. Light colors emitted were not power balanced; predominant colors were white, yellow, red, and green.
20. Plasma tail was conical in shape and light blue/white in color with white/yellow sparkles and was visible more than 150' behind the craft.
21. Flat black opaque area on the disks were bordered with a short lip on the top and bottom.
22. Craft disks had a mostly symmetrical cross section with perfect blending to the rectangular shaped center beam area. There were no visible blend lines to the disk section.
23. Light colors on the exterior worked in groups of four.
24. Electrical field of the craft had to be high frequency AC since I did not feel anything or have my hair standing on end even at very close proximity to the craft of possibly 400 feet.

25. Electrical disturbance was great enough to scramble operation of cell phones and cameras and powerful job site radio that typically worked up to 20 miles away to home base, yet did nothing to the truck engine or lights of the late model 2014 Dodge 4×4 truck as it approached us.
26. Immense speed as was demonstrated by the fast mover craft which covered the entire sky horizon to horizon in 41 seconds as was documented in our captured voice comments in the audio of the video with the Sony camera.
27. Further study of the captured HD video has proven to be VERY interesting, using a component Analog HD video cable to capture and study the recording with a 2Ghz spectrum analyzer. I have found embedded in the video Sync and on each color RGB channel electrical interference patterns of the electrical field of the Craft's propulsion system. There appears to be two massive electrical fields in a poly-synchronous phased interaction, the interval between cycles is very obvious at 457-478ms which is roughly 2x the visual speed of the circular light patterns of the craft. Several control circumstances were recorded with the same camera/memory-chip/battery in a location with no known electrical fields. Confirmation of the no electrical fields for the control recording was determined with my Protek 2Ghz Field analyzer model 3201 meter.[13]

During my visit with the witness, I verified what he described in item #27. We used an oscilloscope made by Instek to examine the signal outputs from his Sony Cybershot camera. The camera was in normal operation when the witness took video of the black bears. This could be seen on the oscilloscope.

The witness still has his original camera. He has been unwilling to part with the electronic data in hopes that he will someday be able to gain valuable information recorded by the camera.

The barbell UFO sightings are anecdotal accounts. Their strength lies in their ability to minimize the concern that a witness misidentified a common aerial object. The shape is completely non-aerodynamic and quite unique. Why would a fabricator of a UFO sighting choose such an unbelievable shape? Your brain initially says "no" to the existence of these barbell sightings because if you were to accept that they are real then think of the implications. These are sighting reports of objects that were built by an intelligence far in advance of our own.

It's not known if Dr. Hynek had ever heard of a barbell-shaped UFO sighting, as they are rare. Surely, he would have dropped them into his bucket of "strangeness" and marveled at their potential reality.

PLAYING WITH THE MIND OF THE WITNESS

This next category of strangeness is difficult to grasp, and it causes many investigators to wonder about the veracity of a witness's testimony. When a witness indicates that they just "knew" to look in a certain direction and witness a UFO, it is only natural for the investigator to ponder the reality of the witness testimony. What do you say when the witness says an unknown light would circle around Polaris, the north star, and draw a cross with its sudden movements? One must be highly skeptical. But what do you conclude when you hear these types of stories from multiple witnesses of good character? You likely begin to doubt the sanity of your fellow man, but soon after, if you're honest, you may also begin to wonder if there is some hidden truth to their stories.

October 27, 2011, 5:25 a.m.; Sealy, Texas. I will begin with a UFO report that I personally investigated. The sighting involved a husband and his wife. The husband has a degree in forestry and his wife has an educational degree and taught math at the local school. I asked them some astronomical questions prior to my interview. I wanted to get a feel for their knowledge of the night skies. Both witnesses were aware of the major stars and constellations in the sky. They also were aware that a star should not rapidly brighten and dim unless it was a variable or pulsating star. They were knowledgeable witnesses.

Their early morning routine was well established. The couple lived in the country forty miles to the west of Houston near a town called Sealy, Texas. There were no streetlights, and the pre-morning sky was dark. The wife would always walk her husband down their driveway at 5:25 a.m. for him to make his carpool. The couple often looked at the night sky during their stroll. The early morning hours of October 27, 2011, were different.

They had been paying more attention to the stars the last few nights because the wife saw a pulsing light in the constellation Orion several nights before. The morning of October 27 they noticed that the star Rigel, in the constellation Orion, would brighten and dim in a pulsating fashion. They described the color of the star as pure white. At its brightest they indicated the star was brighter than Sirius and almost as bright as the planet Jupiter. The husband first thought that perhaps Rigel was a pulsating star, but after researching the topic he realized that was not the case. He described the pulsating feature as about three seconds of gradual brightening; the star's brightness would hold steady for about ten seconds and then this was followed by three seconds of dimming to its normal brightness; the light would hold steady at the lower magnitude for about two to three seconds and then the cycle would repeat. This process was repeated about five times.

Now it gets even stranger. Near the last pulsating-cycle an orange-red orb appeared at the 9 o'clock position of Rigel. The orange-red orb was only seen by the husband, as the wife had turned away to scan other areas of the sky for unusual star activity. The orb appeared when Rigel was at its maximum brightness. The orb was not bright, and the witness described its size as large enough to be easily discernible as a circular object, not a star. The orb disappeared after about two seconds. About two seconds later either the same or a similar orange-red orb appeared at the 3 o'clock position of Rigel. It was equidistant in location from where the orb had appeared at the 9 o'clock position. He indicated that the orb was 1 to 1.5 orb-diameters from Rigel. The second orb appearance also remained visible for only about two seconds and at 1 to 1.5 orb-diameters distant. Rigel made no more pulsations after the orb disappeared.

There is no known phenomenon in astronomy to explain the changes in Rigel reported by the witnesses. Based on the witness testimony, Rigel was pulsating from its normal magnitude of +0.3 to somewhere in the range of –2.0 in a matter of seconds. This is an unheard-of change in brightness of a star. The star Rigel has no history of this type of pulsation, and for that matter, there is no visible star in the sky that pulsates in such a manner. Rigel is a variable star, and its magnitude can vary from 0.0 to +0.3, but over the course of twenty-two to twenty-five days. This was not the case in this incident due to the time period of seconds needed for two orders of magnitude in brightness change. There is no known astronomical event that could explain this. Likewise, it does not seem plausible that the star Rigel could be responsible for the changes in magnitude seen by the witnesses. Although the witnesses feel confident that they were observing Rigel and not an object near Rigel, it is still a possibility that what they saw was near Rigel. That possibility would at least remove the problems involved with explaining a rapidly pulsating Rigel, but it does not make a prosaic explanation any easier.

The witnesses' description of this event was of sufficient detail that one must either discount the story as fabricated or accept the description of the event as provided. I do not believe this story can be explained by assuming the witnesses misinterpreted what they saw. Meteors, satellites, Iridium satellites, aircraft, atmospheric effects . . . none of those can come close to explaining this event. It is almost as if the orb that circled Rigel was beckoning to the witness by making a point about the silliness and impossibility of what the witness was observing. As if it was saying, "Look at me. This cannot be an astronomical event, you closed-minded human." But such speculation cannot be proven. We are left with no rational explanation for what occurred.

This type of story is not uncommon. The book *Grassroots UFOs* by Dr. Michael Swords is filled with such reports from the last twenty to forty years.[14] Even today, these types of unusual reports continue. Veteran military and airline pilots recently reported that during August 2022, three to five bright objects flying in a circular motion like a "racetrack" would do so for hours. No matter where in the world the pilots were located, the lights would appear in the lower right-hand corner of the Big Dipper.[15] If the objects are always seen in the Big Dipper, then this indicates the objects had to be far out in space. Their unusual movements and brightness would also have been visible to everyone on the ground. Yet no one has made such a report. And how can they be making rapid movements covering an area the size of the Big Dipper?

It would require enormous velocity and acceleration. This is nonsensical. Or are the objects closer to the Earth and they simply align themselves between the pilots and the Big Dipper, every time they're seen? This would indicate that the lights are interacting with specific witnesses. Again, a nonsensical explanation to our way of thinking. Yet this is what the pilots have told us.

The work of Professor Harley Rutledge also highlights these types of incidents and what at least "seems" like an interaction between the observer and the observed. Some of his comments are so extraordinary that it is important to document the qualifications of Professor Rutledge as well as the science that he brought to the study of the phenomenon.

Harley Rutledge was the chair of the Physics Department at Southeast Missouri State University. His PhD was in solid state physics from the University of Missouri. He is probably the first scientist to do extensive field studies of the UFO phenomenon. His interest was initiated by a UFO flap that started in the Missouri area during 1973. His own words best describe his decision to investigate the phenomenon:

> In March 1973, as more and more UFO reports poured out of Piedmont, my interest increased, in spite of my original skepticism about the UFO enigma. But my decision to become actively involved did not come easily. Because it would mean placing my career in jeopardy.[16]

Professor Rutledge spent 1973–1979 in the field using instrumentation to measure the phenomenon. He obtained permission from his university to collect a team of scientists to do the work. The main participants were Dr. James Sage of the Electronics Department; Professor Milton Ueleke, an astronomy instructor; and several students. At least thirty-five scientists, engineers, students, and lay persons assisted in the field research at one time or another. The instrumentation that they used in the field included electromagnetic detectors in the visible region of frequencies, the S-band radar frequencies of 2–4 GHz, and lower frequency ranges of 1 to 1,800 MHz. Their optical equipment included binoculars, an 800mm camera system, and three Questar telescopes. The S-band radar set would be used to fix the location of a UFO and to determine its distance.[17]

Professor Rutledge and his team spent seven years in the field examining the UFO phenomenon. They took photos and measurements and documented their findings. Their work was extensive and cannot be properly covered here. It is summarized in detail in Professor Rutledge's book, *Project Identification: The First Scientific Field Study of UFO Phenomena*. The professor's personal experiences and conclusions in his book also hint at what seems to be a possible interaction between the observer and the observed. He must have felt confident in his thoughts to have put them in print. He was the head of his university's Physics Department, and he knew anything that he wrote would be scrutinized and could reflect on his standing at the university.

Harley Rutledge had a personal sighting that is reminiscent of the event near Sealy, Texas, which was just discussed. This sighting occurred at his home on June 20, 1977, at about 10:30 p.m. The professor had been watching a dim light traveling toward Alkaid, the first star in the handle of the Big Dipper. When the light came within three degrees of Alkaid, it disappeared. Rutledge looked around for the missing light. Then suddenly the star Merak, the lower pointer star of the Big Dipper's pan, flared brilliantly. It took one second to reach maximum brilliance and then another second to return to normal. Rutledge knew that the star Merak could not have flared; something in his line of sight of Merak must have brightened. He was surprised once more when the light flared again a few seconds later. This time it was about three degrees away from Merak. He knew this wasn't a plane at high altitude reflecting the sun's light because it was too late at night. He knew it wasn't a satellite because the path of the light was erratic. There was no viable explanation; the light source remained unidentified.

This was not Rutledge's only unusual sighting. He lists many such events in his book. Often the professor would see what he referred to as a pseudo-star that would be out of place in a constellation. While being observed, the light would just fade away. The professor began to question whether these sightings were coincidental or planned. Fortunately, these pseudo-stars were documented by other team members as well. There were many occasions when two or more members witnessed these events and were able to compare notes to establish that they were not "seeing things." The strangeness of these events is best measured in Professor Rutledge's own musings:

> Would these events have occurred had I not been looking in the direction of the event at the time of occurrence? Were events occurring in other directions as well? Many of the sightings occurred near prominent stars, planets, and constellations where, presumably, a person familiar with the sky would look. Was the location of these events accidental, or by design?

The questions being asked by Professor Rutledge indicate that he was considering the possibility that the phenomenon he observed in the sky was cognizant of his presence and was possibly interacting with him. Already, we have laser systems capable of listening to human conversations at a distance of one mile.[18] Scientists are working on artificial intelligence programs that will read thoughts by measuring electrical activity in the brain.[19] *If* the professor was dealing with an advanced intelligence, would it be too unreasonable to consider the possibility that it could be aware of, and reacting to, his actions and intentions? This potential scenario taints the scientist's expected role of the impartial observer in control of the experiment and places the scientist squarely in the unobjective role of being a participant in the experiment. Professor Rutledge is careful to separate what he can prove versus his opinion. Professor Harley Rutledge states near the end of his book:

> In my opinion, the dynamic behavior of the lights and craft we observed indicates an advanced technology rather than an abrogation of the laws of physics. Perhaps modification or extenuation of some physical laws will be necessary. But I am concerned with the number of bizarre reports from sane, respectable persons, like that from a Bloomfield farmer. One day, out looking for his cows in a field, he suddenly encountered a landed disc. When he stepped back two paces, the disc was invisible; he could see trees beyond, in line with the disc's position. Two steps forward, and the disc was visible again. One doesn't need much imagination to think of the possibilities of such technology. In cases like these, it would be difficult for me to accept the objects as a creation of man.

The thoughts of a scientist who spent seven years actively studying the phenomenon are worthy of consideration.

This chapter began by discussing the strangeness that pervades many of the UFO reports that have been made over the decades. How do we find acceptable explanations for disks that sometimes fall through the sky like a falling leaf or tumble through the atmosphere as if resistance from air molecules made no difference? What do we make of possible witness interactions with the phenomenon; is it a figment of their imagination or is it real? Our view of the improbability of any advanced intelligence finding us first is met with the age-old phrase, "When pigs fly." Or perhaps we should change that phrase to, "When barbells fly."

These strange characteristics are not the only ones that have been displayed by the UFO phenomenon. There are other, more quantifiable parameters that lead us to entertain the possibility of an advanced unknown intelligence operating in our vicinity. We've heard the stories of UFOs that make sudden ninety-degree turns and can stop on a dime. Such reports suggest acceleration forces that we are incapable of producing. Other reports of automobile engine failures indicate an electromagnetic component to the phenomenon. The technology to stop an electrical device is available today. What we don't have is the ability to stop some electrical devices and not others. These unusual characteristics and others will be discussed in the upcoming chapters. Hopefully, these next chapters will stimulate your thoughts and curiosity. We should listen to the words of Dr. Harley Rutledge: "Although I had always maintained a skeptical attitude about the existence of UFOs, the hallmark of all scientists is their curiosity."

Chapter Four

Extreme Acceleration

Extreme acceleration has been the hallmark of UFOs since the beginning of the modern phenomenon that began in the Second World War. Witnesses have reported objects that: made sudden turns without slowing down; moved at high speed before making abrupt stops within a split second; and stationary objects that suddenly accelerated such that they disappeared from sight within the blink of an eye. These are not characteristics of any man-made aircraft whether in the 1940s or in the twenty-first century. Today we can generate high accelerations with missiles, artillery shells, and magnetic rail guns, but these cannot make sudden turns and they cannot come to a controlled stop. These are also not the characteristics of any natural phenomenon. Meteors can move at extremely high speeds, but they cannot accelerate. There is no natural phenomenon that can mimic the stop/start actions of UFOs. The accelerations of UFOs reported by witnesses is more akin to the movement of a laser pointer on a wall. UFOs some-times zip up and down and side to side as if there was no mass associated with its movement. This is something Hynek would have called a "strangeness quality."

UNDERSTANDING ACCELERATION

Acceleration is usually measured in units called g-forces. One "g" of force is equivalent to the pull of Earth's gravity. You are experiencing one g-force on your body as you sit in your chair reading this book. If you felt two g-forces on your body, then your weight would feel twice its normal amount; if you weigh 200 pounds, now you feel like 400 pounds. You would be uncomfort-able. A roller coaster may allow you to experience four to five g-forces for a brief moment. If you sustain that level of g-forces for several seconds, then you are likely to black out. A trained military pilot wearing a special suit that keeps the blood flowing to his brain and extremities can withstand eight to ten g-forces for several seconds before passing out. Increase the g-forces further and the wings of his jet will rip away somewhere between thirteen to twenty g-forces, while the pilot would be long dead. These types of high acceleration can be achieved by sudden starts or stops (linear acceleration) or sudden changes in direction (angular acceleration) or a combination of both. The g-forces provided by either method are the same.

How many g-forces do UFOs produce as they stop, start, and make sudden turns? And remember, a sudden stop creates g-forces just as a sudden acceleration. The g-forces you experience if your car traveling at 60 miles per hour (mph) crashes and comes to a stop in half a second are the same g-forces experienced if your car increased its speed from 0 to 60 in half a second. Accelerations produced by UFOs have been measured in a number of ways: sometimes based on radar data and sometimes by how long it takes for the UFO to disappear from eyesight. Calculations based on these methods have resulted in acceleration values of hundreds to thousands of g-forces.

How long does it take a jet to disappear from sight on a clear day with an unobstructed view? It's important to have a grasp of this. If someone tells you that a UFO zipped off and was gone in only a second, you should realize the implications of such a statement. Let's use an F-16 as an example. It is 50 feet long, with a wingspan of 32 feet, and a height of 16 feet. It can accelerate from 200 mph to 750 mph (Mach 1; the speed of sound) in seventeen seconds, generating 1.5 g-forces. You're at an airshow and an F-16 is directly overhead at a height of 10,000 feet and moving at 200 mph when it begins to accelerate to a speed of 750 mph. How long will it take to disappear from your sight? Assuming you have slightly below average eyesight, forty-two seconds will pass before the F-16 reaches a distance of about 8.5 miles or 45,000 feet and disappears. If it can reach Mach 2, then it will fade to a dot and disappear in twenty-five seconds. Imagine the acceleration and speed for an object to disappear in one, two, or three seconds.

Acceleration forces of this magnitude and the ability to stop, start, and change direction indicate that there is a controlling intelligence. Furthermore, whatever intelligence is controlling these objects is far ahead of us in terms of aerospace capabilities. We still depend on Newton's Third Law for our aerospace capabilities: for every action in nature there is an equal and opposite reaction. This is why our jets and spacecraft have exhausts and why our helicopters push air in order to move. But UFOs have no exhaust, no visible means of propulsion, nor any wings, and often there are indications that they don't interact with the atmosphere. The qualities they exhibit support this last contention: a lack of sound, no air movement, no heating of the UFOs outside surface, and no sonic boom when breaking the sound barrier. There is no natural explanation; this indicates a controlling intelligence.

It is difficult for many people to consider the possibility that UFOs are intelligently controlled. If these objects exhibit controlled, high accelerations, then intelligence is implied. Think of the reasons why examples of high UFO acceleration are not valid, if you have difficulty considering the possibility of intelligent control. If there were only a few cases where high acceleration was witnessed, then it's easier to ignore the reports; but there are hundreds of reports that indicate high acceleration.

HINTS OF HIGH ACCELERATION

This chapter will concentrate on UFO reports with sufficient detail and data to provide the best opportunity to calculate an object's acceleration. But there are many other reports that describe sudden movement changes that would imply very high acceleration forces. These sightings began in the 1940s for those who think that these incidents can be explained by modern hypersonic missiles. So before looking at stronger reports in depth, let's examine less detailed reports to get a feel for what is being seen.

November 22, 1944; Trondheim, Norway. RAF 9 Squadron was returning from a mission against targets in Norway. They described the movements of a shiny pink spherical object that was flying behind their bomber: "The object was changing speeds violently, accelerating and decelerating with swift and jerking movements."[1]

March 1945; Santa Rosa highway, New Mexico. An Air Force sergeant and another man spot a grayish and metallic-appearing object shaped like an upside-down canoe. It is motionless and about fourteen feet above the ground. The sergeant's friend described its sudden movement: "It suddenly swept away—like a dragonfly over water—no turning. . . . All too fast—out of sight in seconds."[2]

April 1, 1948; Luzon, Philippines. An Air Force pilot flying a P-47 sighted an unidentified object flying at about 1,000 feet below him and at about 200 mph. He described the object as having a turtle-like back, a dorsal fin, and a half-moon shape. The pilot turned his plane to get closer to the other craft in order to identify it. The unknown object made a ninety-degree turn to the left and accelerated. It disappeared from view in five seconds.[3]

May 31, 1952; Chorwon, South Korea. A U.S. F-94 military jet as well as guards on the ground sighted a disk-shaped object that was engaged by the F-94. As the jet dived to meet the disk, the disk moved upward toward the F-94. It was a game of cat and mouse and, as the pilot testified, the object had superior speed, maneuverability, and climbing ability than his F-94. The guard on the ground who witnessed this engagement stated that the disk moved in jerky motions and turned seemingly instantaneously. The guard described the disk's climbing ability and departure: "From the time from when it first started climbing until it disappeared, took approximately three to four seconds."[4]

November 14, 1956; Jackson, Alabama. A pilot and his co-pilot witnessed a UFO while flying at 25,000 feet over central Alabama. This incident is listed in the Condon Report. His description follows: "darting hither and yon, rising and falling in undulating flight, making sharper turns than any known aircraft, sometimes changing direction 90° in an instant." The pilot described how the object disappeared, "shot out over the Gulf of Mexico, rising at the most breath-taking angle and at such a fantastic speed that it diminished rapidly to a pinpoint and was swallowed up in the night."[5]

May 18, 1962; Pompano Beach, Florida. Mrs. Elizabeth Scott saw a hovering, cigar-shaped UFO. The object remained motionless for about nine minutes before it began to move. When it accelerated, it moved "like a flash of lightning," she said.[6]

October 11, 1964; Brockton, Massachusetts. David Hanson, an engineer, was with two friends when they heard two sonic booms. They looked up and saw two jet fighters. A whitish, dome-shaped object was behind the two jets. The object descended slowly and leveled off onto a horizontal path. Suddenly, it accelerated straight up and out of sight in seconds.[7]

September 3, 1965; Damon, Texas. A sheriff and his chief deputy were driving their patrol car at about 11 p.m. when they saw a bright, purple light several miles away. They pulled their patrol car off the road and viewed the light through binoculars. Suddenly the light began moving toward them at a rapid speed. Within seconds there was a huge object in front of them and only 150 feet away. It was the size of a four-story warehouse and it just hovered in the air.[8]

October 25, 1973; Northwest Cape, Australia. A U.S. Navy captain stood for several minutes watching a black sphere hovering in the sky. The sky was clear and pale green-blue. The object was completely stationary except for a halo around the center, which appeared to be either revolving or pulsating. It was about thirty feet in diameter and hovering at about 1,000 feet. After watching it for about four minutes, it suddenly took off at tremendous speed and disappeared in a northerly direction in a few seconds.[9]

May 17, 1977; Memphis, Tennessee. Multiple policemen in the Memphis area described a triangular object seen in their metropolitan area. One of the policemen gave a statement on the triangle's high rate of speed: "it sped away at a tremendous rate of speed and just disappeared over the horizon in just a second to a second and a half."[10]

July 21, 1977; Porter, Texas. Officer John W. Bruner, a deputy sheriff, was on duty and was the first person to observe the phenomenon. Officer

Bruner and his partner Officer Coogler were parked west of the object, which appeared to be approximately one half to one mile away. The two officers observed the UFO for approximately forty-five minutes. During that time period, the UFO appeared to stand still in midair, pulsated, traveled at incredible speeds, and flew with erratic mobility.[11]

February 9, 1981; San Jose, California. Gary Rounds and Charles Shackleford were flying a Cessna 150, making touch-and-go landings at the airport. As they were climbing away from the runway on one of the passes at about 500 feet (150 meters), they saw ahead and above them a bright, round red light, which they changed course to avoid. At one point, the object approached head-on, then instantly appeared behind their plane. Air traffic controllers Randy Blount and Rich Gutterud observed the performance from the tower and saw the object make "very tight turns." The object hovered, then accelerated away at an "extremely high rate of speed."[12]

June 10, 1982; Madbury, New Hampshire. Three witnesses saw a wedge-shaped UFO with bright white lights and smaller blue-green-red body lights hovering about fifty feet over a reservoir, its lights reflecting off the water surface. They tried to drive to a better viewing location, but the object suddenly moved away. It seemed to move from one location to another almost instantly.[13]

July 3, 1988; Montgomery, Ohio. A police officer describes the extreme rate of acceleration that was displayed by a barbell-shaped UFO that he saw: "And when it moves, I mean it's really going. And it stops and hovers and it zig-zags a couple of times and then it went up and down. It's like if you blink, you'll miss how fast it takes it to get there."[14]

March 21, 1990; east of Moscow, Russia. Gen. Igor Maltsev, the Russian Air Defense Forces commander, summarizes the UFO acceleration viewed by Russian witnesses. Notice the similarity to reports of UFOs from around the world.

> I am not a specialist in UFOs, and therefore I can only link the data together and express my own hypothesis. Based on the data collected by these witnesses, the UFO was a disk 100 to 200 meters in diameter. Two lights were flashing on its sides. In addition, the object turned around its axis and performed an S-shaped maneuver in both the vertical and the horizontal planes. Next the UFO continued to hover above the ground, then flew at a speed two to three times greater than that of modern combat aircraft. The objects flew at altitudes ranging from 100 to 7000 meters. The movement of the UFOs was not accompanied by any type of noise and was characterized by an astounding maneuverability. The UFOs appeared to completely lack inertia.[15]

1993; Stuttgart, Germany. Capt. Paul Coomber had an amazing encounter piloting a flight over Germany. He described three white spherical objects that he encountered: "All three were stationary for a few seconds, then they all disappeared with great acceleration in different directions. It was such great acceleration that I doubt whether any human could have stood it."[16]

October 1996; South Yorkshire, England. A police officer reported seeing a triangular UFO with a dull matte black color and three red beacons twirling at each corner of the triangle. The object hovered directly over his vehicle and shone a bright blue beam that illuminated his patrol car for a few minutes. The beam ceased and the object took off at a terrific speed and executed several incredible maneuvers, including instantly going into reverse, before disappearing over the horizon.[17]

January 30, 2007; Bastrop, Texas. Brian Tietje was driving from Bastrop to Austin, Texas, when he noticed a small object in the sky about thirty degrees to the left of his direction of travel. It was just above the treetops. Within a second, the object was suddenly 200–300 feet from his car. It was shaped like a bullet and about the size of a car. Its altitude was less than 100 feet, and it remained stationary for about one second. Then, a hinge or flap on the back of the object dropped down and the object headed north at an extremely high rate of speed. It was gone from sight within about a second.[18]

March 25, 2012; Cleburne, Texas. A triangular-shaped object was sighted by two correctional officers at the Johnson County Correctional Facility in Cleburne, Texas. The dark object with white lights around its perimeter made no sound as it moved very slowly in the sky. The officer described it as "slipping through the sky." He said it appeared to jerk as it moved like it was jumping from one location to another as it sped up. When it sped up, it was gone in a second. The officer said he was looking directly at it at the time it accelerated.[19]

June 4, 2015; Marengo, Iowa. Two friends pulled their car into the gas station to observe a triangular object that was directly south of their position and extremely close and low to the ground. Measurements taken at the site by investigators suggested that the object was only 278 feet in land distance and 288 feet above the ground. The two witnesses watched the object for a moment or two and then, "in a blink of an eye," the object traveled about four miles east in a straight-line path and hovered once again. A moment later it vanished from view.[20]

There are hundreds of UFO reports from over the last seventy-five years that indicate these objects have the capability to almost instantly accelerate. You have just read many examples that have occurred from the beginning of modern UFO reports in the 1940s to reports from the last decade. Most of these reports cannot be used to calculate a reasonable approximation of the object's acceleration. The reports lack enough detail from the witnesses on time and distance or they lack supporting data such as radar or video. Nonetheless, one must begin to consider the possibility that these reports of extreme acceleration may be real when they're reported from all over the world and for eighty years. Fortunately, there are UFO reports with sufficient information that accelerations can be approximated.

CALCULATING ACCELERATION

What is meant by acceleration? It is the rate of change of velocity with time. If your velocity changes in a positive direction, then the rate of change is referred to as acceleration; if velocity changes in a negative direction, then the rate of change is referred to as deceleration. Another way to think of it is that acceleration involves an increase in speed while deceleration involves a decrease in speed. But remember, a car traveling at 60 mph that crashes and comes to a stop in half a second is the same g-forces experienced if your car increased its speed from 0 to 60 mph in half a second.

Linear acceleration will be the way accelerations are calculated in this chapter. It is the measure of a change in velocity without any change in direction. Angular acceleration measures the directional change of an object's velocity, such as a sudden ninety-degree change in direction. Angular acceleration is a more complicated calculation and will not be used for two reasons. First, it requires that a witness reliably estimate the change in angular movement of an object in the sky over time. Did the object make an actual ninety-degree change in direction, or was it gradual and over what time period? Linear acceleration is much more straightforward. The witness needs to provide sufficient information to know the object's approximate distance, its apparent size in the sky, and the length of time it took to disappear. Secondly, angular acceleration isn't needed because there are plenty of examples where linear acceleration can be calculated.

The formula for linear acceleration is straightforward. It is the change in velocity (dv) divided by the change in time (dt), which can be expressed as, $a = dv / dt$. The change in time can be as simple as how many seconds the witness thought it took for an object to disappear from sight. It's important that there is confidence in the witness's measurement of time and that there is an estimate of the possible variation in a witness's estimate of time. If a fighter pilot tells you that an object disappeared in two seconds, then you might calculate based on the actual time being anywhere from one second to three seconds. If the witness is less experienced, then it would be prudent to use a value from one to five seconds. The change in velocity is a little more complicated to determine. It requires that you know the distance to an object. You can determine the distance to an object in the sky if you know its size and its angular size (apparent size in the sky). This involves trigonometry and will be discussed in specific cases as needed. But for those readers who enjoy the math, the basic formula is, a = 2 * arctan (d / [2 * L]) where a = angular size in degrees, d = actual size, and L = distance. When using this formula, it is important to include variations in the accuracy of a witness's estimate of an object's actual size and its apparent size in the sky.

DETAILED INCIDENTS OF EXTREME ACCELERATION

May 26, 1952; North Korea.   It was during the Korean War that two AF pilots flying an F-94 jet had a very strange UFO encounter. This report comes from Project Blue Book files but with missing pages that might have provided even more information. One of the documents contains sixteen pages and the other has four pages. However, only a total of ten pages are available in the Project Blue Book files. Missing was the information from the ground radar and any interviews with the ground-based radar operators. Nonetheless, there is sufficient information to calculate the g-forces generated by the UFO during its acceleration. The Air Force calculated twenty g-forces of acceleration. The report was approved by Brig. Gen. Charles Y. Banfill, the USAF Deputy for Intelligence. Clearly, this UFO report went up the chain of command.[21]

The event began in the middle of a war zone. It was 3:20 a.m. local time. Ground radar detected an unknown target and requested an F-94 to investigate. The F-94 proceeded to the location provided by ground radar and descended toward the target coordinates. The F-94 was manned by two experienced pilots: one officer as the pilot and the other officer operating the jet's radar. The pilots saw a brilliant object above and in front of them as they descended to 2,500 feet in altitude. They made a pass within 600 feet of the object but due to its brilliance, they could not identify its shape. They made six more close passes with their jet in an attempt to identify the light, but without success. Their aircraft radar could not detect the object despite their being able to visually see the UFO, and the ground radar being able to track the target. After their last pass, the F-94's radar operator turned his head and thought he saw something following them. He mentioned this to the pilot.

It was at this same time that ground radar told the F-94 there was an unknown target on their tail. Whether this was the same object or a new object is not completely clear, although the pilot and his radar operator believed it was a different object. The pilot turned his jet to the right to come around and get behind the target. This time the jet's airborne radar locked on the object, as it was now ahead and above the F-94. The target was 7,000 yards distance, the F-94 was traveling at about 250 knots, and it was closing on the target at a rate of 50 knots. In less than a minute, the F-94 was within 6,000 yards of its target. This is when the target began to accelerate. The object began a

FROM (Agency)	REPORT NO.			
Det 1, 6004th AISS, APO 970	52-85	PAGE 4	OF 4	PAGES

with the F-94 following up to and passing 10,000 foot altitude until lock-on was broken.

f. Size of Object: The radar set was on long range and therefore it was not possible to determine the size of the object. It is possible to get sighting in short range only up to 5000 yards when a comparative size can be obtained from the pip. The object was never closer than 6000 yards and at long range the pip usually remains the same in size except for a slight fading until the lock in broken.

COMMENTS OF REPORTING OFFICER:

From the information obtained it would appear that the two objects might have a relationship to each other, although no size or shape of either one could be obtained. The point of interest is that the bright light was above our present bomb line and the unidentified high speed object was to the rear of our front lines.

VINCENT A. GOSKEY
Captain, USAF
Investigating Officer

D/I FEAF COMMENT:

1. The distance covered by the object is approximately 68,500 feet. Acceleration is 650 ft/sec/sec, (or approximately 20 "G" acceleration, (which is much more than the human body can stand for more than a fraction of a second). The final velocity is found to be 9450 ft/sec, or approximately 5580 knots (6420 mph).

2. The radar sets are checked before and after every mission, and in this case appeared to be working normally. Even if it were assumed that the operator's timing, or the APG-33 calibration were off as much as 50%, the speed is still above any known type of missile.

3. No information has yet been received from the ground controller at Bromide as to the returns plotted or the length of time that object was held in contact by the ground radar.

4. The phenomenal acceleration reported leads to the belief that the APG-33 was not operating correctly at the time of contact, despite checks before and after the mission.

CHARLES Y. BANFILL
Brigadier General, USAF
Deputy for Intelligence

Figure 4.1. Project Blue Book, Air Intelligence Information Report.
Source: USAF, Project Blue Book

shallow climb and in 14 seconds reached a distance of 24,000 to 26,000 yards from the jet, at which time it broke the jet's radar lock.

Let's calculate the object's velocity and acceleration. (I'll go through this step by step in this example but will minimize repeating this process in future examples. So, jump to the end of this paragraph if you want to skip the math.) Once completed, we can compare it to the values reported by the Air Force. Our formula is, a = dv / dt. We first must calculate dv, which is the difference between the initial and final velocity. The initial velocity of the object was about 200 knots, as the F-94 was at about 250 knots while closing in on the UFO at a net value of 50 knots. Let's assume an error of 10 percent in the object's initial velocity. Since one knot is equal to 0.514 meters per second (m/sec), the initial velocity of the UFO was 102.8 m/sec with a variation of 10 percent. The average velocity of the UFO, using potential reporting error, is calculated based on the distance traveled (18K–20K yards) in 13 to 15 seconds. We will convert to m/sec. The average velocity is 1,252 m/sec with a variation of 12.4 percent. Using the average velocity, we can now calculate the object's final velocity as 2,401 m/sec with a variation of 13.4 percent. That is a speed of 5,371 mph! The value of dv is 2,401 m/sec – 102.8 m/sec, or 2,298.2 m/sec with a variation of 14.3 percent. All that's left is for us to calculate dt, which is the change in time. This value was reported as 14 seconds. We know that the radar operator in the jet was tested by the Air Force and his measurement of time was accurate to within 2 seconds when counting to a minute. An error of 1 second in either direction when counting to 14 would be reasonable. So, dt will be between 13 to 15 seconds. The UFO's acceleration is 2,298.2 m/sec divided by 14 seconds. The result is 164 m/sec^2, which is the same as 16.7 g-forces. Once we include variations and possible errors in the values, we are left with a range of 12.8 to 20.6 g-forces.

The calculations demonstrate an object capable of traveling at a speed of 5,371 mph and sustaining 16.7 g-forces. The Air Force estimated a speed of 6,240 mph and approximately 20 g-forces as can be seen in figure 4.1. There was no nation with an aircraft or missile that could begin to approach these speeds and accelerations in 1952.

Do you wonder what the Air Force concluded regarding this event? The conclusion of the Air Force at the bottom of figure 4.1 was, "The phenomenal acceleration reported leads to the belief that the AFG-33 [aircraft radar] was not operating correctly at the time of contact, despite checks before and after the mission." The key word in their explanation is *belief*. It is the Argument from Incredulity—it is too difficult to believe, therefore it cannot be. There is nothing scientific in the Air Force conclusion.

October 24, 1968; Minot AFB, Minot, North Dakota. One of the best documented cases in Project Blue Book is the UFO sighting over Minot Air

Force Base in 1968. Minot AFB was, and still is, a critical part of the U.S. nuclear deterrent with B-52 nuclear bombers as well as control of multiple intercontinental ballistic missiles (ICBMs). Any sighting of an unidentified object over a nuclear facility is taken seriously. Project Blue Book released 107 pages of documents as well as thirteen photos of the radar imagery of the UFO sighted that day, more than enough information to calculate acceleration and velocity. Over a dozen Air Force servicemen on the ground and seven crewmembers of a B-52 witnessed the UFO at various times. In addition to a Blue Book investigation, there was an outstanding civilian investigation.[22] Thomas Tulien and James Klotz interviewed many of the UFO witnesses in person: seven B-52 crewmembers, three servicemen in missile security, two servicemen in missile maintenance, and three of the original Minot Air Force investigators. They have put together several hundred pages of information. This chapter deals primarily with acceleration, so the reader is urged to read more on their own about this interesting case that includes a drawing by one of the B-52 crewmen of the UFO on the ground, statements from witnesses, reactions by the Air Force, and more.[23]

The incident began at 2:15 a.m. on October 24. A two-person security team reported an unusual glowing object go down behind some trees near a nuclear missile silo. Two missile maintenance men reported an unusual light shortly afterward. More reports from more security teams began to pour into headquarters.

The base's weather radar detected a UFO at 3:52 a.m. and three miles from an approaching B-52. Radar Approach Control (RAPCON) alerted the plane to the unknown object on radar. The B-52's radar operator also detected the unknown object on their aircraft radar at three miles. In the next sweep of the radar, less than three seconds, the unknown object had moved within a mile of the B-52 and had come to a complete stop. At the same instant as the unknown object's abrupt movement on radar, the B-52's two UHF radios ceased transmission on all frequencies with the control tower. The B-52's radar operator turned on the plane's radar recording system, which took an image of each three-second sweep of the radar. They obtained fourteen radar scope photographs.

Let's begin with the easiest calculation: the movement as stated by the radar operator, "two miles in one 3-second sweep of the radar and coming to a complete stop." We can't know the exact time that it took the object to move two miles because it had already moved and come to a stop before the radar system had time to even make a single sweep. It could have traversed that distance in two seconds, one second, or even less. We will err on the conservative side and assume it took a full three seconds. The average velocity required to cover two miles in three seconds is 2,400 mph. But that is an "average" velocity. The initial velocity was zero because the object was stationary. The object must reach a velocity of 4,800 mph (2145 m/sec) in 1.5 seconds and then slow back down to zero in the next 1.5 seconds to have an average velocity of 2,400 mph. The acceleration reached during such a maneuver would be equal to dv / dt, or (2145 m/sec – 0) / (1.5 sec – 0). There is a minimum acceleration of 1,430 m/sec^2 or 146 g-forces. There was no aircraft in 1968 and nothing today that can create or withstand those types of g-forces. What did the radar scope photographs indicate for velocity and acceleration?

This incident and the radar photographs were studied by French astrophysicist Dr. Claude Poher. His credentials are well established. He worked for the French Space Program, the National Center for Space Studies (CNES), and became the director of the CNES Rockets-Probes division. Claude Poher received the French National Order of Merit, the CNES medal, and the Astronautic Prize from the Aeronautical and Astronautical Association of France in 1974. He is well qualified to study the incident at Minot AFB, and he completed a 174-page report on the event along with a mathematical analysis of the radar photographs.[24] An example of one of the radar photographs is shown in figure 4.2.

The range of velocities and accelerations of the UFO as detected by radar vary considerably. Much of this information is discussed on pages 71 to 75 of Dr. Poher's paper. The velocity of the object varied from stationary to 12,716 mph. There were four times when the object exhibited rapid changes in movement from radar track to radar track. Those four documented instances result in acceleration values of 18, 48, 60, and 449 g-forces. Those are in the same range as the 146 g-forces that I calculated based on the radar operator's recollection of the object's movement when first encountered prior to turning on the radar recording system. It is noteworthy that Dr. Poher states on page 74 of his report that, "All of these accelerations are compatible with the performances necessary for an interstellar voyage."

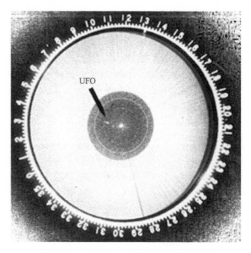

Figure 4.2.   Radar image, October 24, 1968, Minot AFB. *Source*: USAF, Project Blue Book

There is an additional bit of interesting information on page 40 of Dr. Poher's analysis of the radar images. The UFO's size was 200 x 50 meters: twice the length of a football field.

July 1975; Gulf of Mexico, south of Panama City, Florida. There are two witnesses involved in this story. They're brothers. One is an electrical engineer who served in the U.S. Coast Guard; the other has a master's degree in industrial design and served in the U.S. Army. The key to determining the approximate acceleration of the two UFOs observed in this case is whether you believe that these two witnesses can reliably state that an object disappeared from sight in one to two seconds. If these were the only witnesses to have made such a claim, then it would be easier to dismiss their claim. The study of the history of UFOs finds these types of claims over and over and over.[25]

The two men were eighteen miles south–southwest of Panama City, Florida, and were fishing from a small boat. It was a clear, cloudless, and hot summer day. Their boat was anchored at about a twenty-five-foot depth and approximately 200 feet from a U.S. Navy undersea research platform. The platform was a military, gray-painted square, flat-roofed building, maybe 100 x 100 feet, and elevated about 75–100 feet above the ocean on pilings or columns. They knew the pilings would attract fish.

Just after 1 p.m. they spotted in the distance two metallic craft approaching slowly from the south-southwest and heading directly toward the platform. Both brothers were very familiar with commercial and military aircraft and as the objects got closer, they knew these were not any aircraft they had ever seen before. The craft stopped and hovered about 200 feet above and next to the platform, and were about the length of a Boeing 727, or near 150 feet in length. "Hovered" doesn't seem like the right word, as the craft seemed to be planted in the air without the slightest sound or movement. The objects were circular when seen from below and elliptical or cigar-shaped when viewed from the side—the classical "flying saucer," with no bubble on its top or bottom. What initially stood out were two things: their utterly smooth metallic surface tones—matte silver on the top of the horizontal center line and matte purplish on the bottom. There were no markings, seams, rivets, portals, or anything of the sort. And secondly, how effortlessly they moved with no sign of propulsion. The two brothers described how the objects departed as "a few minutes later, both crafts suddenly shot upwards at a 45-degree angle and at an astounding speed." One brother described it as like "a bullet fired from a gun" and that the two disks disappeared to dot size in one to two seconds. The other brother described the disk departing "in the blink of an eye."

Let's calculate the acceleration of these disks using, a = dv / dt. We need the initial velocity, the final velocity, and the change in time. We know the initial velocity is zero since the disks were hovering above the Navy platform.

The change in time will be the time at which the disks first began moving until they disappeared from sight. We have two witnesses with slightly different descriptions of when the disks disappeared from sight. We have "dot size in one to two seconds" and "in the blink of an eye." The latter description is somewhat vague, but it wouldn't be unreasonable to assume that zero to two seconds would be the range for someone to state "in the blink of an eye." The first description is more specific, and we can be safe in saying that if the object became dot size in one to two seconds, then another second would place it out of sight—so we could be confident with two to three seconds for it to completely disappear. Using the statements from both witnesses, we can use a target value of two seconds with an error of plus or minus one second for the amount of time that it took the two disks to disappear from sight. The last variable left is that we need to know the final velocity of the object when it disappears from sight. This is more complicated, but it can be done.

First, we need to know the limits of human vision. How small must an object in the sky become to disappear from sight? It depends on your eyesight. If you have 20/20 eyesight, then you can see an object in the sky as small as one arc minute; 20/40 eyesight can only see down to two arc minutes; and 20/80 eyesight is four arc minutes.[26] We will use the worst case of 20/80 eyesight or four arc minutes for the smallest object they could see in the sky.

Second, we need to know the size of the disks. The witnesses stated the disks were about 150 feet across. They used the reference of the 100-foot Navy platform that the disks were hovering above. We need to consider witness judgment error in our calculations, so we will use a size of 125 to 175 feet.

Now we can calculate the distance the disks traveled before disappearing. We have the size of the object and the angular size at which it would disappear, so using trigonometry, $d = s/(2*\tan(\alpha/2))$. The distance that the disks would have needed to travel to disappear from sight would be 128,270 feet, or 24.3 miles with a range of 28.3 miles to 20.2 miles.

We can now calculate the disks' average velocity since we know the distance and the time it took. Using two seconds as the travel time to disappear from sight in 24.3 miles, we get an average velocity of 43,740 mph. That's comparable to the speed of a meteor traveling through the atmosphere. Even if we use our minimum distance of 20.2 miles and a maximum time of three seconds, we are still left with an average velocity of 24,240 mph. The final velocity at the time the object disappeared, assuming a linear increase in velocity, is 48,480 mph, or 21,672 m/sec.

The two disks accelerated at, $a = dv / dt$, or 7224 m/sec^2. This equates to 736 g-forces. This was a conservative calculation. We assumed poor eyesight for the witnesses and that the disks were smaller than they had thought. The only way to ignore these high g-forces is either not to believe the witnesses or to assume that the object was only forty feet in size and took fifteen seconds to disappear from sight.

It is worth pausing for a moment before examining additional high acceleration UFO cases. Consider some important characteristics that are occurring in these UFO reports of high acceleration:

1. There is no obvious method of propulsion such as wings, rotors, or rocket exhaust.
2. There is no air displacement that would be expected with an object moving through the air at high speed.
3. There is a lack of sound.
4. There is no friction with the atmosphere. A meteor traveling at 25,000 mph burns up in our upper atmosphere, yet UFOs are traveling at these speeds in our lower atmosphere without any obvious heat generation due to friction.
5. There is what appears to be the ability to initiate an almost instantaneous change in direction at high speed.

All the above characteristics suggest that the UFO is not interacting with the atmosphere, or, if it does, then there is some new technology at play that minimizes atmospheric interaction.

November 14, 2004; eighty miles SW of San Diego, California. The incident with unknowns involving a U.S. carrier strike group is perhaps one of the best documented incidents in recent UFO history. It involved dozens of witnesses, radar tracks, and video. This event resulted in three incidents where acceleration values could be calculated for the unknown objects.

U.S. Carrier Strike Group Eleven, led by the USS *Nimitz*, was conducting training exercises off the southwest coast of California prior to deployment to the Middle East. The strike group consisted of the USS *Nimitz*, a nuclear-powered aircraft carrier; the USS *Princeton*, a missile cruiser; two destroyers; a nuclear attack submarine; dozens of F/A-18F "Super Hornets"; early warning aircraft; and several support ships. The USS *Princeton* provided the air defense protection for the strike group. It had the world's best radar, and it was the unit that would direct aircraft to a target.

Unusual targets had been showing up on the *Princeton* radar system for several days: objects at over 80,000 feet and moving at a very slow 100 mph. The radar operators checked the radar systems for the possibility of false returns. They recalibrated systems, checked with other vessels, and found no indication of errors. The flight paths of the objects changed on November 14. The anomalous aerial vehicles (AAVs), originally at 80,000+ feet, were observed to descend in as little as 0.78 seconds to various altitudes from 28,000 feet to as low as just 50 feet or less above the ocean surface. (This is the first incident of high acceleration.) The USS *Nimitz* also detected the unknown objects as did an E-2 Hawkeye airborne early warning aircraft. The unknown objects were now a safety hazard for the F/A-18s operating in the area. In only a few hours an air defense exercise was scheduled to commence which would involve the launch of as many as thirty aircraft from the USS *Nimitz* as well as from Marine Corps Air Station Miramar in San Diego. The captain of the USS *Princeton* came down to the Combat Information Center (CIC) and was briefed on the radar contacts. He authorized the interception of the closest target on radar.[27]

The closest unknown was sixty miles due west of the USS *Nimitz*. Two F/A-18F jets, each with a pilot and weapons officer, were directed to the coordinates of the object on radar at 20,000 feet. There was clearly no error with the radar, as the pilots encountered the UFO at the radar coordinates.

Piloting the lead F/A-18 was the commander of the squadron, David Fravor, and Lt. Appezzato. In the second plane's backseat was the lieutenant commander (LCDR) of the squadron, James Slaight, with Lt. Alex Dietrich as the pilot. Both Fravor and Slaight were graduates of the U.S. Naval Academy. All four pilots saw what Commander (CDR) Fravor described as a white "Tic-Tac"–shaped object, with perhaps two small appendages hanging below its belly, moving just above the water. The object had no wings or exhaust, and its movement had no observable effect on the calm ocean surface such as that of a rotor wash from a helicopter. CDR Fravor estimated the object to be fifty feet above the water, and he described its movement as follows: "It's almost like a ping pong ball. So, when it goes right it can stop instantly, and it goes back left, it goes straight forward, it is randomly moving around, very erratic." CDR Fravor decided to descend toward the object to investigate.

CDR Fravor dropped his plane from 20,000 feet to 12,000 feet. Lt. Dietrich and LCDR Slaight remained at 20,000 feet to observe both Fravor's aircraft and the "Tic-Tac" during the engagement. Fravor continued to drop toward the object, when he saw it turn one of its ends toward him. The "Tic-Tac" began to ascend toward Fravor's aircraft. The two craft began a pirouette toward each other. Fravor's jet was on one side of a circle as he moved downward, and the "Tic-Tac" moved upward on the other side of the circle. The two were less than a mile apart. Fravor commented about the object, "It's about the size of an F-18. So, you know, 47 feet long. But it has no wings." CDR Fravor decided to cut diagonally across the circle to intercept the "Tic-Tac." The next movement of the object surprised Fravor.

CDR Fravor described the object's reaction to his attempt to intercept it. "It starts to accelerate. It has an incredible rate of acceleration. And it takes off like nothing I've ever seen. It literally is one minute it's there and the next

minute it's like, poof, and it's gone." Fravor tried to put the object's acceleration in perspective. He described how even a jet at Mach 3 can be seen for
at least ten to fifteen seconds before it fades from sight, but the "Tic-Tac" in
CDR Fravor's own words, "This thing disappeared in a second; it was just
gone." (This is the second incident of high acceleration. It is therefore important to provide the observations of LCDR Slaight at 20,000 feet.)

LCDR Jim Slaight described the object that CDR Fravor engaged. He also
recounted that the object resembled a giant "Tic-Tac," 40 to 50 feet long, 10
to 15 feet wide, off-white in color, no audible noise or sound, no markings,
fins, vents, or exhaust type of ports. As CDR Fravor headed down toward the
"Tic-Tac," LCDR Slaight observed that the object had now started on a direct
path toward Fravor's jet. Slaight's description of the object's ability to suddenly accelerate was like CDR Fravor's. In Slaight's own words:

> It was there . . . then it rifled off, out of sight in a split second. It was as if the
> object was shot out of a rifle. There was no gradual acceleration or spooling up
> period, it just shot out of sight immediately. I have never seen anything like it
> before or since. No human could have withstood that kind of acceleration.

The two F/A-18s returned to the USS *Nimitz* after the "Tic-Tac" had departed.

Upon arriving at the *Nimitz*, CDR Fravor made a request for the next flight
of F/A-18s from his squadron that departed. He asked that they use their IR
camera to record the object if they were able to find it. Lt. Underwood was
successful in obtaining a video of the object. The video shows the object
breaking lock as it suddenly moves to the left of the screen and disappears.
Three still frames that show the object's movement from left to right are
shown in figure 4.3. (This is the third and final incident of high acceleration.)

The first instance where acceleration can be calculated is based on the
testimony of the senior chief in charge of radar who indicated the object descended from 80,000+ feet to 20,000 feet or less in 0.78 and the firecontrol
petty officer who said it descended "as fast as a thought." If we take them at
their word, then the velocity and acceleration of the object would be 104,895
mph and 12,250 g-forces, respectively. But let's assume that it took much

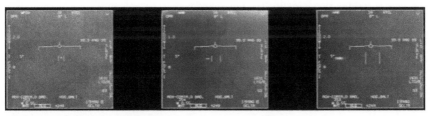

Figure 4.3.   IR video of unknown near the USS *Nimitz* carrier strike group.
Source: Department of Defense

longer, say six seconds. Even then the velocity and acceleration would be 13,636 mph and 207 g-forces. Any reasonable assumptions regarding errors in the testimony still leave us with extreme velocity and acceleration values. One would expect to see a fireball due to air friction at those speeds, and no aircraft would remain structurally intact with such large g-forces.

The second instance of high acceleration involves the testimony of the Navy pilots that the object disappeared from sight in one to two seconds. There are four experienced Navy pilots in two separate jets who viewed the object from separate altitudes and angles. During the engagement with the "Tic-Tac," it accelerated from stationary to "out of sight" within one second according to one pilot, and "like a bullet shot from a rifle" according to the other pilot. Both the CDR and the LCDR estimated the length of the "Tic-Tac" to be 40–60 feet along its major axis, and about 15 feet along its minor axis.

The limit of a human's visual acuity is one arc minute and can be used to calculate a distance at which an object is no longer resolvable. A 60-foot diameter object will reach the limit of human perception at 39.1 miles. Using a time to disappearance of one second results in a peak velocity of 281,520 mph and a maximum constant acceleration equivalent to 12,823 g-forces. Let's use a worst-case situation. Take 15 feet as the lower bounds of the object's size and the limit of human perception drops to 9.8 miles. Instead of one second, let's use two seconds. This results in a velocity of 35,280 mph and a minimum constant acceleration equivalent to 803 g-forces. The resulting velocity and acceleration derived from the pilots' testimony is consistent with that derived from the ship-board radar operators' reports.

The third and final instance of high acceleration is in the information provided by the video. It is the least extreme of the three methods, with an acceleration of 41 to 81 g-forces. This is still well beyond the capabilities of any known aircraft. For example, the F-35 aircraft breaks apart at around 13–15 g-forces. The calculations involved in the analysis of the IR video are intense, but they are detailed on pages 196 to 225 of the report referenced for this event.[28]

How do we explain these extreme accelerations that have been reported for the last seventy years? We can find a way to dismiss each case individually with an explanation that is often as nonsensical as the high accelerations; or we can consider the possibility that what has been reported is a reasonable approximation of the truth. If we consider the latter, then we need to look at possible explanations based on what we know of science. Let's do that for a moment and look at the implications.

One of the first implications is that we're dealing with an object that is intelligently controlled because of its ability to accelerate, decelerate, and change directions. High accelerations can occur in nature. They are normally generated by uncontrolled actions such as: the extreme deceleration of a meteor as it impacts the Earth, rocks hurled outward at a high acceleration due to a volcanic eruption, matter launched outwards during a nova, and so on. But none of these are controlled movements; there is no sudden change of direction without an impact or explosion. The types of acceleration exhibited by UFOs are more nuanced. They are similar to the type of acceleration that we can create with our own technologies—they appear to be intelligently controlled.

The second implication is that the intelligence controlling UFOs has developed a technology that we don't possess. As discussed previously, the objects' extreme velocities and accelerations are accompanied by a lack of any obvious interaction with the atmosphere. Is there an explanation that fits the facts that we have at hand: high velocities, extreme acceleration, little to no atmospheric interaction, and a craft that can survive the experience? If we're dealing with a technology that is hundreds of years advanced of us, then imagine Isaac Newton trying to explain the operation of a cell phone—that's the likelihood that we can answer that question. But let's give it a try.

One possibility is a technology that can lower the inertial mass of an object so that it is near zero. Inertial mass is the mass of a body as determined by its momentum rather than its gravitational mass. As far as we know, an object's inertial mass is always the same as its gravitational mass. No one has established that the inertial mass of an object can be changed, other than an unproven Navy patent filed by Dr. Salvatore Pais.[29] But imagine if it was possible to lower a spacecraft's inertial mass to near zero; this could explain many of the characteristics of UFOs. If the mass of an aircraft was near zero, then there would be no interaction between the air molecules and the surface of the aircraft, no frictional heating, no sonic boom, no air movement, and no sound. High, velocities would be simple as you would not be powering a ten-ton aircraft because it could weigh as little as a picogram. The aircraft's survival of high g-forces, or an occupant, would not be a problem because the mass of the aircraft is minimal. Reduced inertial mass is a possible explanation—but whether it is possible is another question.

A second possibility is technology that allows the craft to warp spacetime. This is done by warping space with an extremely strong gravitational field. This is theoretically possible but would require enormous amounts of energy. There is even a NASA paper on the general concept.[30] An aircraft or spacecraft would move by "falling" toward the gravitational field that is created in front of the craft. The extreme acceleration created would not affect the craft because it would be in freefall. When you free-fall from a plane, Earth's one g-force is no longer acting on your body; the same would be true if you were falling into a gravitational field 100 times that of Earth. Someone on Earth would see the craft accelerating at 100 g-forces but there would be no g-forces exerted on the craft. The craft's velocity would be very high as it continued to accelerate in the artificial gravitational field. How the craft would avoid interacting with the atmosphere is not known nor is how that artificial gravitational field would avoid causing all sorts of disruptions to the Earth.

The last and most likely possibility is one that we have not yet imagined. The same problem that Sir Isaac Newton would have had with explaining the cell phone.

Chapter Five

Electromagnetic Interference

Close Encounters of the Third Kind is an iconic American science fiction film written and directed by Steven Spielberg in 1977. Richard Dreyfuss is an electrical technician who encounters a UFO while on call for a widespread electrical power outage. He stops his car near a railroad track to look at a map and then everything begins to go wrong as a UFO pulls up behind him. His truck flashlight goes out and his truck loses power as its light, engine, and radio go out. Once the UFO leaves, the flashlight comes back on, and the truck inexplicably starts back up. Spielberg didn't need to use his imagination to create this scene in the movie. He used the types of events that had sometimes been reported when people encountered UFOs. This movie was based on the lore from the previous three decades.

Electromagnetic interference (EMI) is the scientific term used to describe the events experienced by Richard Dreyfuss in the movie. It is normally caused by an outside electromagnetic (EM) source that impedes the normal operation of an electrical circuit. EMI can occur when you're in the presence of strong electrical or magnetic fields that induce an electrical current into your phone, camera, car, or any other electrical device that you're operating. This is the same reason you may get momentary static on your phone or radio when driving beneath a high voltage transmission line. EMI can also occur when an EM signal that you're trying to receive is overwhelmed by a stronger signal. This is what happens when your radio station fades out and is replaced by a stronger station's radio signal. EMI can be unintentional, such as interference with your TV or radio during a strong electrical storm, or it can be intentional when someone jams a GPS signal to your phone. We cannot easily determine if EMI that occurs in the presence of a UFO is intentional or unintentional. It could be a byproduct of a UFO's propulsion system or something else entirely. There is no easy way to determine if there is intent.

Could claims of EMI caused by UFOs be a consequence of the public watching too many science fiction movies, such as *Close Encounters of the Third Kind*? It is possible, but how likely is it? If UFO reports related to EMI were rare, then we might dismiss an incident as a coincidence of a witness happening to have an electrical interference on the radio or his car suddenly stopping when he spotted an aerial object that couldn't easily be identified. Yet there are literally hundreds of such reports.[1] Ignoring such a relationship without thought and spurting out the word "coincidence" is not science. What is the likelihood of you seeing a UFO? What is the likelihood of your car stopping? The likelihood of one such coincidence is the multiplicative of those two possibilities. So, if the likelihood of seeing a UFO today is one in a million and the likelihood of your car breaking down during a given five-minute time period is one in a million, then the likelihood of your car breaking down during the five-minute period when you see a UFO today is $1 / (1,000,000) * (1,000,000)$, or one in a trillion. The statistics involved are more complicated than was just explained, but the concept is the same. The large number of EMI events related to UFO sightings cannot be ignored. Coincidence piled on top of coincidence soon forces a realization that the possibility of a causality must be considered.

There were a few reports of what might be considered EMI related to UFOs prior to the Second World War, but they were rare. The first ongoing reports of EMI during a UFO sighting began in earnest in 1942 and they have continued ever since. It involved a military aircrew. There were no previous reports of such interference in the news media that could have instilled in the airmen a preconceived notion to expect EMI with a UFO encounter. This case and a few other select cases follow.

RADIO AND PHONE INTERFERENCE

November 1942; Bay of Biscay, England.   An anti-submarine squadron was patrolling off the coast of England. The tail gunner spotted a strange craft that had no wings and no visible means of propulsion. Others in the crew also spotted the object. The distance to the object was unknown. The assistant engineer indicated that the intercom began to malfunction and became "a jumbled mess of incoherent squawks" while the object was in sight. Fifteen minutes later the object executed "a 180-degree angle turn and disappeared."[2]

July 24, 1949; Mt. Home, Idaho.   The pilot of a Piper Clipper aircraft was flying due west and at 10,000 feet when he spotted seven delta-wing-shaped objects approaching on his left side. He was able to see them clearly as at closest approach they were about 500 feet below his altitude and 1,500 feet away to his left. They were the size of fighter planes but much thinner, about two to five feet thick. He estimated their speed at 450–550 mph, much faster than most aircraft of the time. As soon as he passed the objects' flight path, he noticed that his engine began running rough. His aircraft and engine were brand new. Soon after he landed, he had one of his mechanics check the engine. It was found that all his spark plugs had been burned.[3]

September 1950; Yalu River, Korea.   Three U.S. Navy fighter bombers took off from their aircraft carrier to complete a bombing mission during the Korean War. It was an early September morning, and the sun was just rising. The airmen were alert as they headed toward North Korean territory. The radar gunmen in one of the planes saw large shadows moving along the ground. He looked up to see what was creating the shadows. Above him were two large disk-shaped objects. He estimated their speed at 1,000 to 1,200 mph and his radar indicated the objects were a mile and a half away. Using the distance, he estimated their size at 600 to 700 feet. The objects suddenly halted and began to jitter. The radar gunman readied his guns to fire. The airman stated:

> When I readied the guns, however, the radar went haywire. The screen "bloomed" and became very bright. I tried to reduce the brightness by turning down the sensitivity, but this had no effect. I realized my radar had been jammed and was useless. I then called the carrier, using the code name. I said the code name twice, and my receiver was out; blocked by a strange buzzing noise. I tried two other frequencies but couldn't get through. Each time I switched frequencies the band was clear for a moment, then the buzzing began.

The objects reversed course back toward the planes. They began to maneuver around the planes, circling above and below. The airmen got a good look at these unusual craft and described them: "The objects had a 'silvered mirror' appearance, with a reddish glow surrounding them. They were shaped somewhat like a coolie's hat." When the objects finished their inspection of the Navy planes, they took off in the same direction from which they had come and disappeared at a high rate of speed.[4]

These first instances of radio interference are typical and have continued over the decades. In earlier chapters we discussed radio interference that occurred in 1968 with the B-52 bomber at Minot AFB, the 1973 Army reserve helicopter in Ohio whose radio interference was across all frequencies, and the 1986 Japan Air Lines incident over Alaska. In the latter case the plane's radio communication, both transmitting and receiving, was extremely difficult for ten to fifteen minutes whenever the UFOs came close to the plane. NORAD even offered to send a military interceptor.[5] These types of incidents have continued into the twenty-first century. During Operation Iraqi Freedom in 2004, a security guard at a U.S. forward operating base near Baqubah, Iraq, noticed a bluish light hovering over their base. He tried to call it in by handheld radio without success. He then used his military radio that hops across different FM frequencies. The results were the same. He was not able to contact either the sergeant of the guard or the battalion radio center.[6] A more recent event happened on August 21, 2013, in Kitchener, Ontario, Canada. A perfect sphere with well-defined edges was moving just above the treetops and was 400 feet distance from the witness. He was able to estimate the object's distance because it was at the tree line. The witness estimated its size at 30–40 feet in diameter. When he tried to take a photo with his cell phone, it wouldn't operate. Once the object left the area his phone would operate again.[7]

These are just a handful of the many hundreds of cases involving radio or phone interference. It is important to note that EMI is not an inherent characteristic of UFOs. They can be sighted without interference. But once a witness is in close proximity to a UFO, then the likelihood of interference is much greater. This would be expected based on the inverse square law, which indicates that the drop in intensity of an electric field is inversely related to the square of the distance from the source. One would expect that such an electric field could interfere with more than just radios and phones—and it does.

STOPS AND STALLS OF COMBUSTION ENGINES

It requires a stronger electric field to interfere with the operation of an automobile or aircraft engine operation than it does to interfere with a low-power radio or phone transmission. One of the earliest examples of UFO interference with a combustion engine was in 1952.

March 29, 1952; Baltimore, Maryland. Buried in the Project Blue Book files is an interesting report that most have not seen. The report was written for Gen. John Ackerman, the Deputy Director of Air Force Intelligence, and with a comment that the investigation was "to be given top priority." This incident went beyond Blue Book and all the way to the Pentagon. The Blue Book files on this incident span twenty-two pages and include not only investigations of the UFO incident but also a background check on the witnesses by the FBI and interviews of other acquaintances of the witnesses to confirm their credibility. The names of the witnesses were redacted in the AF report.

The two witnesses were driving toward Baltimore when they heard a roaring sound overhead. Looking out, the driver saw a large disk, shaped like a pancake. As he watched, the disk suddenly plummeted toward the ground at high speed and stopped 200 feet over his car. He described the disk as being at least fifty feet across, having a bubble-like aperture, and that its edges were a "pale green luminescence and a luminous after trail [that] pulsated." The automobile's engine stopped, and the object hovered above the car for about two minutes. The witnesses noticed another car on the highway had also stopped moving. Suddenly, the disk turned on its edge and moved away rapidly as it appeared to roll across the sky. The witnesses were then able to start their car and continue toward Baltimore. The car's engine developed a rough rattle and a car mechanic said that the metal appeared to be magnetized.

The Air Force investigation revealed additional witnesses who had heard noises that night, but they had not gone outside to see the cause of the noises. Further interviews of individuals who knew the driver led to mixed results. Some thought he may have made up the story while others believed him. A check with the mechanic shop did not reveal any unusual problems with the car, but it is unclear which mechanic indicated the metal was magnetized.

Did this incident happen or not? This is the question one is left with after reading the full report. It was the first Project Blue Book report of a car's engine stalling. So, if it was made up, the witness had a unique imagination. One strange event that was described argues that the case is real—the object flipping up on its edge as it moved. Military pilots in the Korean War and two commercial pilots in Virginia reported the same strange behavior of a disk flipping on its edge. Their reports were made three months after this report, which lends credence to the validity of this report near Baltimore. The other two incidents were discussed in chapter 3. Lastly, if someone was making up a story, why would anyone add such a crazy tale of a non-aerodynamic movement?[8]

This type of automobile interference in the United States would increase significantly in 1957. But before moving to 1957, let's jump across the ocean to France, where a myriad of UFO sightings related to EMI of combustion engines began to be reported.

Although the year 1954 was not a significant year in the United States, it was a peak year for UFO reports in France. There were nineteen UFO reports with EMI in the last three months of that year, with ten of the reports between October 11 and 21. The sightings were scattered across all regions of France. All these reports involved autos, tractors, and motorcycles whose engines had stopped in conjunction with a UFO sighting. The UFOs sighted were usually close by. There was one added EMI feature in the French cases that had not been reported in the United States—seven of the reports indicated some level of physiological effects. The electrical impacts on the witnesses included: a tingling feeling, a mild electrical shock, or some level of temporary paralysis.[9]

An important question arises regarding the validity of the reports in France. Is there a simple explanation for the sudden rash of UFO reports accompanied by EMI issues? Some have argued that it is just a coincidence of seeing a UFO simultaneous with an EMI vehicle issue. This is a nonsensical argument to make when there are ten reports within ten days. A better argument might be whether these reports have been influenced by media reports of UFOs and EMI. The French reports came predominately from small villages. They would not have heard of the one or two American reports related to automobile stoppage. This was 1954, and there was no rapid media communication regarding local stories from across the world. International news consisted of major events. There is also no indication of media coverage of a unique French case that set off those ten reports within a ten-day period. It is difficult to find an explanation that argues for ignoring these reports. In three more years, the United States would experience a similar sudden jump in UFO-related EMI reports.

The number of UFO-associated EMI reports hit a crescendo in the United States during the last three months of 1957. Reports of automobiles that suddenly stalled in the presence of a UFO reached a record high in November that has never been exceeded since. Twenty-five reports of stalled cars were reported to Project Blue Book and various newspapers that month, with fifteen of the twenty-five occurring in Texas. Most witness reports described an egg-shape to torpedo-shaped object.[10] The following provides an overview of what was happening:

1. **October 30, Casper, Wyoming;** a couple saw an egg-shaped object sitting on the road ahead. They tried to turn around and their car stalled.
2. **November 2, evening, Petit, Texas;** engines failed on two grain combines when a UFO passed overhead.
3. **November 2, 8:30 p.m., Seminole, Texas;** car engine failed as the driver approached a bright light on the road ahead. The light ascended and his car engine started.
4. **November 2, 11:00 p.m., Levelland, Texas;** a torpedo-shaped object passed over the truck of two occupants and their engine failed.
5. **November 2, midnight, Whitharral, Texas;** a 200 foot-long object was sitting in the road and the driver's engine stopped as he approached. It departed and his car started.
6. **November 2, midnight, Levelland, Texas;** a 200 foot-long, egg-shaped object was in the middle of the road and the driver's engine stopped as he approached.
7. **November 3, 12:05 a.m., Smyer, Texas;** a college student saw an oval object in the road ahead and his car came to a stop. After the object left, his car started.

During the next hour, four more reports came out of Levelland, Texas, regarding an object on the road that caused their car to stop until it departed.[11]

These incidents made for a great opportunity. A lot of investigative science could have been accomplished with so many cases of automobile stalls in such a short period of time, and within a confined geographic location. Scientists could have taken detailed measurements of magnetic fields on the affected metal in the cars. Measurements could have been taken of any trace EM fields on the roads where the object supposedly landed, and trace evidence could have been analyzed with sophisticated analytical chemistry tools. The Air Force did none of this. Instead of investigating, they threw out the first explanation they came across—ball lightning.

These incidences continued into the 1960s and 1970s. Today these types of reports still occur, but they are much less frequent. One of the best recently documented incidents of UFO and EMI occurred in 2009.

November 25, 2009; Port Jervis, New York. A car's engine needs to be restarted once it has turned off. This is the case with most UFO-related EMI cases. But there are a few reports of the car engine restarting on its own after the UFO moves away. The incident that took place in Port Jervis, New York, is a recent example of such a case.

A mental health professional had left work at 12 a.m. in Unionville, which is approximately fifteen minutes from Port Jervis where he lived. He was driving on the Minisink turnpike when he noticed lights in the sky. At first, he thought it was a plane until he noticed it had five lights on it end-to-end that were blue-white-red-white-blue. The strange aspect of this object was that it was turning slowly clockwise. The witness slowed his car down to around 20 mph so that he could more carefully observe the object. He then stopped his vehicle and put it in park. The object was cigar-shaped, about 200 feet in length, and he could hear a faint sound like a cat purring. When he looked at the lights, they seemed very bright, but they didn't illuminate the ground; the witness said he can't explain this aspect as it doesn't make any sense to him. As the object passed over the witness's vehicle, the engine just stopped as if someone had turned off the ignition. The witness tried to use his cell phone, but it wouldn't work even though he always kept it charged. He also tried to roll down the electric window, but it wouldn't work either. After about a minute and a half the craft's lights blinked out and the witness's vehicle started up without any action on the part of the witness. The car radio and the lights came back on, and his cell phone began to boot up. By now the witness was in a state of panic. He put the car into drive and drove home in a hurry. He never looked back.

An investigator from the Mutual UFO Network arrived within thirty-six hours of the event. The witness's phone was tested using an EM meter and was normal. All exterior portions of the witness's car pegged out the EM meter at a reading of 100 microtesla whenever the meter was within three inches of the car. The witness was driving a new 2009 Mitsubishi Gallant, so the investigator found the same model at a new car dealership and tested it with the EM meter; it was normal. This was a very unusual finding, and it is unfortunate that more testing was not done on the car. It would have been valuable to have a detailed diagram of the car and its metallic structure along with multiple magnetic readings across its surface and with detailed readings at distances from the surface, and then repeating all the tests for accuracy as well as any degradation in the magnetic readings over time.[12]

What type of EM emission would cause an automobile to stop, and why did such reports drop off after the 1970s? It might be that the switch to electronic ignitions in the 1970s reduced susceptibility to certain EM frequencies, but that needs to be investigated. And what types of EM emissions would be required to shut down an automobile's electrical system? What power level would be required at the distance that these objects were from the automobile? There have been hundreds of these cases, yet we know next to nothing about the phenomenon. The failure to know is because of our failure with science. These incidents were never investigated by scientists; they were ignored. It's not a perfect laboratory setting for science, but information and possible patterns could have been studied. If these had been reports of a large white woodpecker that had never been seen before, then ornithologists would have been camped out to get a glimpse of a possible new species of woodpecker. But the term *UFO* contains the stigma that a scientist might be investigating the possibility of an extraterrestrial craft. That is *verboten* and The Great Taboo. Thus, we are left with two possibilities: that these car stoppages were all hogwash or that the reports are real, and we have failed to seek to understand the phenomenon.

RADIO EMISSIONS

Automobile-related cases that indicate EMI from UFOs are just part of the story. There have been reports by military pilots that a radio signal was being emitted by a UFO. Six such events occurred in 1957 and are all documented in Project Blue Book. Brad Sparks identified these incidents in his review of the Blue Book files.[13] The first interesting case was further documented in detail by Dr. James McDonald. It is an instance of a radio signal emission from a UFO that overpowers the original airport landing signal.

January 16, 1957; northwest of Ft. Worth, Texas. Lt. Colonel Howard Wright was flying a B-25 bomber from Birmingham, Alabama, to Reese AFB in Lubbock, Texas. The plane also carried a co-pilot, a navigator, and a crew chief. All were experienced airmen. The co-pilot was in control of the aircraft at the time that the pilot spotted a white, round object to the right of the aircraft. Its angular diameter was somewhat smaller than a full moon. Wright noticed that the plane's radio compass was pointed directly at the object and was tracking it. (The radio compass points toward the direction of a radio signal. In this case it was tuned to the radio landing signal from Reese AFB.) The plane was 100 miles northwest of Ft. Worth and 150 miles southeast of its Reese AFB destination. The radio compass followed the object as it rapidly accelerated from the plane's one o'clock to three o'clock position. The object began to blink at a varying rate. The entire object was blinking, not just a beacon light. It was so strange that Wright called the navigator and crew chief into the cockpit so that they could witness it too. The men tried to signal back to the object using a light and morse code, but to no avail. Wright took out a pen and stopwatch and began to record the sequence of the blinks. The object continued to follow the plane for an hour. As they neared Reese AFB, the object suddenly moved toward them as it more than doubled its angular size. It hung motionless before them for five seconds, and this time it was not blinking. It accelerated away from them and disappeared in twelve seconds as measured by a stopwatch.

The next day five individuals from the 4602nd Air Intelligence Service Squadron stationed at Ent AFB in Colorado Springs came to Reese AFB in Lubbock and took detailed statements from the airmen and confiscated all their notes. Ent AFB was the home of NORAD in 1957. Lt. Col. Wright, a West Point graduate, provided a full report that included the object's blinking variations, the radio compass tracking of the object, its sudden acceleration, and supporting statements from a second B-25 that landed thirty minutes after them with a similar story. None of this information made it into the Project Blue Book files but was captured in Professor James McDonald's interview with Wright.[14, 15]

July 17, 1957; south-central United States. Another radio signal is detected coming from a UFO six months after the B-25 bomber incident. This time it is an RB-47. It is the precursor of the modern AWAC aircraft. Its electronics surveillance systems allow it to identify the exact frequency of any signal that is emitted. A UFO had been following the research aircraft for over an hour. While over Mississippi one of the electronic technicians detected a 2,800 GHz emission from the UFO. The pulse repetition frequency and the pulse width matched that of a CPS-6 radar system. But the signal intensity was so strong that the engineering technician pointed out that "it would have to have an antenna bigger than a bomber to put out that much signal." There was an even stronger reason why the signal had not come from a ground radar system: the signal was moving. The RB-47's radar sweep indicated that the source of the signal had flown a circle around the RB-47 at 30,000–35,000 feet altitude while the aircraft was flying at about 550 mph.[16] This is one of the most perplexing events in the history of the UFO phenomenon. The Condon Committee Report listed this case as an unknown.[17]

July 16, 1957; near Las Vegas, Nevada. An equally baffling radar sighting occurred only one day prior to the RB-47's encounter. An Air Force officer was monitoring airspace with an AN/FPS-3A radar system near Las Vegas. His radar detected an incoming object, and standard procedure was for the radar system to automatically send out a military Identification Friend or Foe (IFF) code 1. This is a military method to determine if an approaching aircraft is friendly. The radar sends out a code at a given radar frequency and, if friendly, the aircraft radar sends back an encrypted response at a different, and specific, frequency. The inbound object sent the code indicating it was friendly, but there was a problem. The inbound target was moving at 6,200 mph. It came to an abrupt stop and remained stationary for twelve seconds before accelerating outbound at a speed of 7,000 mph. The acceleration and deceleration forces for such a sudden stop and start would have been astronomical. There is no aircraft or missile that exists today that can move at those speeds, come to a stop, and then accelerate again. There certainly was nothing that we had in 1957 with those capabilities. Maintenance immediately checked the radar system for any issues and found none.[18]

The Air Force tried to explain this as a temperature inversion. A temperature inversion occurs when atmospheric conditions are such that a radar beam will bounce back from a distant target and cause errors in the location and speed of a target. This radar event cannot be explained by any type of cloud inversion or other types of radar anomalies. Why? Two reasons: a radar anomaly cannot reply with a military IFF code 1; and the object remained motionless on radar for twelve seconds before accelerating away. The implication is that an intelligently controlled target knew the military IFF code and had technology far in advance of anything we have today.

The year 1957 had more of these instances. An Air Force radar station near Mt. Lemmon, Arizona, detected a stationary object near Williams Air Force Base that was emitting a civilian mode 3 code. A slight strobe came from the object appearing like electronic counter measures (ECM) jamming. This was only two days after the Las Vegas incident.[19] Not far away, McClellan AFB in northern California had been detecting a military IFF code for several days from a target that would not show up on primary radar. This means the object is sending a signal to the radar station, but the radar is not receiving a return when its beam is bounced off the target. The object finally showed up on primary radar on August 3 before taking off at a speed greater than 1,800 mph.[20]

The last event in 1957 involved an Air Force radar site near Albuquerque, New Mexico, on November 26. It detected a UFO emitting a civilian mode 3 signal while traveling at a speed of 3,500 mph.[21]

Six instances of UFOs emitting IFF codes and/or other EM signals during 1957 with four of those events happening within two weeks of each other. It would have been prudent to bring in Air Force scientists to investigate. Instead, the Air Force wrote it off as anomalous radar propagation.

November 16–24, 1964; northwest of Puerto Rico. The U.S. Navy and Air Force were conducting exercises in the Caribbean during mid-November. Bogeys had been detected on radar off and on for several days. The bogeys were supposedly ours, as they had replied with the military Identification Friend or Foe (IFF) code 1, when interrogated by Navy radar. This happened several times. Checks with Navy command and the Air Force indicated no other aircraft in their military training area.[22]

These incidents culminated when the guided-missile destroyer, USS *Gyatt*, requested a Navy jet interception of one of the "friendly" bogeys. A Navy F-8C was already flying at an altitude of 30,000 feet over Puerto Rico. The pilot of the F-8C, Lt. Cmdr. Woodbury, made visual contact with the target. He described the object as delta-shaped and about the size of a fighter. Its color was black or gray and it had no lights. It had no contrail but had a light source emitting from the tail during periods of acceleration. The pilot pursued the bogey but could not intercept it. The target accelerated out of sight and climbed through 50,000 feet at about an 18°–20° angle of climb at more than Mach 1. The executive officer of the squadron, Cmdr. T. D. Fosdick, sent a report on the incident to the Navy commander of the Caribbean. He summarized the incident as follows:

> There is no reasonable explanation of this target. Its speed, acceleration, ceiling, and ability to decelerate exceed any aircraft I have ever seen or heard of . . . I would evaluate target as aircraft, very high performance, maneuvered as an aircraft and performed no unusual maneuvers except extreme acceleration and deceleration at will, plus a very extreme climb angle in excess of 50,000 feet at high speed.[23]

There were aircraft in 1964 that could match the speed and altitude capabilities of the unknown such as the XB-70 and the SR-71. There were no aircraft in 1964 that could match the high acceleration and deceleration, the high attack angle of the aircraft, and the combination of low and high speeds. And why would any advanced U.S. aircraft have played games with a Navy–Air Force exercise?

How many more military detections of UFOs transmitting an IFF signal happened after 1964? We don't know because the Air Force shut down Project Blue Book in 1969. Information on additional radio emissions by UFOs, if they occurred, remained locked away in military files, or even worse—was simply discarded as time went by. Nonetheless, recent information indicates that the military is still detecting radio emissions from UFOs. The Office of the Director for National Intelligence released a preliminary assessment on Unidentified Aerial Phenomena (UAP) in June 2021. This report summarized new government investigations into UFOs, now referred to as UAP. Within the nine-page report was the statement, "In a small number of cases, military aircraft systems processed radio frequency (RF) energy associated with UAP sightings."[24] Perhaps more information will be released in the future.

Entertain the possibility that UFOs are controlled by an advanced intelligence of unknown origin. This is what science does. Science doesn't assume something is true, but it does consider all the possibilities and evaluate them. If this is true, then what would we deduce when a UFO sends an IFF signal that is known only to us? We would consider the possibility that they had monitored our aircraft's interaction with each other using radio/radar signals at various wavelengths and that they had determined that this was some type of signaling method. We would also consider the possibility that this was an attempt to communicate with us. In the case of the latter, we would design experiments to send out different radio frequencies to communicate. But none of this ever happened because we have steadfastly refused to consider the possibility that a UFO could be controlled by an intelligence more advanced than us.

Steven Spielberg considered that possibility in *Close Encounters of the Third Kind*. And science considers such possibilities all the time. Scientists have considered the possibility that a raven could utilize a tool in its search for food and then set about to prove it. We've considered the possibility that life exists in the cosmos and created the Search for Extraterrestrial Intelligence (SETI) to investigate it. Let's take a lesson from Spielberg. It is time that scientists rather than the military be the agents that investigate the UFO phenomenon.

Chapter Six

The Edge of Physics

There are aspects of some UFO reports that bring us to the edge of what is or is not possible based on our understanding of physics. This does not mean that they "defy the laws of physics." It is beyond our engineering capabilities. We have already touched on one such instance when we discussed extreme accelerations in the atmosphere. Energy and time are the other two. A witness states that their car headlights were bent by a nearby UFO or that a beam of light slowly pushed outward from a UFO. Two witnesses state that they observed a UFO and when they reached their destination an extra two hours had passed. These types of reports make us question the veracity of the witness story, as well we should. Such reports don't neatly fit into our current understanding of physics. At the same time, we must be open to the possibility that the witnesses have accurately reported what they experienced.

LIGHT THAT DOES NOT ILLUMINATE

In the last chapter we discussed a UFO event that happened in Port Jervis, New York, in 2009. A cigar-shaped craft caused the witness's car to stop when it flew over and there were magnetic traces on the car. There was another strange and interesting part to that UFO sighting. The witness also stated that the lights from the craft were very bright, but they didn't illuminate the ground, which didn't make sense to him. He was correct to be in wonder. The witness said the object was the size of a baseball at arm's length. This puts the object's relative size seven times the appearance of the full moon in the night sky. Why wasn't the ground lit by an object this close? We might try to explain this away if we assume that the witness made an error in the apparent size of the object and that it was much farther away. But the magnetic traces on the car argue that the object was near enough to impart a field onto the car, and this is not the only report of such a strange light characteristic.

July 25, 1983; Flushing, Michigan.   A Michigan state highway patrol trooper interviewed four witnesses who had seen a disk-shaped object that had come within a few hundred feet of them. In their descriptions they stated that the disk was stationary and silent as they observed it for two to three minutes. There were two oversized bright white lights on the craft, each about two feet across. The witnesses found it odd that the bright lights did not hurt their eyes and did not appreciably light up the surroundings.[1]

July 1991; Copperas Cove, Texas.   A boomerang-shaped object was at an altitude of 150–200 feet when it flew directly over two students who were home from college. The entire surface of the object glowed a very bright white. The two men thought it was strange that the light from the object did not light up its surroundings.[2]

August 29, 1992; Batavia, New York.   A father and his two children were returning from a trip to Canada. They were driving east on the New York State thruway to the west of Batavia. They had noticed a distant flashing of light and thought it might be lightning. The light came closer to them. Perhaps it was a helicopter or blimp. The father and his children were now very alert and startled because the object was less than 150 feet away and following them along the highway at their speed. The object was very close, and the witnesses could see a lot of detail. The object was the length of a tractor trailer truck, elliptical in shape, and gray. The father described its surface as clean, smooth, and without any seams or rivets. It was silent, gave off no heat, and did not create any turbulence to stir the surrounding brush and trees along the road. It had very intense circular lights, and the father stated that it was strange that the lights did not illuminate their car or the immediate area. The close encounter did not last long. After several seconds pacing their car, the object retreated and moved away much faster than it had approached.[3]

This time we can't explain away the strange behavior of light by saying the object was much farther away. The object was right alongside the car as it traveled down the highway. We are left with the choice of believing the witness or deciding that he has made up the story and has convinced his children to go along with him. Perhaps we need more witnesses.

December 24, 1992; Monroe, Louisiana.   A triangular-shaped UFO was seen on Christmas Eve night by dozens of witnesses. Over a dozen firemen and deputy sheriffs were among the witnesses. It occurred near Monroe, Louisiana, and the UFO was seen off and on for two and a half hours. It was first seen about five to ten minutes before 7 p.m. The two deputies to encounter the UFO described the object as "enormous" with two large, blinding lights in the front. They saw the object up close. Deputy Johnson was ex-military and was familiar with aircraft. He stated, "The craft traveled on over me [his law enforcement vehicle]. It was just over tree top high. No sound and we had all the windows down." The craft then proceeded to display extreme acceleration. In the words of the same deputy, "With both of us sitting there looking at it, the craft speeded up a little bit, and then it accelerated and, zip, it's gone. It was gone within just—maybe one second." A UFO with the same description was spotted again about half an hour later and five miles to the southeast. It was just south of Monroe near Philpot Road. A dozen witnesses saw the object. Several witnesses stated that the two bright lights in the front did not light up the ground or the trees that were in front of the object. Deputy Knight was in the same area and saw the object at treetop height. His statement was similar: "There were three or four large lights in the center of it, shining straight down, but they didn't illuminate the ground."[4]

Were the witnesses correct in their view that the bright light from the UFO did not illuminate the ground or its surroundings? To answer that question, we need to measure the wavelengths of the light and the intensity of the light at various distances from its source. If we were dealing with a streetlamp, then we could set up our instrumentation and measure the light intensity as it propagates from the streetlamp. But we can't do that with the UFO unless it cooperates and shows up for our experiment, or we happen to be at the right place at the right time with our light meters and spectrometer. Neither of these possibilities is likely. If the witnesses are correct and an intense light did not light up its surroundings, then we are left to speculate as to a possible explanation. Perhaps the light emission was directional and at a very specific wavelength such as a laser. Perhaps the light did light up its surroundings, but it was too dim for the witnesses to notice. We will not know the answer unless we study the phenomenon. Or we can ignore the question and find reasons not to believe the witnesses.

CONTROL OF A LIGHT BEAM

Light is a critical element of everyday life. Its control is paramount to our industries, our cities, and our technologies. We're all familiar with light whether it is from a flashlight, a room light, a laser pointer, or car headlights. There are properties of light that we instinctively know from experience that need not be taught in school. When we turn on a flashlight or a laser, we know that the light is "instantaneous" to our eyes. We can't see the light as it moves. It doesn't slowly leave the flashlight or slowly roll back into the flashlight if it's turned off. Nor can we change the direction of the light once it has left our laser pointer. If we want to change the direction of a beam of light, then we move the source of the light, the flashlight or laser. If light were to act differently, we would take notice—and that is what has been noticed in some reports of UFO sightings. Light has been reported to act in strange ways that make no sense to the witnesses. That critical element of everyday life has gone astray.

April 4, 1966; Burkes Flat, Victoria, Australia. Mr. Ron Sullivan, a construction businessman from Maryborough, was traveling at 60 mph. He was approaching St. Arnaut when he noticed a far-off light in the field. He initially thought it was a tractor. Mr. Sullivan describes the strange event that happened next:

> Suddenly my headlights pulled hard over to the right for some unaccountable reason. Instead of lighting the road, they lit up the fence as though they were being attracted by a magnet. I braked as hard as I could and glanced over to the right. In the middle of the paddock [meadow] was a column of coloured light about 25 feet high and shaped like an ice-cream cone. It would have been about three feet wide at the bottom and ten feet wide at the top.[5, 6]

The car's lights were inexplicably bent toward the cone-shaped object and were no longer trained on a dark road at night. The driver avoided an accident by braking his car to a stop. It was only moments later that the object, along with its column of light, departed upward. Once the object had departed, Mr. Sullivan's lights returned to normal and lit the road in front of him. Was there other evidence of this incident? Two days later a nineteen-year-old driver was killed when his auto left the road and struck a tree only twenty feet away from where Mr. Sullivan's car headlights were bent away from the dark road.[7] Was this accident caused by the same phenomenon experienced by Mr. Sullivan two days earlier at the same location? There is no way to know. It would only be speculation, but this event makes you wonder.

November 22, 1968; Newton, Georgia. This incident drew a lot of attention from the United States Air Force. The Project Blue Book report consists of forty-five pages of investigative material, and it was personally investigated by the Air Force's chief scientist, Allan Hynek.

It was about 8 p.m. as the bank adjuster traveled east on Georgia highway 91. He was eleven miles west of Newton. As the driver took a sharp curve and topped a hill, his radio went out and his car lost power and came to a stop. Straight ahead was a bright yellowish oval-shaped light about 200 feet away and about 75 feet off the ground. The light emitted from the object was odd. It was so bright that it lit up the road, the ditch, and all the surrounding trees. The witness found this strange because he was able to look directly at the light without it hurting his eyes. Emanating from the light was a beam that was five to six feet wide and shone down to the ground in front of the car. The witness was frightened, and he estimated that he sat in his car for two to three minutes. The object then changed from its yellowish tone to a reddish-orange color and the beam slowly retracted back into the light. The witness described the eerie event thus: "It seemed like that you could actually see the bottom of the light, the end of the beam itself, going back up into the main body of light." Once the beam fully retracted itself, the object moved straight up and was gone within seconds.[8]

August 13, 1970; Haderslev, Denmark. Police constable Eval Maarvp reported that a disk-like object with a dome about thirty feet in size came within sixty feet of his patrol car. It emitted a brilliant, conical light that surrounded his car. After a few seconds, the light began to draw back into the disk in a very odd manner. The light beam slowly rose from the bottom gradually, leaving darkness in its wake. It took about five minutes for the light to recede back into the disk. The officer then stepped out of his patrol car and the object began moving and vanished vertically in a few seconds.[9]

May 21, 1977; Poole, England. Several different and unrelated witnesses reported unusual disk-shaped objects emitting beams of light. Two witnesses gave identical accounts of a light beam with strange qualities. It was about two feet in width with very clear-cut edges. It seemed to "cut through" the terrain while illuminating nothing. The end of the beam was clearly visible, and it was circular.[10]

November 29, 1989; Eupen, Belgium. The famous Belgium triangle sightings also had incidents of a controlled light beam. Gendarmes Hubert von Montigny and Heinrich Nicoll were only 450 feet away from the triangular craft that hovered motionless and silent in front of them. They estimated the length of each side at 100 feet with an enormous white light at each apex and a dimmer red light in the center. Three very luminous beams emerged from each of the white lights. The beams had sharply defined boundaries and their internal volume was luminous. Later they saw two narrow red-light beams that emerged from the craft and became progressively longer in a symmetrical way. Then the red beams suddenly disappeared, while two red-orange balls appeared at the end of where the beams had been. These balls went back to the object, moved around it, and disappeared. After a pause, the same process was repeated, and this happened about every five minutes several times.[11]

July 1999; Campo, California. A man's car was stuck in a rut while the man was returning home from a fishing trip. He got out to dig the back tire out of the rut. He finished the work and as he got back into his car, he noticed a bright white orb about forty to fifty feet away. It was only four to five feet in diameter and only twenty-five feet above the ground. The man took about ten steps toward the object, when it shone a bright blue beam at him for a few seconds. The final ending of this story is best described by the witness himself:

I lowered my hands in time to see the beam do something very strange. It did not cut off or wink out like a normal light would, it actually retreated back into the bottom of the orb as if it was on a string. I know it sounds crazy and light is not capable of doing this, but nonetheless I witnessed it, and I don't think my description is doing it justice. As soon as the beam retreated back into the orb it began to slowly glide away.[12]

These are but a few of the witness reports of light beams emitted from UFOs and behaving in very inexplicable ways: light that has edges to it and with the inner portions defined by those edges and seemingly filled with light, and light that doesn't appear to move at its usual, almost instantaneous-like speed but instead slowly moves back into its source. It's as if you took a flashlight and when you turned it on, a light beam slowly came out and lit the wall across from you. The descriptions sound more like the movement of matter than of energy, or at least as we understand energy.

There is one potential explanation that could be put forth that might explain light behaving like this. It might not be light as much as it could be controlled plasma. Plasma is the fourth state of matter, and it occurs when the electrons in a gas are stripped from the atom and the gas becomes highly conductive. When lightning strikes this is because of the properties of plasma, which allows a large electric discharge through a gas that is not very conductive under normal circumstances. The light is one of the byproducts of the plasma discharge. Unfortunately for our theory, extreme heat is also a byproduct. Heat is usually not reported by witnesses as a characteristic of the light beams related to UFO sightings. However, in the last few decades research has been done on what is referred to as "cold plasma." Unlike what the name suggests, cold plasma is not truly cold. The difference is that only a fraction of the molecules have been energized in cold plasma, and it seems cold because the gas molecules near you are not energized. Cold plasma has already been used in medicine for dermatology treatment of bacteria at a wound site and also to speed up the healing of a wound. Small beams of cold plasma have also been produced in controlled laboratory conditions. Could cold plasma explain what the witnesses described?

Plasma is a potential explanation. It can appear to have well-defined edges if the method of exciting the atoms in the atmosphere is well defined. It will appear to look like a light beam because of local emission of light by the excited atoms. It can move at a slow speed because its speed of propagation is not controlled by light but by whatever method is used to excite the atoms in the atmosphere. Now there are still issues with how to excite atmospheric gas in a controlled manner so that the plasma front slowly moves backward and forward, but it is something that is technologically possible. However, we don't currently have the ability to do that outside of a laboratory environment on a large scale, such as moving a six-foot-wide plasma slowly through the atmosphere.

Whether plasma is the explanation for the UFO light beam observations that we've discussed in this chapter, we cannot know. We can only speculate as to whether a plasma might match the properties observed. There is, however, one property that would be difficult to ascribe to plasma, and that was the Australian case that involved the bending of a car's headlight beam. If this happened, it was the car's own light beam that was bent, and we know the car's beam was not generated by plasma. So, what caused the light to bend?

There are two ways that light can be bent or at least appear to be bent in the macroscopic world. Light can be refracted as it passes from one medium into another. This is what happens when you put a pencil in a glass of water and it appears bent, or if you shine a strong flashlight into a glass of water at an angle and the light appears to bend. The light doesn't truly bend, but it appears to bend because of the difference in the refractive index of the water and air. The other way that light can appear to bend was first explained by Einstein in his general theory of relativity. A gravitational field warps spacetime so the light follows the curvature of space and appears to bend. These are the two ways that light can be bent other than at the quantum level with diffraction. If the Australian report is true, then there is much that we do not fully understand about light.

SLOWING OF TIME

Some readers may be familiar with the phenomenon of "lost time" by individuals who claim to have been abducted by some type of extraterrestrial entity. Often, they don't see a physical UFO but only entities. This is not what will be discussed here, not because this author has judged them to be invalid but because they require expertise in psychology to make a proper judgment. This discussion will center around incidents where time has slowed down for the witness when they were near a UFO. It is one of the strangest claims made by some witnesses.

Time is simple to monitor when intentionally measured. An experiment is planned out and the appropriate time-measuring equipment is on hand. Measuring time is problematic when no planning has occurred. For example, when time is measured after a sudden emotional event such as a car accident, a robbery, or a UFO sighting, it is more difficult to assess. Time seems to slow down, although we know that is only our perception.

These next reports are from incidents where the witness's perception of passing time is supported by a clock, watch, or some reason that supports the witness's story. The reader can decide if time has been lost after reading these reports.

October 30, 1967; Boyup Brook, Western Australia. This UFO sighting has a lot of unusual characteristics that we have already discussed in other sighting reports, plus the additional strangeness of lost time. The witness was a married man with three children. He was a sheep-shearing contractor and had sixty men who worked for him. There is an extensive report on this incident that includes a recorded interview; a twenty-three-page evaluation of the witness by Dr. Paul Zeck, a psychologist from Perth; and a police report.

Mr. Harris was driving along at a speed of about 65 mph. It was a little after 9 p.m. and he was headed to his next job site when suddenly his car stopped. He stated, "My machine just stopped dead and all electrical systems, motor, radio, everything went dead. I had no feeling of deceleration at all . . . the car just instantaneously came to a stop . . . I didn't feel any—no feeling of deceleration, no thrust or anything I was just like, I, eh, stopped." Everything was dead quiet as Mr. Harris stared at a football-shaped object directly in front of him and about ninety feet off the ground. The object was about thirty feet in diameter and glowed a light iridescent blue similar to the color of lightning. A small hollow tube of light descended from the object toward his car and stopped on his windshield. He was able to look up the length of the tube as there was no glare. He continued to look up at the tube for several minutes before the light went off. The object then departed at a terrific speed and was gone in seconds.

Mr. Harris had kept his hands on the steering wheel during this entire event. The moment the object left, his car was again going at the same speed that it was doing before it had stopped. Again, Mr. Harris had no feeling of acceleration. His car was back to moving at 65 mph. It was as if time had stopped for those few minutes, and that is exactly what Mr. Harris's Omega chronometer indicated when he looked at it upon reaching Boyup Brook; it was running five minutes slow.[13]

Dr. Zeck interviewed Mr. Harris to look at the possibility of a hoax, a dream, or temporal lobe epilepsy. A hoax was deemed the least likely possibility. A dream has altered states of consciousness which could fit with Mr. Harris's story. Arguing against that was the five minutes of lost time on the chronometer. Mr. Harris had no medical history of epilepsy, but it might be possible for such an event to have occurred. The last possibility is that his story was true.

October 1981; Hesperia, Michigan. The young couple was traveling west on Michigan state highway 20. They had just passed through Hesperia, and it was about 8 p.m. Directly in front of them was a distant lime-green light in the sky. Suddenly, the strange light dropped its elevation and came directly at them. The couple feared a head-on collision of some sort as the light reached them in only a few seconds. The green light engulfed their pickup truck and blocked their view of anything outside the truck. They were terrified and in shock. What happens next is even more strange and is described by the husband:

> My next memory and hers seems like literally a second later from one of sheer terror is one of "Hmmm that was weird," and looking at her being totally calm and myself the same way. Our truck was in the exact same place on the highway going 60 miles per hour just as it was when we were in total terror what seemed like only a split second before. There was on my part no swerving or even time to react before we went from complete shock to Hmmm that was interesting. We both watched the green oval object fly off in a southwest direction, more southerly than it had approached, over the trees and off into the far distance and up into the sky disappearing from sight as it seemed to climb far off in the distance. We continued the last three miles to our house on Loop Rd.

The couple did not have a watch or a car clock. When they got home it was 9 o'clock. Where had the hour gone? It was only three miles from where the event occurred to their home.[14]

November 2, 2001; Portage la Prairie, Canada. Steve Chmara and his wife, Donna, were driving west on the Trans-Canada highway toward Regina. It was a clear night and Donna was driving. They both noticed a bright and seemingly distant light. Donna looked over at the car's clock, which read 12:10 a.m. She looked back toward the road and saw that the distant light was getting much brighter and closer. Suddenly it was immediately in front of their car. The light was extremely bright, but it didn't hurt their eyes. It was there for a second and then it was gone. They wondered where it had gone. Donna glanced up through the sunroof and spotted it at about the height of a telephone pole and just to the right of their car. Donna was confused and continued to drive as her mind raced about trying to determine if this was a prank, some projection from a nearby field. She watched the object for what seemed like a minute or so. It had a highly polished metallic surface and was shaped like a boomerang. It was traveling with the car and faced the direction from which it had approached, so it was flying backward. The object turned to the northeast and the couple could see round thruster-like engines at the end of each wing. Steve opened his window. There was no noise and no heat as the object began to move away. Donna checked her car's clock; no time had passed, it was still 12:10 a.m. Steve summarized their experience: "We know some people are going to say we're whacked, but we're really not nuts. We don't attend UFO conventions, none of that. Whatever we saw, it inspired both fear and wonder and was truly the experience of a lifetime."[15]

We know that time can slow down based on Einstein's theory of relativity. The faster an object moves, the slower time will pass within that object. The stronger a gravitational field, the slower time will pass for everything within that gravitational field. Science has verified these phenomena as real. A minute though important change in time on moving Global Positioning Satellites (GPS) is considered when your smartphone tells you where you are located. But these are very tiny changes in the order of a few microseconds of lost time in a day, or a second lost every several hundred years. Although it is theoretically possible, we don't have the technology to cause time to change in any significant manner. For example, if we had the ability to send a spaceship into the cosmos at the speed of light, then time would stop for those onboard the spaceship. But how does time slow down for an observer who is simply in the vicinity of a UFO? Is there a field around the UFO and everything within that field is in a different space–time reference? Is that also why light might bend? All of this is interesting speculation but well beyond the bounds of this book; it is at the edge of our understanding of physics.

Chapter Seven

Our Collective Reaction

Arguably, curiosity is the human trait that drove the development of mankind. It is what caused early man to experiment with sticks, stones, and fire. These early tools allowed humans to begin to control the environment around them. More powerful animals could be kept at bay with fire and sharpened sticks, shelters could be built, and soil could be plowed. This innate curiosity matured and developed structure as humans added experimentation to their curiosity tool kit. Science was born. With science came the ability to control our environment even more. The further our science advanced, the more we were able to control the world around us. Curiosity begat science and science begat control. As Carl Sagan noted, "Curiosity and the urge to solve problems are the emotional hallmarks of our species." NASA scientists even named one of our rovers sent to the planet Mars *Curiosity*.

It would be reasonable to expect curiosity to be a key component in how humanity reacts to any mystery such as UFOs, and it has. We wonder about any object in the sky that we cannot identify. Witnesses report what they have seen, the military sometimes investigates, the media relay stories about UFO sightings to the public, and sometimes a scientist will examine whatever information is available. Yet we all feel a certain barrier to discussing the subject of UFOs and what the topic may imply. We're happy to sit at a coffee shop with a friend and talk about our view of UFOs. It is enjoyable to contemplate the "what ifs" and the implications that those thoughts bring. But we begin to hesitate in our conversation if more friends join us at the table. Why is that? Don't you find that odd? It makes one wonder how society in general deals with this subject. How have witnesses, members of the public, the media, the military, the government, and the science community reacted to UFOs? This is the question that we will explore in this chapter.

THE WITNESSES

How have witnesses reacted to UFO sightings? There have been over 300,000 people who have witnessed a UFO over the last eighty years: the National UFO Reporting Center has over 130,000 sighting reports;[1] the Mutual UFO Network has over 125,000 sighting reports;[2] Project Blue Book had over 12,000 reports;[3] and tens of thousands of reports have been filed with UFO agencies in Great Britain, Canada, Australia, France, China, Brazil, Belgium, Italy, and New Zealand. Most of these witnesses misinterpreted a known object or saw an object at a far distance that they could not identify. Those are not the witnesses of interest. The witnesses of interest are those who saw a UFO that was nearby, usually less than 500 feet distant, or who saw a UFO perform sudden turns and accelerations that cannot be explained by anything man-made. Their reactions are often life changing. They have witnessed an event that they will remember for the rest of their lives. When they tell their story, it often begins with, "I will never forget . . ."

Imagine for a moment that you had witnessed a UFO at a close distance. How would you react and how would it affect you? You look at a distant object moving in the sky when suddenly it moves toward you and within a second, maybe two, that speck is only 500 feet away and hovering in front of you. It is a silver, metallic disk-shaped object with no obvious form of propulsion. Curiosity has momentarily left, and you feel more like a deer in headlights. You are stunned and wondering if you're really seeing this. By the time the initial shock to your mind wears off, the object begins to move and disappears from your sight as quickly as it appeared. One part of your brain tells you this object was made by someone much more advanced than humans and the other part of your brain tells you that is not possible. You begin to wonder if you really saw that object or if you were hallucinating. What will you do next; who will you tell? You consider relating your experience to a couple of your closest friends, or maybe not because they might think you were crazy. This is the very quandary that most witnesses find themselves facing when they witness a UFO up close.

My experiences with witnesses of UFO sightings have been somewhat unique and have given me a personalized view of how witnesses react. In the sixteen years that I have investigated this phenomenon, I have personally interviewed over 200 witnesses, and in addition to those I have interviewed over the phone several hundred more witnesses. I have also read thousands of reports sent into MUFON by witnesses. This has given me an insight into how people react not only to the phenomenon itself but also how they interact with other people when they describe what they have seen.

Most witnesses will never forget their UFO sighting, and for most it is only a short-term distraction in their lives. Not everyone reacts in that manner. Some are not able to just view a UFO sighting, file it away in their minds, and go about their lives. I've seen two other ways that witnesses react. And these extreme reactions tell the investigator that whatever the witness saw, it must have been something that was difficult to fathom.

One very unusual reaction comes from a small group of around 5 percent–10 percent of witnesses. This group does not want to talk about what they saw. They are so shocked by what they have witnessed that they react like some individuals who have returned from a war—a condition known as post-traumatic stress disorder (PTSD). They refuse to talk about it or discuss it. They compartmentalize the event in their memory and separate it from their normal life. The only way we know about this group is when there are a group of two or more witnesses; there will often be one that their comrades will say has refused to discuss the experience with them or anyone else. But sometimes they will finally talk if they find someone who is not close to them emotionally but will listen to them and not judge them. Once they've told someone in authority of their story, they often don't want to talk about it again. It is cathartic for them. There is one such story that sticks in my mind.

I was contacted by a woman who was ex-Navy and was now thirty-seven years old. She wanted to tell me a story that she had never told anyone. She began her story and then paused. She said it was giving her chills to tell this story for the first time in sixteen years. When she was only twenty-one, she was stationed on a Navy ship and had observation duty late that night. She went to her post to relieve a male sailor. As she approached the other sailor, she saw a large object sitting off the bow of the ship just floating in the air. It was cylindrical in shape and the size of a large tractor trailer. She asked the sailor if he could see it and he replied, yes. His next statement and action were flabbergasting. He told her that his shift was over, and he walked off, leaving her alone with the object still hovering over the bow. I could tell from her voice that sixteen years later, she was still traumatized by that event. She thanked me with sincerity for listening to her story. I tried to contact her again because I had some additional questions that I had forgotten to ask. My repeated calls were never answered—she had said what she wanted to say.

The final group is also a small percentage of people whose UFO sighting changes their lives. They do the opposite of compartmentalizing the event. They become obsessed to varying degrees with a desire to investigate and understand what they have seen. This can vary from someone who becomes a devoted student of the subject, and sometimes in a very scientific way, to others who become so obsessed with trying to find the answer to this enigma that their normal lives are overshadowed. They sometimes lose their jobs, withdraw from society, or get divorced; their experience totally changes their lives. Sometimes they begin to see UFOs everywhere and may even lose touch with reality. Some may believe the UFOs picked them out as a special person to witness the event and they sometimes think that the UFO has given them special abilities to recognize what is going on with mankind. It is likely this is some type of coping mechanism, like the individuals who pigeonhole the event in the recesses of their minds and won't discuss it further. But I am not educated as a psychologist, so I can't provide any in-depth analysis of these human conditions. It does tell all of us one thing—these people have experienced a traumatic event, and it was so "in their face" that whatever they saw was not a simple misidentification of a common object.

I have given about two dozen presentations at public libraries regarding the subject of UFOs. Sometimes it is about the history of the subject or sometimes about a particularly interesting case that I have studied. Usually, anywhere from twenty to forty people show up. I always ask the audience how many of them have seen a UFO. Almost every hand goes up. Then I ask how many of them reported their UFO sighting. Ninety percent of the hands drop and only two to four hands remain. Dr. Allen Hynek also did this in his presentations to audiences, and with the same result. You might ask, "Why?"

The stigma associated with the UFO phenomenon has much to do with the reluctance of individuals to report on what they have seen. Many of the witnesses that I have interviewed who saw an object up close are very reluctant to report it as they feel people will laugh at them or think they're crazy. Some witnesses are even reluctant to tell what they saw to their spouse. Examples of this type of behavior abound. In the famous Chicago O'Hare disk sighting of 2006, one can hear over the released audio tracks an airport air traffic controller state, "If I did see it, I wouldn't admit it." The Phoenix Lights sightings of 1997 saw that same type of behavior in the highest elected official in the state. At a press conference, Arizona Governor Symington had someone dress up as an alien and come on stage. You would think that this indicated he thought the Phoenix Lights were some kind of joke. It didn't. Ten years later, he admitted that not only should he not have staged such a parody but also that he himself had seen one of the large triangular UFOs along with everyone else. This is truly perplexing human behavior to make fun of something that you yourself had seen. How does a subject become so stigmatized that people are willing to deny what they have seen? Much of the answer to that question lies with the media.

THE MEDIA

The stories of a small percentage of witnesses are reported in a newspaper, radio, television, books, or in the modern world through a social media platform on the internet. How those stories have been reported by the media has varied over time; sometimes factually, sometimes dramatically, and sometimes with ridicule and disdain. It is the media that both provides and influences the public's view of reality.

Newspapers in the 1940s and early 1950s reported on UFOs in a manner that reflected what they had heard from Air Force sources as well as individuals from both the military and the public. The *Miami Herald* showcased the front of their July 16, 1952, newspaper with the headline, "Miami Pilots Spot 8 Saucers Flying in Formation." The front page of the *Washington Post* on July 28, 1952, led with the headline, "Saucer Outran Jet, Pilot Reveals." These news stories were the result of flying saucer sightings all along the U.S. Eastern Seaboard during the summer of 1952. The media stayed in the thick of things. *Life* magazine had reporters in the National Air Traffic Control Tower in Washington, D.C., watching the action as it happened. The media coverage was so intense that the Air Force sent their director of intelligence, John Samford, to calm the media and the public. He held a press conference about the UFO sightings that were occurring up and down the East Coast. It was then that he was forced to give in to the concerns and make his famous statement that indicated some UFO reports were made by "credible observers of relatively incredible things."

The Air Force were now aware of the power of the media to affect both the public and elected government officials. The media's effective coverage of the wave of sightings in 1952 made this abundantly clear. Apparently, the CIA was also aware of the use of media in influencing a situation. Together, the Air Force and the CIA took action through the establishment of the Robertson Panel, which was discussed in the opening chapter of this book. Their solution was to use the power of the media to their own advantage. The key recommendations from the Robertson Panel match the recommendations made by the CIA's assistant director of scientific intelligence, H. Marshall Chadwell. The recommendation related to the media was for the government to both debunk UFO reports and educate the public on UFOs through education that could be accomplished by mass media such as television, motion pictures, and popular articles.[4]

The ties between the media and our government are historical. Famed investigative journalist Carl Bernstein of the Watergate scandal noted that more than 400 American journalists have secretly carried out assignments for the CIA for over twenty-five years, based on CIA documents. These assignments included, but were not limited to, planting disinformation and propaganda in media outlets. The CIA documents indicated that the most valuable of those were the media giants: CBS, *New York Times*, and Time, Inc.[5] It should therefore not be a surprise that the CIA could also influence the narrative about UFOs.

Beyond the influence of the media giants, the CIA's additional control of the UFO narrative may have come via the purchase of the tabloid magazine, *National Enquirer*. Gene Pope was the first publisher of the *National Enquirer*. He graduated from the Massachusetts Institute of Technology (MIT) with a degree in engineering in 1946. Five years later, he joined the CIA. Pope described his job as working in the "CIA's psychological warfare unit." Pope left the CIA one year later and the twenty-five-year-old purchased the *New York Enquirer* from the Hearst publishing empire for $75,000. He renamed the magazine the *National Enquirer* and converted it to a sensationalist tabloid newspaper. It was estimated that another $250,000 would have been needed to make the paper profitable. This was quite a sum of money in the early 1950s, and especially for someone so young. Where Pope obtained those funds is open for debate, but the CIA is a prime candidate.[6]

The *National Enquirer* damaged the UFO subject through sensationalism and the accentuation of any crazy stories on the subject that could be found. Story lines were written as outlandish facts that were so beyond the pale that anyone reading them would associate such a subject with craziness. Examples of front-page headlines published by the *National Enquirer* included "UFO MURDERS, 4 Men Killed by Deadly Rays from Spacecraft" (Dec. 29, 1981), "Aliens on Moon When We Landed" (Sept. 11, 1979), and "Mystery Blasts Linked to UFOs" (Jan. 24, 1978). These UFO headlines were often seen by the average citizen when they walked through their local grocery checkout center. Other tabloids competed for attention with stories of space aliens backing George Bush for president, lizard-like aliens, and alien abductions to harvest human embryos to save a dying alien planet. The *National Enquirer* was effective in minimizing serious thought being given to UFOs, whether the CIA was behind it or not.

The disdain for the UFO subject shown in large media outlets and the craziness displayed by the tabloid magazines ostracized the topic. By the end of the twentieth century the media's handling of the UFO subject had reached its death knell. The subject was dramatized even by mainstream media to capture headlines. Claims of photos of aliens or wild statements that used to be reserved for the tabloids became more common in the main media networks. This effectively pushed back any thoughtful conversation on the subject and the UFO subject became known as the Great Taboo.

Attempts were made to break through the taboo. Investigative journalist Jon Hilkevitch was not aware of the world of UFOs until the Chicago O'Hare sighting of 2006. His report of a thirty-foot disk hovering over a departure gate made the *Chicago Herald* and the national news, but the reaction to the story was minimal. As noted by investigative journalist Leslie Kean: "This thing was hovering over Chicago O'Hare Airport at rush hour. Lots of people saw it . . . the U.S. government never said a word."[7] Kean herself went on to try and puncture the Great Taboo with a National Press event held in 2007 in Washington, D.C. Former Arizona governor Symington was her guest speaker along with famous witnesses from many of the major UFO sightings of the previous thirty years. The results: nothing. Kean was disappointed but did not give up. She used those witnesses to write individual chapters in a book that became a bestseller, *UFOs: Generals, Pilots, and Government Officials Go on the Record*. Although she had lost the battle, she had not yet lost the war. The battle that Kean fought was one that was perfectly described by Dr. Allen Hynek twenty years earlier:

> How is it possible that in the United States where even trivial events are flashed across the world, only one national TV and radio network carried an account of these utterly astounding sightings? [He was referring to the Hudson Valley UFO sightings of the 1980s.] Was no one minding the store? Was everyone asleep at the switch?

This refusal to report news that didn't fit a popular narrative would be reversed in 2017, and it is a story unto itself that will be examined in the next chapter. A key reason for that reversal is related to two of the other key protagonists and members within the military and the government.

THE MILITARY

Before discussing the military's reaction to UFOs, it is important to state what is meant by the military. The military is an arm of the government and historically is the primary part of government that has dealt with UFOs. Any unknown object in our skies is a potential threat to national security, and that is the primary responsibility of the military. They are the frontline of our government's defense, and they are responsible for the executive and legislative branches of our government that provide the military with its direction and funding. The Air Force has historically been the primary branch involved in the investigation and tracking of UFOs. But all branches have been involved at one time or another. These along with our intelligence agencies constitute our military response to any threat.

By now, you should have a good understanding of the overall government reaction to the UFO phenomenon across the last eighty years. But governments are rarely transparent. Secrecy has become a key component of our government as we have evolved as a nation. There are three basic levels of secrecy in the government: confidential, secret, and top secret. There are 4.9 million people with secrecy clearances and of those, 1.3 million have top secret clearances.[8] We are a nation of secrets, and this lack of transparency affects almost all information held by the government, including UFOs. Consequently, our government's reaction to UFOs has varied from intense interest to blatant disregard of the subject. It was like Charles Dickens's *A Tale of Two Cities*: "It was the best of times, it was the worst of times, it was the age of wisdom, it was the age of foolishness, it was the epoch of belief, it was the epoch of incredulity, it was the season of Light, it was the season of Darkness, it was the spring of hope, it was the winter of despair."

Maj. Gen. Charles Cabell, the director of intelligence for the U.S. Air Force, best personified this Dr. Jekyll and Mr. Hyde mentality. It was early in the era of UFOs, then referred to as flying saucers. The press had been hounding the Air Force for more information regarding these unknown objects in our skies. Something needed to be done. In October 1950 Cabell had his aide, Brig. Gen. Moore, send a letter to the Commanding General of Air Material Command at Wright-Patterson Air Force Base. In that letter he instructed them to answer press inquiries regarding UFOs with the following statement: "We have investigated and evaluated _____ incident and have found nothing of value and nothing which would change our previous estimates on this subject." A copy of that letter can be seen in figure 7.1. But this attitude toward the press and the public was just one side of the coin. Only a few months later, Gen. Cabell chastised his subordinates for not taking the UFO subject seriously. He said, "I want an open mind, in fact I order an open mind. Anyone that doesn't keep an open mind can get out, now." He went on to say, "I've been lied to, and lied to, and lied to. I want it to stop. I want the answer to the saucers, and I want a good answer."[9] The story the general gave the public was completely different from the seriousness with which he addressed the UFO subject internally.

A common statement from the military over the decades has been that UFOs are not a threat to our national security. Additionally, they have implied to varying degrees that there is no conclusive evidence that UFOs are real. But the actions of the military are not in alignment with these statements and indicate an incongruity between statements and actions. There are a dozen known instances when orders to fire on UFOs have been given. It is likely that there are even more instances that have never been released to the public. These actions do not mesh with the view that there is no threat to national security and that the phenomenon is not real.

June 6, 1950; Grenier AFB, New Hampshire.   Although orders to fire on unknowns have been documented in the Second World War and in 1947, these were during an era when there was a suspicion that UFOs might be an enemy weapon. The first clear order to fire on unknowns over U.S. territory happened in New Hampshire. We knew these were not enemy aircraft flying

OCT 1 ~ ' 50

AFO1V-TC

SUBJECT: (Restricted) Releasing Results of Analysis and Evaluation
of "Unidentified Aerial Objects" Reports

TO: Commanding General
Air Material Command
Wright-Patterson Air Force Base
Dayton, Ohio
ATTENTION: Chief, Intelligence Dept

1. This headquarters is cognizant of press interests in the so-
called "flying saucers" reports, referred to by this headquarters as
"unidentified aerial objects." Your headquarters has previously been
advised as to the release of information concerning Air Force interest
in this subject. Your attention is invited to USAF PIO release of 6
September 1950 and Hq USAF letter, subject "Reporting of Information
on Unconventional Aircraft," dated 8 September 1950.

2. In a recent telephone conversation between Colonel Watson,
Hq AMC and Colonel Harris, this headquarters, Colonel Watson requested
guidance in the matter of releasing results of investigation, analysis,
and evaluation of incidents brought to his attention. This headquarters believes that release of details of analysis and evaluation of
incidents is inadvisable, and desires that, in lieu thereof, releases
conform to the policy and spirit of the following:

"We have investigated and evaluated _____ incident
and have found nothing of value and nothing which would change
our previous estimates on this subject."

3. Results of analysis and evaluation of incidents possessing
any intelligence value will be forwarded to this headquarters for information and for any action relative to possible press releases.

BY COMMAND OF THE CHIEF OF STAFF:

S/
E. MOORE
/Brig. Gen., USAF
Assistant for Production
Directorate of Intelligence

VX-COC.76 GENERAL - Press Release

OFFICE SYMBOL	1 AFOIV	2 AFOIA	3 AFOIN	AFOIC	5 AFOIP	6 AFCPR
SIGNATURE OF RESPONSIBLE OFFICER					Col. Wilson	Gen. Patterson
INTERNAL OFFICE COORDINATION	4 Col.	USAF		Brannon		

CONFIDENTIAL   16-29242-1   U. S. GOVERNMENT PRINTING OFFICE

Figure 7.1.   Letter from Gen. Charles Cabell on how to reply to the press.
Source: USAF, Freedom of Information Act

over the United States. The orders went out. F-86s assigned to the 654th Aircraft Control and Warning Squadron "were directed to fly with 'hot' guns for certain missions involving interception of unidentified tracks."[10]

Summer 1952.   The summer of 1952 was the time when UFOs were being sighted visually and on radar along the Eastern Seaboard. An Air Force Information Officer, Lt. Colonel Moncel Monts, confirmed orders to fire on UFOs when he stated in July 1952: "The jet pilots are, and have been, under orders to investigate unidentified objects and to shoot them down if they can't talk them down."[11] How a pilot was to coax a UFO to land is anybody's guess. These orders to fire on a UFO were also confirmed in an Air Force memorandum where it was stated: "General Garland advised that he is considering making arrangements for a guided missile to be fired at one of the objects [UFOs], and of having camera equipped all-weather interceptors stand by to attempt to intercept and photograph them."[12] Yet through the other side of their mouth, the Air Force was telling the public that UFOs were not real and not a threat to national security.

During that same summer an F-86 pilot fired on a UFO accelerating away from him at a rapid speed. The large-caliber bullets from his guns either missed or never reached the target, as there was no effect.[13] Sadly, this incident or a similar one is described in a 1970 USAF Academy textbook as if firing on a UFO was appropriate. The story of a F-86 incident begins with, "We too have fired on UFOs . . ."[14]

These orders to fire on UFOs are further supported by a 1967 audio interview of a Boeing engineer who had been stationed as an Army radar specialist on the East Coast in the summer of 1952. The details of this incident were described in chapter 1.

May 1957; Kent, England.   Decisions to fire on UFOs continued. In 2009 Dr. Milton Torres stated that he was ordered to fire on a UFO in 1957. Then USAF pilot Torres was stationed at RAF Station Manston in Great Britain. He knew when he took off that he had orders to fire a twenty-four-missile salvo at the UFO once he was in range and had a radar lock. He obtained a radar lock twenty-five miles from the UFO. He was preparing to fire in twenty seconds when the UFO took off at what he estimated must have been a speed over 7,000 mph.[15]

Spring 1972; Langley AFB, Virginia.   The 48th Fighter Interceptor Squadron was headquartered at Langley AFB and equipped with F-106 Delta Darts, capable of 1,200+ mph speeds, and armed with four air-to-air missiles. Often, they would escort Soviet bombers out of U.S. airspace. During the spring of 1972 an intrusion was detected in U.S. airspace and two F-106s were scrambled. About forty-five minutes after being airborne, the pilot chatter began about a disk-shaped object that possessed extreme speed and maneuverability. One of the F-106s fired a missile and the pilot reported that it went right through the disk as if it wasn't there.[16]

November 14, 2004; 60 miles southwest of San Diego. The USS *Princeton*, a Ticonderoga-class guided missile cruiser, detected an unknown target on radar at 20,000 feet and to the west. The *Princeton* directed the nearest aircraft, an F-18 Marine Hornet, to investigate. The pilot was asked if he had any ordinance available on his aircraft and he replied that he did not. A few minutes later the *Princeton* called off the Marine Hornet as two F-18 Navy Super Hornets from the USS *Nimitz* were also on their way to the target. The lead pilot was also asked what type of ordinance he had aboard, and he replied, "None."[17] There is more to this story, but the important point to note at this juncture was what seemed to be the military's desire to engage an unidentified target with weaponry. Whether the Navy jets would have fired if they had been armed, we will never know.

February 10–12, 2023; Alaska, Yukon, and Lake Huron. The U.S. Air Force shot down three unknown flying objects in three days using state-of-the-art F-22s armed with heat-seeking missiles. Whether these objects were truly unknown is open to debate, as the government has not been transparent as to the nature of the three objects that were shot down. What can be stated is this is the first time in history that the government has ever shot down any objects classified as either UFOs or Unidentified Aerial Phenomena (UAP). That the United States shot down three objects in three days stretches the credulity that these were truly UFOs. But a portion of the public believed the military's statements that they did not know what these objects were. The government's and the military's lack of transparency only served to fuel conspiracy theories.

Here is what we do know. The first UFO was shot down over Alaskan waters on February 10. And remember, the term *UFO* means nothing more than an unidentified flying object. The Defense Department stated the object was most likely not a balloon, as it broke into pieces. It was about the size of a small car. The second UFO was cylindrical in shape and was shot down on February 11 over Yukon Territory after permission was obtained from Prime Minister Justin Trudeau of Canada. The third UFO was shot down over Lake Huron, Michigan, on February 12. It was octagonal in shape with strings hanging off it, which sounds potentially like a balloon.[18] A search was mounted for all three of these objects. Before the week was over the searches were called off without finding debris from any of the three objects.[19]

What should be learned from the military reaction to UFOs, whether it was in the 1950s or seventy years later in the twenty-first century, is that we are willing to destroy an object that we cannot identify. The word *we* is used rather than *military* because the military is just an extension of who we are.

Shoot first and ask questions later. This seems to be who we are as a nation and as a species. When we someday encounter an alien intelligence, whether it is here or on another planet, let us hope that our reaction will not be to eliminate any possible threat out of fear and/or our aggressive impulses.

THE GOVERNMENT

The other protagonist with a Jekyll-and-Hyde personality is the government. The government reaction to UFOs has been through the executive and legislative branches. The U.S. president has been the primary participator in a public manner for the executive branch and both the House of Representatives and the Senate have been involved with UFOs at various times in history. All these parts of government are heavily influenced by the public and the media because those entities are what control their reelection and careers. Consequently, their actions are usually taken to ensure reelection whether the subject is UFOs, global warming, overseas military interventions, or any other issue that garners public and media attention. If the public takes UFOs seriously, then those elected officials take them seriously; if the public thinks UFOs are for those in the loony bin, then their elected officials avoid the subject like the plague.

It was 1957 when Congress first became involved with UFOs. A civilian UFO organization, the National Investigations Committee on Aerial Phenomena (NICAP), had requested congressional intervention in the question of UFOs. NICAP had become frustrated with the Air Force's lack of transparency on the subject. They brought in two well-credentialed admirals to urge congressional support in studying UFOs. The first was retired admiral Delmar Fahrney, who was also the former chief of the Navy's Guided Missile Program. Fahrney made national news when he stated at a press conference that there were objects coming into our atmosphere at very high speeds that could not be matched by the United States or the Soviet Union. The second admiral was the first director of the CIA and was now a member of NICAP, retired admiral Roscoe Hillenkoetter. Briefings of Congress ensued and subcommittees to investigate UFOs were initiated. Then in May 1960, Hillenkoetter made an astounding statement to the press when he said:

1. UFOs are guided by intelligence.
2. They are not Russian.
3. We have never properly investigated them.
4. Congress needs to look into this.

Hillenkoetter's statements along with his pedigree stoked the fires in Congress. Wouldn't a former director of the CIA know what was going on over our skies? The Air Force fought back and successfully resisted the congressional attempts for official investigations. The Air Force was also helped by a sudden lull in UFO sightings during the period of 1960–1963. But the lull did not last long. A new wave of sightings hit in 1965 and Congress again entered the fray after the Air Force mishandling of the "Marsh Gas" sightings in Gerald Ford's state of Michigan. As described in detail in chapter 1, this led to the Condon Report and the Air Force was able to avoid any future congressional pressure by dropping out of public UFO investigations in 1970.

Civilian UFO groups filled the vacuum. It was in this period of the 1970s to the 1980s that reports of abductions became more common. Usually there was no UFO involved, but the witnesses claimed the abduction was related to aliens. Problems ensued as these groups were varied in their level of investigative rigor. Books with unsupported facts made claims such as aliens created us, aliens abducted us for breeding purposes, and other such nonsense. Among the books were: *Our Ancestors Came from Outer Space*, *The Space-Gods Revealed*, *UFO: Contact from the Pleiades*, and *Alien Meetings*, to name a few. The UFO subject became associated with craziness and the public pulled away, as did Congress and the executive branch. Occasionally, a government official would tiptoe into the UFO waters, but it was unusual.

Government interaction with the UFO subject waned, although it would still crop up on occasion at a personal level. It happened with the then presidential candidate Jimmy Carter. He was one of our more science-minded presidents. He was educated in engineering, worked on nuclear submarines, and had graduated from the U.S. Naval Academy. Carter stated during the presidential campaign of 1976 that he had seen a UFO in 1969 while governor of Georgia. He described the object as about the size of the moon in the night sky and that the object was very bright with changing colors. He told a reporter that, after the experience, he would never again ridicule anyone who claimed to have seen a UFO. Carter also promised that, if elected president, he would encourage the government to release information on UFOs to the public and to scientists. His admission of seeing a UFO did not prevent him from becoming president, but then again, his opponent did not pounce on that admission. Once president, Carter backtracked on releasing UFO information. He said that national security implications prevented him from releasing such information.[20]

Discussing UFOs during a presidential campaign wasn't always so benign. The Democratic Party's presidential primary of 2008 is a case in point. Candidate Dennis Kucinich of Ohio was asked during a Democratic primary debate if he had seen a UFO, and he replied that he had. His acknowledgment that he had seen a UFO was sufficient to derail his already weak candidacy for president. Candidate Barack Obama was asked if he believed in life on other planets in the same debate. He provided the better political response with, "You know, I don't know. And I don't presume to know. What I know is there is life here on Earth, and that we're not attending to life here on Earth."[21] Answering a question about UFOs and intelligent life elsewhere was knowing whether it was asked by Dr. Jekyll or Mr. Hyde.

Times change. Thirteen years later, and after winning the presidency for two consecutive terms, Obama's answer to questions about UFOs was different. When asked on a late-night TV show in 2021 a question about unknown objects in our skies, he said, "But what is true, and I'm actually being serious here, is that there is footage and records of objects in the skies that we don't know exactly what they are. We can't explain how they move their trajectory."[22] The difference in those two answers from the former president not only reflected a change in his government-based viewpoint of the UFO subject; it also reflected a change occurring within the public that allowed politicians to be more open.

THE PUBLIC

The general public's reaction to UFOs is the wellspring of how we as a society collectively react to the phenomenon. Yes, the media and government may impact the public's perception, but those organizations are made up of the same human frailties and strengths that make up the public at large—the apple doesn't fall far from the tree. The public's reaction tells us a lot about who we are as a species. Are we innately aggressive or peaceful, open-minded or closed-minded, curious or fearful, suspicious or trustful? The human quality or need that reflects how we react to UFOs is the same characteristic that runs through much of our existence as individuals and as a society, our need to control. The need to control also determines how we react to UFOs.

Our success as a species has been our ability to control the environment around us. We learned to control fire, build weapons and objects that protected and housed us, and tame both predators and mother nature. Through that success, mankind has always considered itself the center of all that is important. And for the last several thousand years our ability to control our environment has given us sovereignty over all creatures on the planet. They have all bowed before us—the tiger, bear, elephant, buffalo. We have remained the superior species on planet Earth and all our needs and beliefs have revolved around us. Our anthropocentric position on this planet is centered in our industries, our lifestyles, and our view of who we are.

The UFO phenomenon has the potential to upset the Jenga blocks that we have assembled. The reason is because the meaning of the word *UFO* does have a hidden implication in the back of the public's mind. The public sees or hears of an object that can move from a stationary position to extreme speeds, unbelievably rapid changes in direction, and sudden stops. It is reasonable to consider the possibility that the object is controlled by an intelligence far beyond our own. This possibility clearly implies that we may not be at the top of the totem pole in our capabilities. Like Governor Symington, it is easier to laugh than to think seriously about the implications. Such a possibility implies that we are not in control. A lack of control is something that society as a whole rarely experiences, and is something that an individual does not usually experience until near death.

This lack of control is why one witness will block a close-up UFO encounter completely from their mind or another witness becomes obsessed with a desire to understand if such an event really happened. It is also why our military fires on an unknown target without knowing its identity, just as our ancestors fired their arrows into the rustling sound in the bushes. Our ancestors evolved with the realization that an unknown movement or sound could be a life and death situation. Control was a matter of survival. George Bernard Shaw succinctly described this need when he said, "To be in hell is to drift; to be in heaven is to steer."

The possibility that UFOs are a more advanced intelligence from some unknown origin has always fascinated the populace. A Gallop poll in July 2021 showed that 41 percent of the American population believe that some UFOs may be alien spacecraft. However, the American public's attraction to a subject does not necessarily mean there is an abiding interest in it. The latest ongoings of the Kardashians or the British royal family attract much more public interest than whether UFOs are controlled by an advanced intelligence.

There is a smaller percentage of the population that is convinced that UFOs are visitors from another world and even that they have mingled among humans on Earth. They are sometimes derisively characterized as "believers." This group is very hopeful if not certain that UFOs are interested in saving humanity from itself. They view reports of UFOs shutting down ICBM systems as warnings for humanity to be careful in the use of nuclear weapons. Some have claimed to have been contacted by aliens and told that humanity must do a better job of caring for the Earth. There is no proof of any of this, and even if UFOs are controlled by advanced intelligence, there is no way to reliably interpret another species' intentions. Although this group may not have proof, they do possess a characteristic that makes it difficult to discuss the subject with them; they are certain of their convictions and are not willing to listen to evidence to the contrary.

There is a flip side to the "believer" group—the debunkers. Debunkers possess a similar characteristic of being unwilling to accept any evidence that is counter to their view. They believe there is no possibility that UFOs could be intelligently controlled by something beyond Earth. There is no UFO sighting that they cannot explain. Even Project Blue Book and the Condon Report could not manage to explain all UFO sightings, but debunkers always believe that *they* can. They see themselves as smarter than everyone else. A debunker believes that if the government couldn't explain a sighting, then they just didn't look hard enough. For some debunkers, it becomes a life passion to tear down whatever beliefs that others may have by whatever means necessary. The use of the plural pronoun to refer to debunkers is used advisedly, since debunking seems to be a uniquely testosterone-driven obsession.

Sitting on the side of science is the skeptic. A skeptic acknowledges there are cases, even interesting ones, that are not explainable even if the skeptic harbors doubts that they may have, ultimately, extraordinary implications. The National Aeronautics and Space Administration (NASA) provides a very good explanation of the proper use of skepticism: "Skepticism is the act of suspending judgment (the opposite of jumping to conclusions) when evaluating an explanation or claims. It allows scientists to consider all possibilities and systematically question all information in the course of an investigation."[23] This is easier said than done. We all have preconceived prejudices. A scientist tries to put those prejudices aside and suspends judgment while evaluating the evidence. The public depends on a scientist to be a good skeptic.

THE SCIENTIFIC COMMUNITY

The answer to the UFO phenomenon must come from the world of science and academia. The military has investigated UFOs for eighty years and we still know next to nothing. Science is the respected path that our society recognizes for progress. A Pew Research Center survey in 2015 noted: "Science holds an esteemed place among citizens and professionals. Americans recognize the accomplishments of scientists in key fields and, despite considerable dispute about the role of government in other realms, there is broad public support for government investment in scientific research."[24] The reaction of the scientific community to UFOs may be the most important of all societal segments.

Peter Sturrock was a professor of applied physics at Stanford University in 1977 when he conducted an exhaustive survey of the American Astronautical Society regarding UFOs. He surveyed 1,356 astronomers regarding their views about UFOs. The results were enlightening. Astronomers were positive in their view that the UFO subject deserves scientific study, with 53 percent indicating that the subject either "certainly or probably" deserves scientific study. Only 20 percent of astronomers indicated that the scientific study of UFOs should "certainly not or probably not" occur. Sixty-two of the 1,356 astronomers had either witnessed or obtained instrumental records of an event they could not identify and thought was related to the phenomenon. Most interesting was the relationship between the number of hours astronomers spent studying UFOs versus their views on whether the subject should be scientifically investigated. Figure 7.2 clearly shows that the more knowledge a scientist acquires about UFOs, the more the scientist sees a need for a scientific investigation of the subject. Only 29 percent of astronomers who had spent less than an hour reading literature on UFOs thought it was "certainly or probably" worthy of scientific study. This category jumped to 67 percent of astronomers who had spent more than fifty hours on the subject.[25] This is a very noteworthy fact. The more that scientists study the subject, the more they see the need for a scientific examination. The problem is the scientists who have done no research on the subject.

Why haven't scientists been studying the UFO subject in earnest if additional knowledge breeds the desire for more scientific study? Eighty percent of the astronomers in Sturrock's survey expressed a desire to help resolve the question regarding UFOs. Yet there are very few academic papers that have done any research on the UFO subject. The answer to the question is the

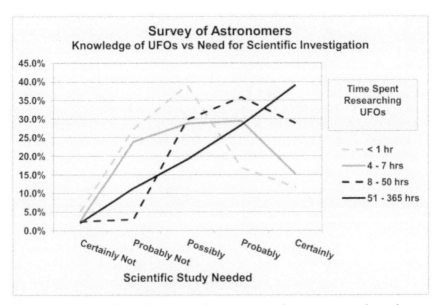

Figure 7.2.   Graph of data from survey by Peter Sturrock. *Source*: From the author

Great Taboo. It is difficult to blame academics when the mainstream media belittles the subject by dramatizing the stories of the zaniest of witnesses and citizens of UFO groups who talk about UFO bases buried beneath Antarctica. At the same time, science has always been expected to remain above the fray and to be society's leader for the source of truth, not the follower of arbitrary social trends.

James McDonald was the senior physicist at the University of Arizona's Institute for Atmospheric Physics. His field of study would be appropriate in ascertaining if the phenomenon was natural or artificial. McDonald interviewed over 500 UFO witnesses and studied the subject in depth. It would be difficult to argue that there was anyone more knowledgeable of the UFO subject than James McDonald.

McDonald was disappointed in the study of UFOs—disappointed that the scientific community had failed in its job. He addressed this issue before the American Association for the Advancement of Science, the world's largest scientific body, with 120,000 members, and the publisher of *Scientific American*. McDonald minced no words when he presented his paper, "Science in Default."

> Only a very small number of scientists have taken the time and trouble to search out the nearly puzzling reports that tend to be diluted out by the much larger number of trivial and non-significant UFO reports. The net result is that there still exists no general scientific recognition of the scope and nature of the UFO problem.

McDonald did not stop there. He went on to condemn scientists who made statements on a subject with which they had done little research other than reading the newspapers.

> Present evidence surely does not amount to incontrovertible proof of the extraterrestrial hypothesis. What I find scientifically dismaying is that, while a large body of UFO evidence now seems to point in no other direction than the extraterrestrial hypothesis, the profoundly important implications of that possibility are going unconsidered by the scientific community because this entire problem has been imputed to be little more than a nonsense matter unworthy of serious scientific attention. Those overtones have been generated almost entirely by scientists and others who have done essentially no real investigation of the problem-area in which they express such strong opinions.[26]

If there was ever a curator of the scientific study of unidentified flying objects, it was Dr. James McDonald. His curiosity was insatiable, and he was not thwarted by any taboos. He was willing to stand in awe of the mysterious and rather than ignore it, he chose to apply science. The study of UFOs needs more James McDonalds.

Chapter Eight

A Change in Attitude

Humans have always desired to be the center of importance, whether in our personal lives or as a species. Our anthropocentric position on this planet is centered in our industries, our lifestyles, and our view of who we are. "It's all about me." We love our smartphones, cars, vacations, money, homes, and whatever else we need. Even in our religions, it is us at the center—God created Earth for all mankind. We're much more comfortable with the concept that Jesus sacrificed himself for us, rather than Jesus's sermons telling us to be humble and minimize our egos. The former makes us important; the latter is harder to accomplish, and it seems to minimize our importance. Our innate tendency is to always put ourselves at the center.

Such anthropocentric beliefs extend even into the world of science. The scientists of ancient Greece believed that the universe revolved around the Earth. It was not until the sixteenth century that the Copernican Theory moved the center of the universe from the Earth to the sun. That change did not come easily. We often solely blame religion for condemning Galileo for supporting a belief that the earth was not the center of the universe, but the Aristotelian scientific community of the time also castigated the renegade scientist. They were happy to see Galileo punished by the Catholic Church for pushing too hard on their beliefs. After all, all their teachings and writings would be obsolete if Galileo was right. But with time and evidence, science finally acquiesced and removed the Earth from the center of the universe. They had a compromise. The sun and our solar system were still considered the center of everything. All was good. It was only 100 years ago that modern science recognized through the work of Shapley and Hubble that our solar system is not even the center of our own galaxy.

Although we may have lost our central location, we still had our uniqueness. Earth might well be one of the very few places, or even the only place, in our galaxy where life could exist. We could be the center of life even if we couldn't be the center of the galaxy. This belief was weakened by Frank Drake in 1961 when he published his now famous Drake Equation that predicted there should be many intelligent civilizations in our galaxy.[1] But that was not the view held by most scientists of the time. It was a common view in the mid-twentieth century that some cosmic roll-of-the-dice gave Earth all the right ingredients for life to develop. The fortunate tilt of the Earth gave us our four seasons of the year. Our solar system provided the giant planet Jupiter so that Earth would not be constantly bombarded by asteroids. Additionally, a key theory that is still harbored to this day is that our moon is unique in that its orbit around Earth provides conditions such as the tides and it blocked powerful solar storms that would have prevented early life on Earth from evolving. Many scientists believed that man existed through coincidental events critical to the formation of life. And with the vast distances between stars, Earth was considered a unique location in the cosmos where life had managed to spring. We were the Pale Blue Dot in the cosmos, as coined by Carl Sagan after seeing a distant photo of Earth taken by the *Voyager I* spacecraft. We were unique.

EXOPLANETS

There were no known planets that existed outside of our solar system prior to 1992. Yes, there was debate among astronomers as to whether our solar system was unique or was a common occurrence in the universe, but the pre-Copernican beliefs of uniqueness were the favored arguments. There was no evidence that other stars had planets, and it was believed that our solar system was likely a rarity in having many planets and even more rare in its development of life. In 1992 part of that veil of uniqueness was torn away when the first planet outside of our solar system was discovered orbiting a pulsar 2,300 light-years away.[2]

In less than thirty years since that first discovery, the ability to detect exoplanets has grown immensely, although with limitations. By December 2009, there had been over 400 exoplanets detected. Because most early methods of detection of exoplanets depended on gravitational interaction between the planet and its star, they were limited in their capability. Those methods were predisposed to detection of very large planets in the size range of Neptune to Jupiter and planets that orbit extremely close to their star. None of those types of planets are likely to harbor life. The ability to detect a smaller planet has improved as astrophysicists have turned to the use of the transit method. This technique measures the decrease in light given off by a star when one of its planets transits between it and Earth.

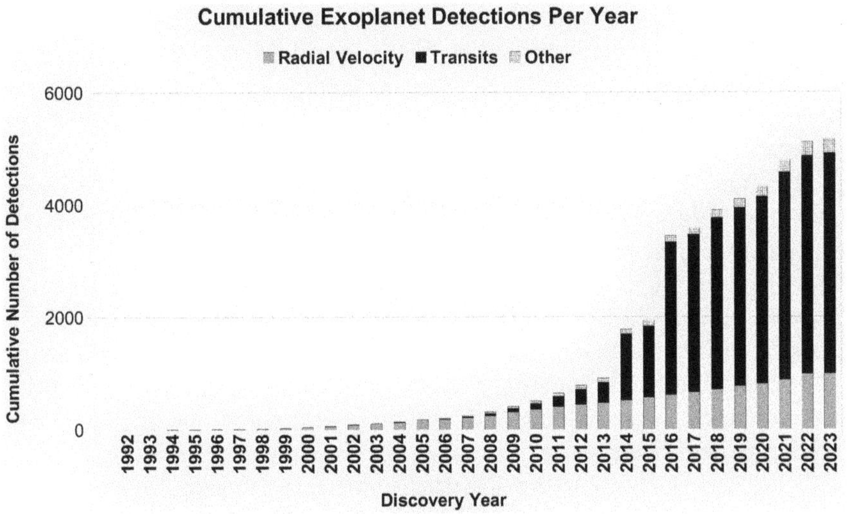

Cumulative Exoplanet Detections Per Year

■ Radial Velocity ■ Transits ▨ Other

Figure 8.1.   Graph of exoplanet discoveries. *Source*: NASA Caltech

The launch of the Kepler space telescope in March 2009 placed a platform in space that used the transit method of planet detection. Kepler's capability allowed for the detection of planets the size of Earth that orbit smaller M-class stars at a distance that could support life as we know it. This capability could not detect an Earth-size planet around a larger G-class star such as our sun, but it was an improvement. By December 2013 analysis of data from the Kepler telescope had increased the number of confirmed exoplanets to over 850 and more than 3,600 potential candidates. These numbers have improved, with more Kepler findings and discoveries from terrestrial-based telescopes. The launch of the Transiting Exoplanet Survey Satellite (TESS) in 2018 and the James Webb Space Telescope (JWST) in 2021 is expected to raise the number of potential exoplanets to beyond 20,000. Already there have been 5,300 exoplanets confirmed as of February 2023, and another 6,000+ candidates are awaiting confirmation. Figure 8.1 shows the rapid rise in the discovery of exoplanets.[3]

Do these planets have the right temperature to support life as we know it and are there the necessary ingredients for life such as water, oxygen, and carbon? The answer seems to be "yes." The more we learn about exoplanets, the birth of solar systems throughout our galaxy, and the chemical ingredients available in space, the more it seems that life may be ubiquitous in the cosmos. Sixty-three of these exoplanets are in an orbit that should allow the right temperatures to support life.[4] Do they have water? We know that the existence of water beyond the Earth is much more common than previously thought. Water has been found in comets, on Mars, and even on our own

desolate moon. Jupiter's moons Callisto, Europa, and Ganymede are all sus-
pected of harboring large quantities of liquid water beneath frozen oceans.
A team of U.S. astronomers, led by Cornell University astrophysicist Martin
Harwit, discovered a massive concentration of water vapor within a cloud of
interstellar gas close to the Orion Nebula. The amount of water measured is
so high that it is enough to fill the Earth's oceans sixty times a day.[5] Astronomers studying the water vapor around infant star V883 Orionis find that it's
chemically similar to water in our solar system's comets.[6] All this evidence
draws us to the supposition that it would not be unexpected to find water on
some of these Earth-like worlds. And more than just water has been found
in space: all five bases that exist in DNA and RNA have now been found in
meteorites. The building blocks for life are likely available throughout the
universe, and it is possible that life on Earth is a result of the seeding of the
right ingredients from space.

We will soon know more than just whether the right ingredients exist in space.
Through the use of its higher resolution and the spectrometer on the JWST, we
will be able to measure the chemical constituents in the atmospheres of some of
these exoplanets. Already an exoplanet 700 light-years away, WASP-39b, has
had its atmosphere analyzed. Water and carbon dioxide were among the several
chemicals detected in its atmosphere. WASP-39b is about the size of Saturn
and orbits as close to its star as Mercury does to our Sun. It's not an Earth-like
planet but what is important is that we have demonstrated the ability to detect
chemicals in another planet's atmosphere. So, the next question is, "When will
we be able to detect what is in the atmosphere of an Earth-like planet orbiting at
about the same distance from a G-type star like Sol?"

A telescope that would allow us to detect an Earth-like planet orbiting a
G-type or K-type star is on the drawing board. This would allow the detection
of a planet like ours that orbits from a similar distance and a similar type of
star. Finding "Earth 2.0" will need a coronagraph that blocks out the light of
the parent sun so that it can be seen with a very large space telescope. The
next generation telescope will be called Diffractive Interfeo Coronagraph
Exoplanet Resolver (DICER). It will be capable of seeing any "Earth 2.0"
out to ten parsecs, or about thirty light-years.[7] There are over three dozen G-
type and K-type stars within that distance. This will be our first opportunity
to determine how common our solar system may be. One wonders if any of
those stars has a planet with telescopes pointed in our direction and measuring the chemicals in our atmosphere. And their telescopes may be so good
that they can detect the emission of artificial light on the side of our planet
facing away from the sun.

The growing realization that Earth-like planets are plentiful in our galaxy
has arguably reduced the taboo about UFOs. There is now a complete generation of people who have lived through a time when the weekly discovery
of new exoplanets is the norm. The argument is no longer whether our solar

system and world are unique; the remaining argument is whether another civilization could reach our solar system in a reasonable period of time. New information has recently become available that has begun to change not only the public's view but also many scientists' views on whether we should more seriously entertain the possibility of intelligent life visiting Earth.

THE *NEW YORK TIMES*

It was the autumn of 2016 when I met with an individual working for the government's program on UFOs, called the Advanced Aerospace Threat Identification Program (AATIP). The conversation that ensued surprised me for a couple of reasons. First, the government had claimed that they had stopped investigating UFOs in 1970 with the close of Project Blue Book. I knew this was not true, as any object that is initially unidentified could turn out to be an aircraft or missile from an enemy nation. An object can't be ignored just because it is not immediately identifiable. But I was surprised that we now had an "official" group that was looking into the type of objects that *remained* unidentified: in other words, UFOs. Second, the UFO story that was relayed to me came from a folder (that I was not allowed to see) that was two inches thick. I was given a lot of details verbally, all of which I needed to confirm. I began that task, which would eventually involve hundreds of hours of research on the most impressive UFO incident that I had ever investigated.

My research began with the review of a military blog site with the name *FighterSweep*. I had done an internet search using some of the key information that I had been told. Nested within that site was an article from March 2015 with the title, "There I Was: The X-Files Edition." The story that was told matched what I had heard from my government contact. It was a story based on the blog author's conversation with a longtime friend who was a Naval Academy graduate with a degree in oceanography and was the commander of an F-18 squadron.[8] The quality of the witness could not have been better, and he was not the only witness. My investigation revealed almost two dozen witnesses. All the witnesses were service men and women either in the U.S. Navy or the U.S. Marines. Their ranks varied from junior seamen to commanders and lieutenant colonels. And the blog indicates that there was one more piece of information—an infra-red (IR) video of the object in question. The blog article provided me with the clues that I needed, and it was just the tip of the iceberg.

I sent a total of twenty-six Freedom of Information Act (FOIA) requests to every department in the U.S. Navy, the U.S. Marines, NORAD, and the Defense Intelligence Agency. I began these requests in late 2016. I asked for two pieces of information: confirmation that the event had occurred along with documentation (logs, reports, and radar data), and a copy of an infra-red video that had been leaked to the internet. By the end of 2017 my FOIA requests had all been denied. Every reply that I received indicated that the government had no information although after an appeal, a string of emails was provided that indicated several Marine officers aboard the USS *Nimitz* were aware of the event and that more information on the event should be available.[9] But I was stonewalled. The government agencies steadfastly maintained that there was no information. Were they telling me the truth? "You cannot depend on the truth from a FOIA submission," is the one thing that I've learned from fifteen years of experience submitting FOIA requests.

It would be an understatement to say that I was surprised to read the front page of the Sunday edition of the *New York Times* on December 17, 2017, with the story, "Real U.F.O.s? Pentagon Unit Tried to Know." The same story that I had been researching for over a year was admitted to by the Department of Defense and the Navy. Included in the story were details indicating that the event had occurred and that the video of the November 14, 2004, event that I had been researching was real.

The story released by the *New York Times* set in motion events and testimonies that would convince much of the public across the world that UFOs were real and would also begin to unlock the taboo in the scientific community. The journalistic objectivity of the *New York Times* led credence to the events. It caused worldwide coverage by other journalistic outlets, and it caused more service men and women to be willing to talk about what they experienced thirteen years earlier. It also exposed the existence of AATIP, a key government UFO investigative group that had been supported and financed by several key congressional leaders including then Senate Majority Leader Harry Reid. The release of this story owes much of its success to the hard work of the three main authors: Helene Cooper, Leslie Kean, and Ralph Blumenthal.[10] I had not been successful in exposing the story, but I was pleased to see the truth come out in America's most trusted newspaper. A summary of that story can be found in the latter part of chapter 4 of this book. It took place in November 2004 in the Pacific Ocean about sixty miles southwest of San Diego, California. It involved Carrier Strike Group Eleven led by the USS *Nimitz*.

This landmark report in a prestigious newspaper would generate follow-up reporting across all the major news outlets, including many of the major media throughout the world. It was highlighted in the *Washington Post*, *Politico*, the *Boston Globe*, *Time* magazine, the *Los Angeles Times*, the *Chicago Tribune*, and more. Stories even showed up in magazines that never discussed the UFO subject such as *Scientific American* and *Astronomy*. Foreign media outlets also picked up on the story: *Le Parisien* and the *Libéracion* in France, the *Guardian* in England, *The Times of India*, *CNN Brasil*, and more.

The impact of that first report in the *New York Times* was instrumental in generating increased attention on UFOs. But it would be remiss not to discuss how the *New York Times* obtained this story. This is a story within itself, and it began one year earlier in the winter of 2016. The principal character was the former deputy assistant secretary of defense for intelligence in the Clinton and Bush administrations: Chris Mellon, a member of the influential Mellon family. He understood well the bureaucratic tendencies of the DoD, and he had many personal contacts in Congress and in the government.

Chris was consulting for the Office of Naval Intelligence in late 2016. He attended a meeting where he learned that restricted U.S. airspace was being routinely violated by unidentified aircraft. He also learned about the *Nimitz* incident of 2004 and viewed numerous classified and unclassified videos of UFOs. He was concerned that the DoD was not reacting to incursions in our restricted airspace. Why were they not concerned? It seemed that because the craft did not exhibit the signatures of typical enemy aircraft that they were being ignored. This was a dangerous assumption, and Chris raised the issue with senior officials to no avail.

Chris continued with his efforts. In the summer of 2017, he obtained the help of Lue Elizondo, who had the lead role at AATIP. They wanted to brief Secretary of Defense Mattis about the UFO problem. They spent months trying to convince Gen. Mattis's White House liaison and his special assistant to arrange for a briefing on incursions in our restricted airspace. Because of the stigma around UFOs and the potential damage to the general's reputation, no briefing was allowed.

Chris Mellon was not deterred. This was an important matter that impacted our national security. History has shown many times that ignoring a potential threat can lead to a catastrophe, especially since the origin of these UFOs was unknown. What if they were Russian or Chinese? Chris put together a plan in the autumn of 2017 to utilize a major press outlet to garner the attention of Congress and put pressure on the DoD to act. He reached out to *Politico* editor Bill Duryea, *Washington Post* Pulitzer Prize–winning reporter Joby Warrick, and Leslie Kean, who had done freelance reporting for the *New York Times*. They were all understandably skeptical of the story and wanted additional evidence of incursions in U.S. airspace.

A hidden source within the DoD provided Chris copies of three compelling, authentic, and official UFO videos taken by F-18 pilots. Chris met with each of these journalists, showed them the videos, and offered each of the three major news outlets the chance for an exclusive front-page UFO story. The *Washington Post* was hard to convince, but the *New York Times* and *Politico* were very interested in the story. The videos were convincing.

Leslie Kean informed Chris that the *New York Times* would agree to his terms. Chris met with the paper's national security reporter, Helene Cooper, in Washington, D.C. Lue Elizondo and Leslie also attended the meeting. Later, the journalists were also introduced to Lt. Cmdr. Dave Fravor of the 2004 *Nimitz* incident as well as other Navy pilots. They also were introduced to Senator Harry Reid. The impetus for the *Times* article was Chris Mellon's actions. Without Chris's dedication, the public would still be in the dark on our military's encounters with these unknown objects and the testimonies received from many Navy pilots would never have been heard.[11]

The reason for the seriousness and popularity of the 2004 *Nimitz* event was because of the quality and sincerity of the key witnesses: U.S. Navy pilots. These were some of the best trained and experienced pilots in the world. There were six pilots directly involved in the UFO sighting by U.S. Carrier Strike Group 11. Their testimonies across multiple media outlets were the type of statements that were expected from highly educated and trained professionals; they were factual and direct without exaggeration. The testimony of Cmdr. Fravor and Lt. Dietrich, now a lieutenant commander and instructor at the Naval Academy, resounded the most with the public. Objects were detected on radar, military jets were sent to intercept, visual confirmation of the target was made, and the commander's jet engaged the target. Their stories not only enthralled the public but also garnered the attention of many scientists in both academia and private industry.

Chris Mellon's plan to bring the *Nimitz* story to light appeared to have worked, or at least for the public. But only persuading the public was not true success. It was in March 2018 that Chris determined that the *New York Times* story had not ignited the furor on Capitol Hill that he had anticipated. None of the congressional oversight committees had requested any briefings or taken any action. He was dismayed with the inaction in Congress.

Chris contacted his former colleagues at the Senate Armed Service Committee (SASC) and the Senate Select Committee on Intelligence (SSCI). He and Lue Elizondo met with staffers on those committees. They next brought in some of the Navy aviators to meet the staffers: Lt. Cmdr. David Fravor, Lt. Alex Dietrich, and Lt. Ryan Graves. The staffers were impressed, and they arranged for briefings by the Navy pilots of the committee members. Bill Nelson, who later would become NASA director, was among the senators who were deeply impressed by the testimony of the Navy officers. Chris Mellon spent the next two years bringing witnesses before senators in the SASC and the SSCI. His efforts received a boost in late 2018 when John "Jay" Stratton, soon to be the head of the government's Unidentified Aerial Phenomena Task Force (UAP Task Force), began providing classified intelligence briefings to the senators. Chris's plan was back on track. His work would lead to the most detailed legislation on UFOs in history, which would stipulate the creation of a new government organization to study the phenomenon as well as stringent reporting requirements.

It was during these Senate committee hearings that the *New York Times* broke another major story on UFOs and again, by the same authors as before. The article came out on May 26, 2019. This report was even more recent and involved Navy pilots off the East Coast of the United States during 2014 and 2015. Again, it was a U.S. carrier strike group that was involved—the USS *Roosevelt* and its accompanying ships and aircraft. It was more difficult this time to bring the witnesses together as many were still on active duty and could not testify. The key witness was a pilot educated as an aerospace engineer, former Navy lieutenant Ryan Graves.

According to Graves, Navy pilots had reported seeing objects that had no visible engine or infra-red exhaust plumes. They were seen at altitudes as high as 30,000 feet and could travel at hypersonic speeds. In the summer of 2014, Lt. Graves was part of a squadron called the "Red Rippers," VFA-11. He and Lt. Danny Accoin were stationed at Naval Air Station Oceana in Virginia and were training for deployment to the Persian Gulf. Lts. Graves and Accoin spoke on the record to the *Times* about the objects, as did three other pilots who wished to remain anonymous. Lt. Accoin told of a time that his radar detected a target, as did his IR camera system, because the training missile locked onto the target, but visually, he could not see it. Graves indicated that these encounters, whether only on radar or sometimes visual, were occurring almost daily.

Then, disaster almost struck. Two F-18s were flying in a restricted military operating area just east of Virginia Beach over the Atlantic Ocean. The USS *Roosevelt*'s strike group monitors the skies constantly with radar. No unauthorized aircraft are allowed into the area during practice exercises for safety reasons. The two jets were flying in tandem about 100 feet apart when an object came within a few dozen feet of each plane. The object looked like a sphere encased in a cube. This near miss angered the squadron. A hazardous air safety report was filed with the Navy. These are taken seriously and warrant a full investigation. The pilots wanted action taken.

The pilots were now convinced these objects were not part of some classified drone program for a couple of reasons. First, government officials would not endanger the lives of fighter pilots training for deployment to the Persian Gulf. Second, the acceleration of the objects was unheard of. The pilots said the objects could move from a standstill to hypersonic speeds and then make sudden stops and turns. Nothing in our arsenal could do such a thing, nor did the pilots believe anyone within those objects could survive such movements. As Lt. Graves pointed out, "Speed doesn't kill you, stopping does. Or acceleration." Graves went on to discuss the multiple capabilities that the objects demonstrated and compared that to our aircraft. "We have helicopters that can hover. We have aircraft that can fly at 30,000 feet and right at the surface. Combine all that in one vehicle of some type with no jet engine, no exhaust plume."[12]

It is hard to imagine these were any type of drone. It is also hard to believe that our government would not be investigating such incidents, especially when it put the lives of our pilots in danger. As noted earlier, the government was investigating these incidents through AATIP. The knowledge of what was happening went beyond AATIP, as was made clear in another *New York Times* article in June of 2021.

The article is titled, "U.S. Finds No Evidence of Alien Technology in Flying Objects, but Can't Rule It Out, Either." The story begins by noting that "American intelligence officials have found no evidence that aerial phenomena witnessed by Navy pilots in recent years are alien spacecraft." Let's dissect that statement. So how would one prove something was an alien spacecraft? The origin of a craft cannot be proven, short of it landing and some aliens getting out and saying, "Hi, we're from Alpha Centauri!" All that can be done is establish that an aircraft displays capabilities that are beyond what any nation on Earth can replicate. But if that is established, then by definition it is "not terrestrial," which means it is not from this Earth. Is there a difference between saying "not from this Earth" and "alien"? The quote provided by the American intelligence officials made at the beginning of this paragraph ends with, "but they still cannot explain the unusual movements that have mystified scientists and the military." Think about that statement. So, we have a craft with unusual movements that cannot be explained. It sounds like these unusual movements were made by a craft not manufactured by Russia, China, or us, if we can't even explain its movements. The article then quotes someone who should know, former President Barack Obama.[13] They quoted him from an answer he gave to a question on the *Late Late Show with James Corden*. Replying to a question about UFOs, Obama said, "What is true, and I'm actually being serious here, is that there is footage and records of objects in the skies that we don't know exactly what they are." The article left out the most critical part of Obama's reply: "We can't explain how they moved, their trajectory. They did not have an easily explainable pattern."[14] Think about that for a moment. We can't explain how they moved. Well, if an object moved like Lt. Graves and Cmdr. Fravor described, then we couldn't explain how it moved. We don't know how any object can suddenly stop, suddenly accelerate, and make instantaneous right-angle course corrections.

These well-publicized events, along with the knowledge that exoplanets are common throughout our galaxy, have changed the perceptions of a new generation of people. The generation that is currently under age forty-five is the one who grew up in the world of exoplanets. Unlike previous generations, they know that worlds like ours likely abound throughout the cosmos. They are less doubtful as to whether it's possible for another civilization to reach our world. A poll conducted in 2021 by the Pew Research Center bears this out. While only 57 percent of Americans over age fifty believed that intelligent life exists on other planets, the poll showed that the belief was much higher in the younger ages, with 69 percent of those age thirty to forty-nine and 76 percent of those age eighteen to twenty-nine.[15] This change in perception has also begun to chip away at other parts of society: academia, the government, and the military. After all, the people within our institutions are people who came from the public, and they would naturally also be part of this new paradigm shift away from our anthropocentric views.

UAP

It is difficult to say which institution initiated the changes that began to alter the view of this phenomenon during the last few years. It does seem like a paradigm shift that moves through society all at once with almost a will of its own, a little bit like a snowball rolling downhill with its own impetus and maybe even purpose. Perhaps the change in attitude began with a change in words. A change from the word *UFO* to the word *UAP*. Before discussing why this change occurred and was important, it's appropriate to discuss how each word represents the unknown objects seen in the skies.

Unidentified *Aerial* Phenomena, and recently changed by the government to Unidentified *Anomalous* Phenomena, is a broad term. "Anomalous" means unusual or not expected, so it broadens the term further from the original use of "aerial." Phenomena is the plural of phenomenon, which means an observable occurrence. UAP therefore represents multiple types of unidentified and unusual events that occur. It is somewhat redundant, as one would normally expect an anomalous event to be unidentified. It is also quite a broad term. A ghost or the Loch Ness monster are both unidentified anomalous phenomena. So was a pulsar for many years until it was finally identified. The same is true in the beginning stages of a new viral epidemic—it is an unidentified anomalous phenomenon. The use of the word *aerial* at least eliminated all of these except perhaps a pulsar.

The meaning of Unidentified Flying Object is much more straightforward. The observer cannot identify what they are observing, it is moving through the sky, and it appears to be a physical object. The term *UFO* was coined in 1952 by the first head of Project Blue Book, Capt. Edward Ruppelt.[16] It doesn't apply to the Loch Ness monster or a ghost wandering the halls of a house or a new viral outbreak. It was a good term to define the unknown objects that people saw moving through the sky. But there was a problem. Over time, the meaning of UFO evolved into something different.

In the early days of UFOs (late 1940s and early 1950s) well-meaning government officials and some scientists hypothesized that based on the propulsion capabilities that these objects appeared to possess, they could be from another world outside of our solar system. There is nothing wrong with this hypothesis, as it is simply a "possible" explanation for something that is observed. A scientist may deal with multiple hypotheses of an observation and still be able to drop all of them when the information that becomes available changes. But the media and the public have difficulty with that concept and what begins as a hypothesis gets expressed as a fact or a likely fact. If a media representative asks a scientist if a UFO could be from an alien world and the scientist says, "It's possible," then the next morning the media headline could be, "Scientist Claims Aliens Are Visiting Planet Earth." The media led with these types of headlines over and over during the history of UFOs. These types of headlines sold news. Ultimately, these dramatizations resulted in the term *UFO* becoming synonymous with the word *alien*. Even worse, the word *alien* began to mean there were little gray beings with large heads and eyes piloting the craft and sometimes abducting humans. Those types of characterizations transformed the term *UFO* into an ugly word that became taboo especially in government and the scientific community.

Although the abbreviation *UFO* better characterized the objects being seen in the skies, that radioactive term was recently jettisoned for *UAP*. The decision to do that was first made in the government by John "Jay" Stratton. Stratton was at an executive level in the Office of Naval Intelligence and had previous experience as the Chief of Air and Space Warfare, Defense Warning Office, Defense Intelligence Agency, and he co-created the effort that later became known as AATIP.[17] Everything that was UFO-related came across his desk from 2008 to 2021. He headed the UAP Task Force that was created to meet congressional legislative demands in 2020. Stratton was the individual who decided to abandon the acronym *UFO* in favor of *UAP*. The reason was because of the stigma associated with the word and that stigma prevented many reports from being made.[18] Career-minded military officers did not want a "UFO Report" as part of their military record. UAP was more acceptable, and Stratton knew that a change was needed. It was a change that probably helped in not only getting the submission of military reports but also in getting the U.S. Congress to accept briefings on the subject.

The first classified briefings of Congress on the UAP subject began in 2018 and over the next few years would involve both the Senate and House Armed Services Committees as well as the Senate and House Select Committees on

Intelligence. The briefings were made and presented by Stratton during his buildup of the UAP Task Force and later as its director. The primary incident of interest was the 2004 incident with the USS *Nimitz* and USS *Princeton* as well as the East Coast UAP incidents. It was called UAP, but everyone involved knew the real interest was in the part of UAP that did not involve nation-states. There was nothing in the 2004 incident that suggested this was Russian or Chinese. If the object Cmdr. Fravor had engaged twenty years ago had been from China, we would be speaking Chinese today. Congress is likely well aware that the part of the UAP mystery involving advanced technology is not from nation-states.

The briefings as well as the public commentaries on the UAP subject involved some of the most prominent senators and representatives in Congress from both parties. The UAP subject was one of the few subjects in Congress where Democrats and Republicans seemed to have found common ground and were able to cooperate. Among the most vocal senators and representatives were Senators Kirsten Gillibrand (D-N.Y.), Marco Rubio (R-Fla.), Mark Warner (D-Va.), Martin Heinrich (D-N.M.), John Kennedy (R-La.), Mitt Romney (R-Ut.), and Representatives Andre Carson (D-In.), Adam Schiff (D-Ca.), Mike Gallagher (R-Wi.), and Tim Burchett (R-Tn.). One must wonder what caused these prominent members of Congress to involve themselves in a subject that can so easily derail a politician's career.

Most likely, there must have been videos in the briefings that made it clear to the members of Congress that UAP were real and were powered by technologies well beyond those of our adversaries. Listen to some of the statements from the senators who were in these classified briefings:

Sen. Marco Rubio: Advanced objects demonstrating advanced technology are routinely flying over our restricted or sensitive airspace posing a risk to both flight safety and national security.[19]

Sen. Kirsten Gillibrand: There are so many of us now on the intel committee and armed services that we're going to stand by the service members who documented this stuff. They have video. They have radar. They have heat sensors. They have everything.[20]

Sen. Mitt Romney: Well I don't believe they are coming from foreign adversaries. Why if there were, that would suggest they have a technology that is in a whole different sphere than anything we understand, and frankly China and Russia just aren't there, and neither are we, by the way.[21]

Sen. Martin Heinrich: If there is a foreign government that had these kinds of capabilities, I think we would see other indications of advanced technology. I can't imagine that what has been described or shown in some of the videos belongs to any government that I'm aware of.[22]

It seems clear that these senators are aware of something that the public doesn't know because of their classified briefings. Was there something more on the videos that they examined?

It was only three days after the *New York Times* article of December 17, 2017, when a military officer contacted me anonymously. He was aware of four other videos that had been taken at the same time as the video released by the *New York Times* and known as the Gimbal video. He knew that the Gimbal video was related to the USS *Roosevelt* carrier strike group because he had been there. No one knew the USS *Roosevelt* was involved or that it was on the East Coast at the time. What he told me next later confirmed that his statements were true. He described the other videos he had seen. One of the four videos he described to me was the Go-Fast video that would not be released for another fourteen months. These four videos he described had been seen by several crewmen on the USS *Roosevelt*. Could these classified videos have been what were shown to and convinced our senators and representatives that what they saw was not made by any of our adversaries? The officer said one of these videos was so convincing that he did not think it would ever be released by the government.

He described a nighttime IR video and a bright white ball approaching an F-18. The pilot initiates radar lock with his dummy missile. It is an "exercise" missile and is not live. As soon as he locks on the object, it makes a quick rotation and then it zips off the FLIR screen like a laser pointer that is skimmed across a wall. There is also radar imagery embedded in this video and the object disappears off radar at the same time.

Was this the video that the senators and representatives were shown? Whatever they saw, it was sufficiently convincing that Congress proposed and passed multiple pieces of legislation on UAP that included whistleblower protection of anyone who reports a UAP from reprisals, the Intelligence Authorization Act of 2021, or the 2022 National Defense Authorization Act, and in late 2022 Congress passed the most extensive UAP investigative and reporting requirements in the history of the United States. It was contained in Section 1683 of the 2023 National Defense Authorization Act. The 2023 act included twenty-six pages devoted to UAP. It created the All-Domain Anomaly Resolution Office (AARO), whose roles would include developing a standardized UAP data collection system, analysis of the data, coordination with other government agencies, scheduled classified and unclassified reports to Congress, periodic briefings of Congress, collection of all public UAP data from 1945 to the present, and the collection of any hidden UAP government data from 1945 to the present.[23] The conclusion that these requirements were onerous would be an understatement. And there was one other item that was clear if one reads between the lines: Congress asked for information back to 1945. There were no such things as UAP across the time frame of 1945 to the present. Clearly, Congress was aware that objects seen in the skies in the 1940s, 1950s, and 1960s were not Russian or Chinese UAP. Congress's interest was and is clearly regarding the unknown high-tech aerial objects formerly called UFOs.

The changes in attitude prevalent in the public have been occurring in both the military and the government. Was the change caused by pressure from the public? Or was the new attitude caused by the same winds of change that were affecting the public? It doesn't make any difference. What was important was the new attitude. This new view of UFOs/UAP was also beginning to be felt in the scientific community and academia.

A CRACK IN THE WALL

There have always been many scientists who have ignored the stigma and studied UFOs. They've included Dr. Hermann Oberth, a father of early rocketry; Dr. J. Allen Hynek; Dr. James McDonald; Dr. Harold Ritchey, father of solid rocketry; Dr. John Mack of Harvard; and French physicist Dr. Claude Poher. These scientists understood the scientific process, and no one should doubt that they used it in their examination of the UFO enigma. Unfortunately, their study of the subject usually came as a risk to their career. Dr. Hynek created a group of academics that were referred to as "The Invisible College." These scientists hypothesized various possible causes of UFOs but did so with each other, and most kept their names hidden so as not to taint their careers. It is sad to think that the halls of science should decide what activities constitute proper scientific study. This appears to be changing as we move into the twenty-first century.

There are now two newly formed organizations in the United States that bring academics together to scientifically study the UFO subject, although as was mentioned it is now referred to as UAP. Those two groups are the Galileo Project and the Scientific Coalition for UAP Studies (SCU). Both groups provide an open atmosphere that allows scientists and academics to share thoughts, ideas, generate academic papers, and work on projects together. Both organizations are in the forefront of making the subject of UAP one that can be investigated in a scientific manner. This would have been unheard of thirty years ago. Times are changing.

SCU was formed in August 2017 just before the *New York Times* article that brought the subject of UAPs to the national forefront. Several individuals and I created the SCU as a 501(c)(3) nonprofit with a mission to promote the scientific exploration of UAP. The organization has grown organically as scientists and academics learn about the group. This slower growth and the

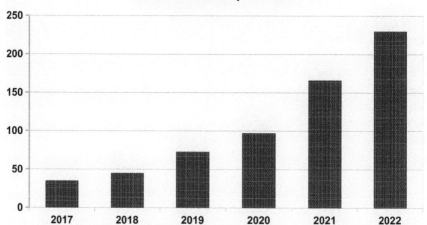

Figure 8.2. Graph of SCU membership growth. *Source*: From the author

establishment of a strong board of directors has helped prevent SCU from encountering any significant structural problems that could thwart the organization's proper development. As of March 2023, SCU had 235 members, of which 30 percent had PhDs and another 21 percent had advanced degrees. The international nature of the UFO phenomenon is reflected in the 20 percent of the SCU members that are outside of the United States. Figures 8.2 and 8.3 show how the organization has grown over time. Engineering has

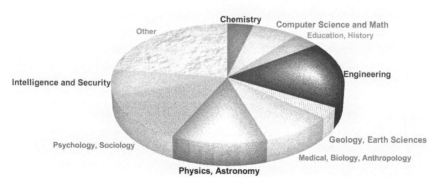

Figure 8.3. Graph of SCU membership makeup. *Source*: From the author

been the leading degree type, although members also have backgrounds in physics, astronomy, chemistry, aerospace, and oceanography. These areas of study include university professors, current and former members of various space programs, the defense and high tech industries, as well as members with government backgrounds.

SCU has three primary goals. One is to establish credible, objective, scientific, peer-reviewed content on the subject of UAP. The organization provides peer review for any papers submitted and self-published, as well as publishing papers in outside academic journals. The second goal is to create scientific and technological partnerships with other organizations and universities. SCU has partnered with the University of Toronto, the French aerospace organization 3AF-Sigma2, the Hessdalen Project in Norway, and several other organizations that are developing automated camera systems for UAP detection. SCU also has members that are part of the Galileo Project. SCU's third goal is to sponsor networking and public environments to aid communication within the serious research community. This has been done through annual conferences that have been held since 2019. This networking is also achieved by the organization's promotion of various projects that scientists within SCU can cooperatively engage in. These projects include characterizing UAP, modeling possible UAP propulsion mechanisms, drone characterization, historical underwater UAP trends, and statistical analyses of UAP occurrences near nuclear facilities.[24]

The Galileo Project (GP) was formed in the summer of 2021 by Harvard University astrophysicist Avi Loeb and Dr. Frank Laukien, chief executive officer of Bruker Corporation. Its name was aptly chosen, as it links the stigma that Galileo Galilei faced in showing that the Earth revolved around the sun to the stigma in science regarding UAP. GP notes on its website that the "multitudes of Earth-like exoplanets" argues that we should look at life elsewhere in the universe. The project argues for the "systematic and transparent scientific methodology to the study of these phenomena." Over 140 individuals are part of the organization and there are at least forty-eight professors and PhDs associated with the project. Most of the PhDs at GP originate from academia as compared to SCU, where most originate from industry. GP has received approximately $1.8 million in donations for its operation.

GP has two primary goals. The first is to examine the possibility of an extraterrestrial origin for unidentified aerial phenomena, by making observations of objects in and near Earth's atmosphere. This is being addressed through the development of an automated camera system that can collect multiple types of data on an aerial object including optical, infra-red, acoustical, magnetic, and spectrographic. Artificial intelligence is used to help discriminate between known and unknown objects detected by the equipment. The second goal is to understand the origins of interstellar objects that exhibit characteristics that differ from typical asteroids and comets. This goal is driven by Professor Loeb's paper on the first known object that originated from outside our solar system and is known as Oumuamua. The object was discovered in 2017 by the Haleakalā Observatory in Hawaii, and its name comes from the Hawaiian word for the lead soldier or scout. Oumuamua was abnormal. Its shape was elongated, it did not have a coma, it was abnormally reflective, and it had non-gravitational acceleration. Loeb hypothesized that the object could be explained by an extraterrestrial craft that originated from outside our solar system. Other hypotheses such as nitrogen ice or a hydrogen-emitting comet have been proposed by other astronomers.[25, 26]

CONCLUSION

Attitudes toward UFOs have changed. This is demonstrated by the existence of organizations such as SCU and GP. The rebranding of the word *UFO* to *UAP* was arguably instrumental in that change. The discovery of thousands of exoplanets in a period of only twenty-five years has made all of us realize that we may not be as unique as we had thought. And the *New York Times* story of a U.S. Navy F-18 squadron's encounter with an object in 2004 that displayed speed and acceleration capabilities beyond anything we can build then or now, has made us wonder and reexamine the question, "Are we truly alone?"

The answer to this question does not lie with the military. The military has wrestled with the UFO question for seventy-five years and, based on what has been stated by our leaders, there is no indication that we know any more now than we knew in 1950. The same objects that zipped past our propellered aircraft in the Second World War are zipping by our jets of the twenty-first century. The military's mission is national security and primarily nation-state vs. nation-state. In 1953 and 1969 the U.S. military concluded that UFOs *were not* a threat to national security and therefore were no longer of interest and need not be investigated. In 2021 the military stated that UAP *were* a threat to national security if they were a "potential adversary."[27] Would the military consider a spacecraft from another world a potential adversary? They have never expressly answered that question. Their concern is defense and not whether we "are truly alone." The military had access to the world's best radar in the year 2004, yet twenty years later we still don't know the speed of the UAP, its exact size, or its acceleration capabilities. Science is not what they do. If we want to solve the UAP enigma, then the answer must come from the scientific community.

The question for science is not so much whether it is possible to solve the UAP enigma as whether we are ready to solve the enigma. Science has shown its capabilities to tackle any problem. The scientists brought together on the Manhattan Project provided the scientific ingenuity to split the atom. When President John F. Kennedy announced a new space effort with the Apollo program, NASA and private enterprise put a man on the moon within eight years. We can solve this seventy-five-year-old enigma if we choose to do so.

But it will require a new attitude for how science approaches a solution to UAP. There will need to be openness and a willingness for scientists to study the history of the subject so that they can understand the basic scope and nature of the problem. The stigma must be removed in the study of the subject. Much of the stigma in the scientific community has been generated by scientists and others who have done essentially no real investigation of the problem area in which they express such strong opinions. As was pointed out in the last chapter in the study by Dr. Peter Sturrock, the scientists with the most opposing views of the UFO/UAP subject are those who have not studied it. That is closed-mindedness; that is not science.

A model already exists on how UAP can be studied and done in a manner that promotes science, no matter the answer to the UAP enigma. The Julius-Maximilians-Universität of Würzburg in Germany, under Professor Hakan Kayal, has begun the study of UAP. There, engineering students work on the development of automated camera systems and micro-satellites with not only the purpose of detecting UAP but with the ability to do other observations of the Earth. Professor Kayal notes a specific example of an offshoot of their studies related to artificial intelligence used in their micro-satellites.

> As soon as you go interplanetary, communication with the satellite becomes a bottleneck. With increasing distance from Earth, data transfer takes longer, you can't keep sending data back and forth. That's why the AI must be able to learn independently on the satellite. And it must only report relevant discoveries to Earth.[28]

As always with science, the study of a subject invariably results in discoveries that we would never have anticipated. The same will be true with UAP.

The study of subject matter related to UAP can go beyond just engineering schools. A university's departments of philosophy, language, or international affairs could study how we should someday contact another intelligence. How do we communicate, and what is ethical in our approach if another intelligence is less advanced than us? Even if the explanation for UAP turns out to be mundane, all these efforts will still be of use. Perhaps in the future or perhaps right now, as how we deal here on Earth with other humans or even the ethical treatment of intelligent animals.

As NASA so succinctly put it for young, budding scientists, "Science consists of observing the world by watching, listening, observing, and recording. Science is curiosity in thoughtful action about the world and how it behaves."[29] It is time that we put aside our anthropocentric view of our universe and allow science to do what it does best—uncover the truth.

Chapter Nine

The Challenge for Academia

You may be familiar with the term *a paradigm shift* at your place of employment or in discussion with friends. This term refers to a groundbreaking shift in how a subject is understood, such as a new idea that fundamentally alters our perception and understanding of an issue. The realization that the Earth was not the center of the universe in the sixteenth century was a paradigm shift in how we viewed our world. Similarly, Einstein's realization that gravity is not a force, but is a curvature of space-time caused a paradigm shift in many scientific fields. However, you may not know that this phrase was popularized by Thomas Kuhn, a professor emeritus and philosopher of science at the Massachusetts Institute of Technology, in his famous book, *The Structure of Scientific Revolutions*.

Kuhn likened science to the art of solving a puzzle. He devoted an entire chapter to the subject: "Normal Science as Puzzle-solving." Kuhn's examination of paradigm shifts can be likened to the paradigm that has marginalized the subject of Unidentified Aerial Phenomena (UAP), which are commonly dismissed as anecdotal reports that can be explained away through careful examination. The scientific community will not consider the UAP subject a puzzle worthy of study until that paradigm is broken. Kuhn states, "one of the things a scientific community acquires with a paradigm is a criterion for choosing problems that, while the paradigm is taken for granted, can be assumed to have solutions. To a great extent these are the only problems that the community will admit as scientific or encourage its members to undertake."[1] In other words, you may look at how UAP reports can be explained but DO NOT think that it is science to look at a hypothesis that might indicate some UAP are real. This approach effectively restricts scientists from exploring hypotheses related to UAPs, thus creating a circular catch-22 situation. Under this old paradigm, it is considered unscientific to collect data on UAPs, perpetuating the notion that there is no scientific data to support their existence. The breaking of this old paradigm and the acceptance of a new paradigm that supports the scientific study of UAP is the first step that must be taken.

This scientific study of the UAP puzzle is sometimes referred to as ufology. But ufology is not a science. Biology, chemistry, physics, psychology, and sociology are sciences. The study of UAP should utilize the sciences just as the study of global warming utilizes many different scientific fields. A solution to the UAP puzzle arguably involves more scientific fields than any other modern issue. A proper study of UAP involves physicists, astrophysicists, chemists, astronomers, geologists, aerospace engineers, statisticians, software engineers, sociologists, and psychologists. It would be difficult to find a scientific field of study that would not be useful in the study of UAP.

The modern study of the phenomenon will be a difficult challenge for academia and the scientific community. It should be noted: there is a difference between academia and the general term, "the scientific community." Academia is a subset of the scientific community. The scientific community is a broad and somewhat nebulous term that includes scientists in academia, in the military-industrial complex, in leading edge technology firms, private industry, think-tanks, and even individual scientists that work on their own. These are the broad organizational areas that scientists choose when deciding their career path. It is the scientists in academia that must lead the study of UAP. These are the scientists who produce open peer-reviewed papers for publication, write competitive proposals for government grants, involve graduate students in their study of interest, and use their academic freedom to do leading edge research. Without the efforts of academia, the challenge will be much more difficult.

HISTORY AND DESIGN OF EXPERIMENT

The scientist's first task is to update themselves on a subject and study the background information on that subject in the literature. The scientist is faced with a voluminous amount of anecdotal data with UAP, of which more than 90 percent is invalid. The remaining data is rarely provided in a scientific manner. The quality of an investigative report is haphazard depending on the investigator or lack thereof. Because of this, most scientists tend to want to start from scratch and discard all the historical data over the last eighty years and begin data collection anew. This would be a mistake.

A researcher does not need to believe background information on a subject. It can be taken with a "grain of salt." Historic data provide a mountain of observations that a scientist can use to provide information on the type of equipment and measurement capabilities that will be needed. A researcher would want to know the details behind the first scientific field study of the phenomenon completed in the late 1970s by Dr. Harley Rutledge of Southeast Missouri State University along with other professors and grad students from the university.[2]

A thorough understanding of the history of the phenomenon can be found in several well-written books. The following books provide a good understanding of the historical background of the subject as well as an understanding of some of the characteristics displayed by UAP: *The UFO Enigma: A New Review of the Physical Evidence* by Dr. Peter Sturrock, *Project Identification: The First Scientific Study of UFO Phenomenon* by Dr. Harley Rutledge, *UFOs and Government: A Historical Inquiry* by Dr. Michael Swords et al., *Unconventional Flying Objects: A Scientific Analysis* by NASA scientist Paul Hill, *The Report on Unidentified Flying Objects* by Edward Ruppelt (former head of Project Blue Book), and *The UFO Experience: A Scientific Inquiry* by Dr. Allen Hynek. In addition to these books, academic papers and monographs have been written on specific UAP cases that an academic should review. Most of these papers have been referenced throughout this book.

Historical reports tell us that it is important to know UAP potential acceleration capabilities so that camera systems can be designed to measure rapid movements and changes in direction that are often initiated from a standstill. There are many historical reports of objects accelerating so rapidly that they disappear from site within one to two seconds. The scientist must design his automated equipment so that the camera frame rates are sufficient to capture such motion on film. If multiple cameras are being used for triangulation to calculate speed, then the timing between cameras needs to be modeled so that it is known that a high acceleration can be captured on the equipment. There are many other input variables and calibration issues that must be considered with equipment. Some initial work in this area has been begun by the scientists in the Galileo Project. Their goal is to build automated systems that can detect this type of acceleration.[3]

The study of history provides more valuable information. The cameras need to be placed in locations that are more likely to lead to the observation of UAP. Are there particular geographical areas or types of facilities where UAP are more likely to be seen? Puerto Rico and Catalina Island, off the coast of southern California, have been shown to be "hot" areas for UAP sightings based on work done by SCU. The less populated New England states and New Mexico have higher than normal reports of UAP. The U.S. ICBM sites have had more than their fair share of reports, but placing automated equipment in those areas is problematic. Nonetheless, the study of the history of UAP helps pin down the best locations for placing automated equipment.

What other equipment beyond optical cameras should be incorporated into an automated system? History again provides some valuable clues. Project Blue Book has several reports of unknown objects emitting military identification frequencies in the 900 to 1,200 MHz range. The French have documented plant damage from UAP due to heating of water that is in the 2,400–2,500 MHz range. Add to this information the reports of electromagnetic interference with compasses, batteries, and other electrical equipment. All this historical information supports the need for the widest band of spectral measurements possible. And let's not forget the lack of sound that is so often reported. This argues for the need for acoustical measuring equipment. All this historical background information is important to know how to best design scientific equipment for measuring UAP.

MILITARY DATA

None of this type of equipment is inexpensive. The costs can quickly reach millions of dollars. Cost is a sufficient deterrent such that a researcher might pause and consider looking for all the information currently available. What data can the military provide? This possibility will likely come to mind for any scientist. After all, some of the best high-quality measuring equipment in the world exists within the United States military.

There are modern radar systems that can measure size, velocity, and acceleration of any airborne object at multiple radar and microwave frequencies with sampling rates in milliseconds. These types of systems detected the UAP involved in the 2004 *Nimitz* incident.

Also available are multimillion-dollar, high-magnification optical and cryo-cooled infra-red camera systems capable of measuring temperature changes as slight as a tenth of a degree Celsius. These same systems are used in our military satellite systems that are the most sophisticated in the world at detecting objects near the Earth's surface or at lower atmospheric altitude. One such system detected an object in 2021 that resembled the Tic Tac–shaped objects seen in 2004.[4]

And let's not forget the many UAP reports that note a total lack of sound. Some of the world's most sensitive sonar and acoustical systems are controlled by the military. These systems can detect the faintest sounds in the ocean or atmosphere. Verification that there is no sound from a fast-moving object in the atmosphere would be important information.

The use of military information for the study of UAP seems like an opportune area for pursuit. Yet the scientist immediately hits another roadblock.

Figure 9.1.   Image of a Chinese spy balloon
Source: USAF

The openness of science is not shared by the military. The desire for se-crecy in the name of national security is more important to the military. The Director of the Office of National Intelligence (ODNI) released two versions of a UAP report in June 2021. One report was for the public and the other was classified and only for select members of Congress. The public version contained nine pages but with almost no usable information.[5] The report noted that the government had data on 144 UAP sightings, of which only one had been identified (a balloon). The congressional version was seventeen pages long. A copy of the classified June 2021 UAP report to Congress was obtained via a Freedom of Information request in March 2022.[6] The classified report contained very little additional information and what was there was heavily redacted. The redactions were referenced against section 1.4 of Executive Order 13526, which states that any infor-mation that can be reasonably expected to damage the national security of the United States may be classified.

The redacted information included: object shape, information on UAP ac-celeration capability and behavior, flight characteristics, number of UAP dis-ruptions of Navy training exercises in a military operations area (MOA), and type of physical sensors used in detection of UAP. It is difficult to understand how knowing the shape or color of a UAP or the speed at which it travels threatens national security. After all, the military recently released photos, shapes, and speed of Chinese spy balloons flying over the United States without any concern for national security. (See figure 9.1.) Nonetheless, that is the position being taken by the military on the release of information re-lated to UAP. It is clear at this point that the only way scientists will get the necessary data to study the UAP subject is to collect it themselves. Civilian science groups such as SCU and the Galileo Project have already committed to the open sharing of information and will not utilize classified data since the release of the information would be in the control of the military.

REPEATABILITY OF EXPERIMENT AND PREDICTABILITY

In most of the sciences, scientific experiments that are conducted can be repeated by other scientists and the expected results can be predicted. But this is not always true. The observation of a nova cannot be repeated in a predictive manner. It is a one-time occurrence. Another example is the prediction of weather. We know how air masses of different temperatures will react with each other and it is predictable. We know that warm water rises to the top of the ocean. But as more and more weather variables enter the equation, the ability to reliably predict the interaction of those variables and an outcome decreases. If predicting weather is difficult, consider the difficulty in predicting how human beings react. There are even more variables that go into a human's opinion including different backgrounds, experience, and even genetics. It is not surprising that a survey of society does not always result in the same findings. There are differences in the various sciences.

What *is* shared across the sciences is the scientific method. It is the process of observing, asking questions, and seeking answers through carefully designed tests and experiments. This gathering and analysis of data is not unique to any one field of science. It is the same in physics, chemistry, biology, sociology, or psychology. The difference is the reproducibility of that data.

The terms *hard sciences* and *soft sciences* are often used in distinguishing the degree of difficulty in the reproduction of experimental data. Unfortunately, those terms have taken on a negative connotation that splits the sciences into rival camps. So, instead, those differences will be referred to as *natural sciences* and *social sciences*.

Physics and chemistry are considered natural sciences. Every experiment is easily reproducible. Mixing vinegar (acetic acid) and baking soda (sodium bicarbonate) produces carbon dioxide as one of the byproducts. Any scientist can replicate those experimental results if the conditions of the original experiment are known. Biology is also a natural science, but part of it also involves social science. An experiment involving bacteria is repeatable while an experiment involving the reaction of dogs is less so. Debates can result as to how a pack of dogs may react to a deer while there is less debate as to what happens when you feed a specific food to a particular bacterial strain in a petri dish at a given temperature, humidity, light exposure, and so on. Sociology and psychology are the epitome of social sciences. They deal with human and societal behavior. How well can you measure individual human emotions or predict the reaction of a society to the discovery of extraterrestrial life? The results are not consistent even when the scientist attempts to control all the input variables. And the results can change over time based on culture. This is the essence of the difference between natural and social sciences. Their similarity is that they are all sciences, and inconsistencies in the results do not make one science more, or less, scientific than another.

What is the common thread that determines whether a scientific field deals with easily reproducible experiments? It can be argued that the study of a living organism drives the uncertainty that exists in the social sciences. The more intelligent an organism, the more the variability in the control of an experiment. The study of bacteria provides repeatable results, while the study of dolphins is less repeatable. Unlike bacteria, each dolphin has a certain uniqueness to it. A rocket will always generate a certain amount of thrust given certain input variables. A monkey will not always generate the same reaction to a set of input variables. The inanimate rocket does not interfere with the output; the monkey may choose to interfere with the experiment. Raise the intelligence of the experimental subject from a monkey to a human and the difficulty of reproducibility increases further. This inability to produce a testable and repeatable experiment is disconcerting to some scientists, especially those whose fields of study are in the natural sciences.

One might argue that the study of UAP has more similarities to the social sciences than the natural sciences. Repeatability is an even larger problem with UAP. It is a nightmare for a scientist drilled in the need for control of experiments, repeatability, testable predictions, and results that can be published in leading academic journals. The subjectivity of the observer as well as the possibility of interference by the observed arguably make this a social science.

How does a scientist best utilize science in the study of UAP? After a scientist has identified the needed equipment, the type of data, how the data will be collected, the procedures to be taken, the real problems begin. Where do you go to take measurements on UAP? This is not like a laboratory experiment or the observation of a particular bird species in a known habitat. One cannot plan a UAP sighting, and one cannot depend on happenstance to provide a sighting. It requires multiple sets of the same equipment in different locations that can be run in an automated fashion with network access. It is somewhat akin to setting up cameras in hope of catching a photograph in the wild of one of the twenty-five remaining Hainan gibbons. And once data is collected on a UAP sighting, how does that work get repeated? Otherwise, other scientists may argue it was just an error in the equipment or some stray EM signal that caused the measurement to coincide with a distant disk-shaped light that was photographed. Scientists interested in the work will insist on replicating what was done. They will want to be able to take a photo of a disk-shaped light that emits an EM signal at that same frequency. And what if all UAP sightings are not the same, just as all jet aircraft are not the same? That makes the problem of duplication of experiment a very challenging task.

Let's pause and assume something about the subject of our experiment. Assume that most UAP were a new Chinese drone. This is a possibility under consideration. If that is the case, the researcher cannot expect to be able to easily collect information. It's unlikely for there to be a certain time or day that they show up. The drone's goal would be to avoid detection. The same technique discussed earlier of an automated camera system would need to be utilized. Let's go one step further. Assume for a moment that UAP are controlled by an unknown intelligence (UI) much more advanced than ourselves. Study the history of UAP and that assumption is not so bold, after all. Many scientists who have studied the subject in detail would support that assumption as reasonable. Those scientists include Hermann Oberth, James McDonald, Allen Hynek, Massimo Teodorani, Claude Poher, Peter Sturrock, Michael Swords, Kevin Knuth, Alexander Wendt, Erol Faruk, David Saunders, Garry Nolan, Jacques Vallée, and many more. They would surely state that this assumption is worthy of consideration.

How does this assumption of a UI affect the data collection, how the tests should be set up, and the repeatability of the data collection? Earlier in this chapter we discussed the social and natural sciences. Running experiments on the actions of advanced intelligent beings would be considered a social science. One would expect variations in the scientific analysis due to the same individual and societal variations seen in psychology and sociology. One would also expect a reasonable likelihood that the experimental subject might choose to interfere with the experiment. Repeatability and controllability of the experiment would be problematic.

Consider the difficulties for a scientist attempting to collect data on a UI. When dealing with humans a psychologist cannot cage the experiment as can a biologist but at least can ask and hope for the patient's cooperation. What type of cooperation would a scientist expect to receive if studying an intelligence far more advanced than the scientist? It is not like the UI will agree to show up at a certain time for the observations and equipment measurements to begin. Even worse, one must consider the likelihood that the UI knows what the experimentalist is trying to accomplish. The experimental subject would have such a high degree of control over the experiment that it would be difficult to determine whether the experiment was conducted properly or not, or even who was the experimenter and who was the subject.

We could be in the reverse situation of a zoologist running tests on a chimpanzee. Imagine the chimpanzee trying to run experiments on the zoologist. The chimpanzee decides it wants to establish if the zoologist knows how to use a stick as a tool. The chimp hands the zoologist a stick but gets no reaction other than the zoologist accepts the stick and then puts it down on the table. One day the chimp notices the zoologist use two sticks when eating. The chimp is excited that the zoologist has demonstrated the use of a stick as a tool and tells its fellow chimps what happened. The chimp tries to repeat the event, but the zoologist will not cooperate and demonstrate a second time the use of two sticks as a tool when eating. How well was the chimpanzee in control of that experiment?

Our anthropocentric tendencies immediately kick in. How could we be the chimpanzee? It just doesn't compare; it's apples and oranges. We are much more advanced than a chimp. The problem is—we have never been in that position. We have always been the dominant intelligence in any experiment involving life. Perhaps we need to put ourselves in the position of the chimpanzee. What could the chimp do that would engage the zoologist such that the chimp had some level of control?

A DIFFERENT TYPE EXPERIMENT

The chimp has little chance of running a standard experiment on the zoologist and certainly even less of a chance of repeating it. The chimp thinks of something that might give it some level of control that it has not had up to this point. It decides to communicate with the human zoologist using patterned movements of the stick. The zoologist recognizes the chimp's attempt to communicate. The zoologist is now very interested and attempts to communicate back to the chimp. The chimpanzee is still not in control of the experiment, but perhaps now there may be a meeting of the minds.

UAP may not be a natural phenomenon but instead may be controlled by a UI. If true, we should attempt to communicate with UAP. There is certainly nothing to lose from that attempt. And there is precedence that indicates communication might be possible.

Possible communication at radio frequencies has been reported. Chapter 5 listed four instances of reported radio communication in Project Blue Book files. Military radar systems send out a code at a given radar frequency, and if friendly, the other aircraft sends back an encrypted response at a different, and specific frequency. This process is called Indication Friend or Foe (IFF) and allows aircraft to determine if another aircraft belongs to the enemy. Military encounters with UAP have occurred where the UAP was reported to have sent back a radio signal indicating it was friendly. No one can be certain that it was the UAP that sent the return code. More recently, Dr. Sean Kirkpatrick of AARO indicated in his April 19, 2023, testimony to a Senate subcommittee, "We get intermittent radar returns, we get intermittent radio returns."[7] He did not indicate if these were related to IFF radar-radio queries. Based on what we know, it certainly is worth trying to use radio codes to entice UAP to a particular site and attempt communication.

There have also been a number of reports where dependable witnesses indicated that the UAP responded to visible light. Two Illinois police officers and a fireman noticed that a UAP hovered in front of them as long as their lights were turned off their patrol car but would move back away whenever the lights were turned on.[8] A reverend and three dozen witnesses in Papua New Guinea claimed they shone a light at the UAP and it shone a light back at them.[9] A family in Georgia also shone a spotlight on a UAP that was about quarter of a mile away and observed a different reaction. The object raced toward them at extreme speed and stopped within seventy-five yards of their position.[10] Independent of UAP sightings, a new MIT study theorizes that existing laser technology could be fashioned into Earth's "porch light" to attract alien astronomers.[11] Again, there is no reason not to attempt to communicate with multiple methods.

In addition to attempts to communicate, what else should be considered if UAP are controlled by a UI? It would be logical to look for indications of a technology far in advance of our own. There are two characteristics of UAP that are outside our current technological capability: extreme acceleration (greater than 100 g-forces) and a lack of interaction with the atmosphere. Examples of the latter include lack of sound, lack of atmospheric heating at high velocities, lack of any aerodynamic surfaces for flight, and the ability to easily transition between water and the atmosphere. These two characteristics should be a key part of any equipment setup that is designed to observe UAP.

Extreme acceleration can be detected using sophisticated phased array radar systems. These are a computer-controlled array of antennas which create a radar beam that can be steered electronically rather than manually. This allows for radar pulse emissions in milliseconds rather than seconds. This is critical for reliably tracking objects moving at speeds of Mach 10 and beyond. Unfortunately, these types of systems are controlled by the military and are not available to academia. This leaves triangulation of a UAP using two or more automated camera systems, as mentioned earlier in this chapter.

A lack of atmospheric interaction can be detected using infra-red (IR) cameras. This requires the ability to measure the speed of the target as well as its IR signature. Any aircraft generates heat as it moves through the atmosphere, and that heat can be measured in the IR portion of the spectrum. The X-15 traveled at speeds of Mach 4–6 and was made of a special alloy to withstand heating on its wings that could reach 1,200 degrees Fahrenheit (F). Even a commercial airliner moving at 600 mph is warmer than the surrounding air. While the outside air at 35,000 feet may be a chilling –67 degrees F, the atmospheric heating would raise its skin temperature to –31 degrees F. All these differences can be measured by an IR camera operating in the 3-to-5-micron wavelength range, and with temperature accuracies to within a fraction of a degree.

Some have argued that these extreme accelerations and lack of interaction with the atmosphere might be some new U.S. black project. There are two reasons why UAP exhibiting these characteristics are not black projects. The first reason is empirical and is because these types of characteristics have been reported for over eighty years. This is far too long for a black project. The second reason is that our technological advances come in gradual increments and not in leapfrog improvements. The speed and acceleration of military jet aircraft improved after the first German jets of the Second World War for about thirty years but have now been stagnant for sixty years. The F-4 Phantom jet reached speeds of 1,600 mph in 1961 and the F-15 is capable of speeds of 1,875 mph, and it was first released in 1972.[12, 13] Modern military jets are slower as improvements came in stealth, jamming capabilities, radar, and weapons systems rather than speed and acceleration.

A very good example of the gradual changes in technology and the difficulty in leapfrogging can be seen in computers and the computer chips that power them. The bestselling computer of 1981 was the Texas Instruments TI-99 home computer. It operated at a speed of 3 MHz, and it had 16KB of memory.[14] A modern laptop is 1,000 times faster and contains ten million times more memory. Could a black project in the 1980s and 1990s create a modern computer? The answer is, "Absolutely not." You could give the best scientists of 1981 a modern laptop along with the blueprints to build it and they could not do it. The reason is because the technological infrastructure to build that laptop did not exist. They did not have the optical systems that could build sub-nanometer-size circuitry to create the microprocessors to run the laptop. They did not have the ultra-pure water, ultra-pure manufacturing facilities, plasma etching techniques, chemical deposition systems, the high-quality silicon nitride transistors, and the thousand other requirements to build advanced microprocessors. Those technologies did not exist in the 1980s. Any black project depends on hundreds of underlying technologies possessed by the scientific world that exist at a given time in history. You can't just leapfrog across technologies. It is a gradual process that a civilization slowly develops over time.

A craft capable of Mach 20+ speeds that doesn't burn up in the atmosphere, is capable of hovering, accelerating beyond 100 g-forces, and then hovering again is not just beyond the ability of any black project; the hundreds of technologies that would need to be developed to manufacture such a craft do not exist.

Much more scientific information is needed on UAP. This is the challenge that must be met by academia. The military has not solved this challenge in eighty years and there is little hope on the horizon that they will solve the UAP enigma in another eighty years. Measuring extreme accelerations and a lack of atmospheric interaction is a challenge for academia and not the military or the world of ufology. It is time for a paradigm shift, and that shift has begun. Stigma related to UAP is dropping and the U.S. Congress is pushing for answers. The next step is for Congress to provide funding so that academia can begin doing what they do best—collecting and analyzing scientific data.

Chapter Ten

The Extraterrestrial Hypothesis

The search for extraterrestrial life in our galaxy has been ongoing for almost fifty years. It began in 1959 with a short paper published in *Nature* by Cocconi and Morrison arguing that the monitoring of radio waves would be a logical way to try and detect the existence of an intelligent extraterrestrial civilization.[1] The paper initiated the modern search for extraterrestrial intelligence (SETI) era. By the late 1970s NASA had begun the search for extraterrestrial intelligence in our galaxy by looking for radio transmissions from other civilizations. Their hope was to detect either an intentional signal directed at our planet or the more likely radio signals that are a byproduct of a developing civilization.

You might think that there was nothing wrong with searching for extraterrestrial life (ET). You would be in error. NASA found it very difficult to obtain a constant supply of funding for SETI. Many people thought it was a waste of money. Senator William Proxmire was famous for his annual awards of government projects that fleeced the American taxpayer. In 1979 he gave his "Golden Fleece" award to NASA for its use of taxpayer dollars to search for extraterrestrial civilizations. The pressure from Congress made it difficult for NASA to fund the SETI effort. Partly because of this impediment the SETI Institute was formed as a nonprofit in 1984 for the purpose of detecting such radio signals. Today there are over 100 scientists working on projects at the SETI Institute.

Many scientists believe it is worthwhile to look for very distant signals indicative of ET, although they are hesitant to look for signs of ET near Earth. It is ironic that while SETI searches for ET, the SETI organization frowns on discussions of whether UFOs or UAP could have an extraterrestrial source. It is clearly stated on the SETI webpage that ET reaching Earth is very unlikely due to distance. SETI dislikes the concept so much that they try to read ET's mind when they state, "Given the difficulty (and cost) of interstellar travel, it seems reasonable that any aliens would need a good motivation to undertake it. Coming here to embroil themselves in the affairs of humankind seems highly improbable."[2] The SETI view is that it is okay to discuss the possibilities of an intelligence much more advanced than us if it is far off and separated by light-years of distance. But a hypothesis that ET will discover us first and could already be in our solar system is *verboten*. Is it physics that denies this possibility or is it our human psyche? When you read about ET, are the discussions couched around when/if/how *we* will discover ET or whether ET will discover us? Which is more likely, a more advanced intelligence discovering us first or us discovering the advanced intelligence? The answer should be obvious. Unfortunately, our ego's feeling of importance does not like the answer. But our egos should not drive science. Science would argue that the possibility of ET visitation of Earth should be examined.

Let's begin that examination with what we think we know regarding UAP. This is based on eighty years of anecdotal reports and a handful of incidents where we have other evidence such as photos, video, radar, or trace physical evidence. UAP are usually physical objects capable of moving through our atmosphere and sometimes our oceans. Their velocity, acceleration, and maneuverability indicate a technology far beyond our current capabilities. They are intelligently controlled based on how they react to our aircraft and because it requires technology to achieve the velocities and accelerations that have been reported.

What we don't know about UAP is considerable. We don't know what is operating the craft, whether it is biological, artificial, a drone, or something else entirely. We do not know the intentions or purpose. We are unable to predict when or where a UAP will next appear. We do not know how they move without any obvious exhaust or aerodynamic features. Their method of propulsion is a complete mystery. We don't know their origin; however, this is the one unknown that we may be able to speculate upon.

There are several hypotheses that have been suggested to explain UAP. One is that UAP are earthly travelers from the future. Another hypothesis is that UAP originate from the depths of the ocean and that they are a hidden civilization that either originated here or traveled here from elsewhere. Some have suggested that they are travelers from another dimension. This chapter will explore a different hypothesis: the Extraterrestrial Hypothesis (ETH). Do UAP originate from another solar system in our galaxy? Are they controlled by an extraterrestrial life form? Why this hypothesis is the best fit for the characteristics observed with UAP and for what we know about the universe is the crux of this chapter.

DOES ET KNOW WE'RE HERE?

What are the steps needed for a civilization to search for other worlds via interstellar space travel? The very first step is to identify potential planets orbiting distant stars. Humanity has already taken this step. We are very early in the process, but our abilities are advancing rapidly. As previously discussed, we have discovered over 6,000 exoplanets. This number will balloon into tens of thousands of planets and more as we develop techniques that allow us to see Earth-size planets orbiting at Earth-like distances from their star. Today, we could not detect our Earth if it was ten light-years distant from us. It is too small and too far from the sun to detect with our current detection methods. Soon that will change as our technologies advance. A more advanced civilization would already have that ability and Earth would be among its catalog of planets.

The second step is to look for planets that have signs of intelligent life. ET would begin by looking for the building blocks for life, assuming they were carbon-based like us. They would examine a planet's reflected light to look for oxygen, water, carbon dioxide, methane, and other chemicals to determine if a carbon-based life could exist. (Humanity is just now taking its first baby steps in this area.) Like us, an extraterrestrial race would be examining planets in their catalog that not only have the right chemical ingredients but that also have signs of intelligent life. These planets would be the ones that ET would carefully observe with their advanced telescopes and spectrometers. ET would look for changes to a planet's atmosphere that might be caused by an advanced intelligent life. They would look for emissions in the various parts of the electromagnetic spectrum that indicate a civilization was expending large amounts of energy.

Let's use our planet as an example of how our atmosphere indicates that an intelligent civilization exists here. What would ET see if they turned their powerful telescopes toward Earth? About 200 years ago ET would have noticed large amounts of hydrocarbons were being emitted into the Earth's atmosphere. This was driven by the coal burning of the industrial revolution in the nineteenth century. Some ET scientists might begin studying Earth as one of the more likely planets to harbor advanced intelligent life. ET would see the complexity of the emitted hydrocarbons increase in the twentieth century as we burned oils, plastics, and garbage that we released into the atmosphere. ET scientists would know that the more complex the hydrocarbons are, the more likely that they were produced by an intelligence on Earth rather than simple vegetative fires. By the 1950s and 1960s our atmosphere contained isotopes of uranium, plutonium, and other radioactive compounds. These were created from our detonation of nuclear bombs on land and in the atmosphere. The ET scientists studying Earth might have been excited when they first detected those chemicals. There is nothing natural about those isotopes. Any civilization that analyzed our atmosphere with a high-quality spectroscope would know that intelligent life exists here.

Earth's EM emissions would also tell ET that intelligence exists on this planet. Our planet began emitting visible light into the cosmos beginning in the early 1930s, when our largest cities began to install nighttime lighting.[3] ET would shield their telescopes from our sun's glare with a coronagraph and would detect our cities' emissions of incandescent light from the dark side of Earth. They would suspect the light was not natural because of the unique frequency emitted by incandescent lights. This would pique their interest and perhaps they would dedicate a telescope to the observation of our planet. Soon ET would detect electromagnetic frequencies emitted by radio, television, and radar from Earth in the 1930s and 1940s. ET would note that our planet had revolved around its sun only a few more times before something else interesting occurred. Nuclear fission explosions had begun on this now very interesting planet. This was 1945, and ET would continue to monitor nuclear explosions on this planet for another twenty revolutions around its sun. There would no longer be any doubt that an advanced civilization was developing on the planet Earth. The only doubt remaining with ET was whether this new civilization would destroy itself or use nuclear power peacefully.

The final step in the search for extraterrestrial life is interstellar travel. Even if ET knew we were here, could they reach the Earth? Toward the end of the twentieth century no one thought interstellar travel was feasible. Most scientists didn't think it would ever be possible. The closest star to Earth, Proxima Centauri, was four light-years away. It would take our fastest spacecraft over 17,000 years to reach a planet in that star's system. Such a trip would be meaningless. Consequently, most scientists believed that if we could not even contemplate interstellar travel, then no one else could either. This view rapidly changed in the twenty-first century.

THE CHALLENGE OF INTERSTELLAR TRAVEL

Humankind's greatest challenge will be our attempt to reach the stars. The distances are immense. It will require the ability to harness enormous amounts of energy to power a spacecraft to within at least 40–50 percent of the speed of light to reach the nearest stars in a reasonable time. This will place about a dozen star systems within an eight to twenty-five year-long trip of Earth. If we can reach speeds at 99.99 percent of the speed of light, thousands of stars are within reach. You might think that it would take four years for a spacecraft to reach the nearest star, Alpha Centauri. That is true from our perspective on

Earth, but it will be different for anyone on the spacecraft. Only three weeks would have passed for the occupants of the spacecraft because time slows down at extreme speeds. This was first theorized by Albert Einstein and has been proven by measuring slight changes in clocks in orbiting satellites. It would only take two hours for the occupants of the spacecraft to reach Alpha Centauri if they could reach 99.9999 percent of the speed of light.

Speed isn't the only barrier. Imagine if their spacecraft impacts an object while traveling to the nearest star. Even the smallest dust grain impacting a spacecraft at near light speeds would be catastrophic. New types of spacecraft shielding will be required. How does the spacecraft maneuver around a small meteor that is detected at a distance of a few miles when the spacecraft's time to impact is measured in fractions of a second? The challenges are complex and will stretch our technological capabilities but we're on the cusp of making such a journey more than imaginary.

Interstellar travel by humans may become a reality in the twenty-first century. Scientists are researching how we can develop interstellar travel. In 1996, NASA launched the Breakthrough Propulsion Physics program. Its purpose was to examine unique space propulsion techniques that could be used for interstellar space travel. They looked at everything from nuclear propulsion to the possibility of traveling through warps in space. The National Space Society has created a roadmap to space colonization of the stars.[4] NASA's Ames Research Center and the Defense Advanced Research Projects Agency (DARPA) collaborated on a project to study the requirements to build a spacecraft capable of interstellar travel. This project was begun with a symposium in October 2011 in Orlando, Florida, that brought together papers from scientists around the nation who were to think "outside of the box" on the topic of interstellar space travel.[5] Already, research has begun at NASA's Johnson Space Center in Houston to look at the possibility of warp travel through space by the end of this century.[6] Warp travel allows for travel at speeds greater than the speed of light by warping space so that two points in space become closer. It's somewhat like pinching a balloon together so that you don't travel in a straight line between two points on the balloon's surface but instead bring the two points together. Whether warping space will ever be possible is still not known. But slower travel is possible. We have already stepped beyond theoretical interstellar propulsion technologies. Interstellar travel is now on the drawing board.

NASA has proposed a plan to launch nano-size spacecraft toward the Alpha Centauri planetary system in 2069. The concept originated in a project called Breakthrough Starshot. It was founded in 2016 by Yuri Milner, Stephen Hawking, and Mark Zuckerberg. The concept is to launch multiple nano-size spacecraft weighing only grams using powerful lasers. The ground-based lasers would push sails only a few hundred atoms in thickness that would be attached to the gram-size spacecraft. These 100-gigawatt level lasers would accelerate the spacecraft to about 20 percent of the speed of light within a few minutes. The spacecraft would reach the Alpha Centauri system within twenty years and would take flyby photos.[7,8] For the first time, we're discussing interstellar travel that is technologically feasible.

Interstellar travel is now more than just a thought. Soon travel between the stars may be a reality for humanity. If we can achieve it, then others can too. What has been achieved by ET civilizations that are 100 or 1,000 years more advanced than us? Can we really continue to state that ET cannot get here? Think about the implications of what we have just discussed. ET civilizations only slightly more advanced than us will know that an intelligent species exists on planet Earth. ET civilizations 100 years ahead of us will be able to send robotic probes to our planet, and if 1,000 years ahead of us, probably more than just probes. There is no technical barrier. Curiosity and desire are the only remaining elements required.

How quickly could another civilization detect us and send a probe? Let's assume that the lighting of cities on the dark side of Earth was the first sign that piqued ET's curiosity. Nighttime lighting of our cities began in earnest in the early 1930s. The first significant numbers of reports of UAP began in 1942, as seen in the graph in chapter 2. If ET can travel at near light speed, then their home would need to be within six light-years of Earth. If ET can travel faster than light using techniques such as warping space, then their home would be within twelve light-years of Earth. This is the farthest that light could travel from Earth's night-lit cities between 1930 and 1942. Could ET be from a star system farther than twelve light-years? Perhaps, if they sent a spacecraft toward Earth when they first saw hydrocarbon emissions in our nineteenth-century atmosphere or if they have some method of communication that is faster than light.

It is possible that an ET civilization has sent a probe or probes toward our planet. This is the extraterrestrial hypothesis. How do we know if they have visited? It is easy enough to hypothesize that they could; it is more difficult to prove that they have.

ET AND UAPS

If ET exists, it is reasonable to expect that ET could at least send probes to Earth. We used deductive reasoning to make this determination. We started from a set of general premises: there are thousands of exoplanets; life develops throughout the universe as it did on Earth; some of that life will evolve intelligence; intelligent life will know our planet harbors intelligence; and that intelligent life will choose to visit us. This is our hypothesis. The next step is to determine whether we have any information that supports that hypothesis. Inductive reasoning can be used for this task. Inductive reasoning involves using specific observations, such as observed patterns, to reach a general conclusion. Usually, in science, experiments are run to try and verify the hypothesis. In this case, we can't run an experiment on an advanced ET. But we can make observations and take measurements. The question we want to answer is whether the observed behaviors of UAP fit our ET hypothesis. Gathering the evidence to answer this question is more difficult than it might seem.

Astronomer Carl Sagan once said on his TV show *Cosmos*, "Extraordinary claims require extraordinary evidence." He made this statement when talking about the possibility of aliens visiting Earth. This is a nice, succinct adage for a TV show, but its value in science is debatable. It is often used as an argument by those who have not thoroughly studied the subject. Science does not have two definitions of evidence: regular and extraordinary. It is not like we're choosing a different grade of gasoline. Evidence consists of a collection of facts. Evidence is evidence and a fact is a fact. And who defines what is an extraordinary claim or an extraordinary fact? This is very subjective, and the goal of science is to reduce subjectivity and enhance objectivity.

The simplest way to prove the ET hypothesis is for an alien spacecraft to land, their occupants emerge, and they tell us they're from Alpha Centauri or wherever. Short of that, it must be proven that unknown objects seen near Earth or in our atmosphere are of extraterrestrial origin. If our hypothesis is correct, we should look for evidence UAP are visiting us from a distant exoplanet. One indication would be that we are able to detect UAP moving in near-Earth space and entering our atmosphere. A second indication would be UAP exhibiting velocities and accelerations that if sustained would reach speeds necessary for interstellar travel. The final indication would be that UAP demonstrate a technology that is beyond that of any technology on Earth. All three of these indications are what we would expect as indicators of an advanced civilization visiting Earth. The gathering of evidence to prove this will require considerable effort.

Can we detect extraterrestrial craft in near-Earth space that enter our atmosphere? The most advanced radar systems that can detect objects entering and leaving our atmosphere are those of the NORAD and the United States Space Surveillance Network (USSSN) operated by the U.S. Space Force. Similar capabilities are expected to be possessed by Russia, China, and our European allies. The primary role of these systems is to detect the launch of intercontinental ballistic missiles, movement of enemy satellites in orbit, and any other orbital or ground activity that threatens their host nation. Consequently, these systems are looking for specific maneuvers from man-made satellites and weapons systems. Their purpose is not to look for extraterrestrial craft. Furthermore, these systems are collecting quantities of data that are so large that they must be filtered to prioritize data that have the signature of a threat from another nation-state. This filtering of data was evident in the early 2023 UAP incidents over Alaska and Canada when the military admitted that they had not detected the objects because their computer systems had filtered out the radar data that did not meet the characteristics of enemy craft.[9] The answer to the question at the beginning of this paragraph is, "Yes." We have radar systems capable of detecting extraterrestrial craft entering our atmosphere if we are willing to utilize our resources for that purpose. Unfortunately, we have not used radar for the purpose of detecting ET. National security concerns related to potential conventional and nuclear war between the Earth's major nation-states have dominated the use of these radar systems.

ChatGPT, a new artificial intelligence system developed by OpenAI, Incorporated, was asked if NORAD and USSSN could detect extraterrestrial craft entering our atmosphere. Its answer was very similar: "While these systems are highly capable of detecting and tracking objects in space, their primary purpose does not include the detection of extraterrestrial craft entering Earth's atmosphere. The focus of NORAD and the Space Surveillance Network is on objects with known orbits and trajectories."

The second question is whether we can establish that some UAP exhibit velocities and accelerations that if sustained would reach speeds necessary for interstellar travel. This was discussed at length in chapter 4. A paper was published in the journal *Entropy* that indicates accelerations reported during UAP sightings are consistent with what would be necessary for interstellar travel at light speed.[10] But to prove the ET hypothesis we need actual measurements that establish the accelerations of UAP. Military phase array radar systems have detected UAP during their rapid acceleration as was reported in the U.S.S. *Princeton* incident of 2004. The military will not provide the radar data that would establish acceleration values for UAP because of national security concerns. The worry is that our enemies would then understand details of how our radar systems work. This claim is debatable. Nonetheless, the military's claim prevents scientists from obtaining information on the acceleration of UAP.

This leaves it to civilian scientists to establish acceleration values for UAP. Developing a suitable civilian phase array radar system of the sophistication of military systems is cost prohibitive. The most effective way to collect data will be through a network of automated camera systems that will track a UAP simultaneously on multiple cameras using rapid frame rates. The exact velocity and acceleration can then be calculated using triangulation. Acceleration or deceleration values greater than 100 g-forces should be an indicator of a non-terrestrial craft as none of our aircraft can survive more than fifteen g-forces. Our aircraft achieve high g-forces through angular turns and not through linear acceleration. Linear acceleration in military aircraft is limited to around two g-forces and deceleration of an aircraft can achieve eight to twelve g-forces for a temporary moment. Any object moving through the sky at high speed that suddenly decelerates to a hovering position for a few seconds before accelerating again cannot be explained by any human aircraft. These are the types of characteristics that need to be captured on multiple camera systems.

The third indication that UAP are of non-terrestrial origin would be that they demonstrate a technology that is beyond that of any technology on Earth. High acceleration is one indicator of non-human technology. There are others. The lack of any visible propulsion system is one. The ability to move through the atmosphere at extreme speeds without generating extreme heat is still another sign of a non-human technology. Currently, hypersonic missiles can reach speeds as high as Mach 10. But at those speeds they must remain well above 50,000 feet altitude to avoid the melting of the metallic surface and shock wave pressures that would crush its structure.[11] UAP have been reported at those speeds near the Earth's surface with no obvious heating of its surface, sonic boom, or any other atmospheric shock waves. This is a capability that we don't possess. In order to measure these characteristics in a scientific manner, an automated camera system should also include an infra-red detection system as well as an acoustical measuring device.

Before we leave the subject of UAP and ET, it is appropriate to touch on a final question. If some of the UAP that are reported are ET, are they all from a single ET civilization? Think about that question for a moment. If there is one ET civilization that has found us and visited us, then the likelihood is that there are others. It is more likely that there are zero ET civilizations that have visited us than there is only one. If we are not unique and that is proven by discovering another civilization, then there will be more than one. If we someday find microbial life on Mars, would we not expect to find more than one species of bacteria? It's possible that would be the only type of bacteria in existence on Mars, but not likely. Where life exists, it is ubiquitous; where there is one, there is usually more.

There are even hints of multiple ETs in the study of UAP shapes. The 1940s were dominated by the disk shape. The 1980s brought the larger, triangular-shaped UAPs. Is this from the same ET civilization just as our aircraft come in different shapes: balloons, helicopters, jets, and missiles? Or do the different shapes indicate a different owner, or planet of origin, if you will? There is no way to know for certain. But to the extent that we would expect there to be more than one ET, we must consider the possibility that the different UAP shape and movement characteristics might be indicative of more than one ET civilization.

WHERE IS EVERYBODY?

Enrico Fermi first asked, "Where is everybody?" at a luncheon conversation with Edward Teller, Emil Konopinski, and Herbert York in the summer of 1950. These men were nuclear physicists who had been instrumental in the U.S. development of the first atomic bomb at Los Alamos National Laboratory in New Mexico. Fermi didn't say who "everybody" was, and that's what caused the other men to laugh. They somehow all knew by the way he asked the question that he was referring to ET. Where was ET?[12]

Some have referred to Fermi's question as the Fermi Paradox. It is an argument that centers around the concept that if intelligent life exists in our galaxy, then it would only take it a few million years to colonize the galaxy; yet we have no evidence that this has happened, therefore the assumption that life exists in our galaxy must be false. However, this is not an argument that Fermi made, so the term *Fermi Paradox* is a misnomer. Fermi's luncheon conversation was a lighthearted discussion. What is called the Fermi Paradox is an argument made in a paper by astrophysicist Michael Hart in 1974. Hart's theory was heavily based on the idea of colonization. ET would spread across the galaxy by colonizing the nearest worlds, similar to how a bacterial colony will spread. The problem with this theory is that it assumes that ET behaves like humans: conquering, colonizing, and coalescing before moving to new territory. The paper also ignored the possibility that ET was already visiting Earth.[13] Perhaps the better question is whether ET has visited Earth, and if it has, why has it not contacted us. A number of hypotheses have been proposed as to why ET has not contacted us directly.

The Rare Earth hypothesis is the first and most common explanation. It is the view put forth by Hart: the Earth is either a rare or singular event such that intelligent life is an anomaly in our galaxy. The hypothesis is supported by the lack of success of the SETI program which has been looking for radio transmissions for over forty-five years without success. But there are several strong arguments as to why SETI has failed. Many of SETI's assumptions are based on an anthropocentric view of ET. Like Hart, SETI assumes ET thinks like us. The radio wavelengths SETI chose to examine are between 1,420 and 1,720 MHz. They chose those because there is less noise at those frequencies and that's what humans might choose if trying to send a signal. There are thousands of other frequencies that they are ignoring. They also assume that ET is beaming their signal directly at us. Talk about anthropocentric! And SETI's decision to look at radio waves was also based on the fact that humans were heavy into the use of radio waves and analog communications when SETI was formed in the 1970s. Today, our electronic society has moved away from analog and to digital. Our radios and televisions are becoming digital. An ET confining their search for intelligent life to a 1,420–1,720 MHz emission from Earth would likely never find us. Although possible and still popular, the Rare Earth hypothesis is becoming less tenable as time passes.

The Great Filter hypothesis is an interesting explanation as to why we may never find ET. The hypothesis is that something prevents an intelligent civilization from ever reaching the point of being able to travel to the stars. Imagine that every civilization develops as we have. The ability to destroy one's own civilization develops long before the ability to travel to the stars. We have had the ability to annihilate our civilization for almost sixty years with nuclear weapons. We have likely had the ability to destroy our civilization with biological and viral warfare for at least the last twenty years. Today we are inadvertently destroying our planet through global warming, with no viable solution available to us. And we're overdue for a solar flare similar to the Carrington Event that last occurred in 1859, before the age of electronics. Such a solar flare today would decimate our electrical grid system by inducing large electrical currents that would short-out our power grid. The power outages would be so massive and widespread that they would last months. The resulting effects on our internet-based economy would affect everything from planning to crop production to delivery of products. Multiply the logistical impacts of Covid by 100 and you will have a feel for the devastation. Any of these calamities (nuclear war, biological war, global warming, Carrington Event, asteroid impact) could be the Great Filter that stops our civilization from ever achieving interstellar travel. Meaningful interstellar travel is likely several hundred years away. Will the Great Filter stop our advance to the stars, and has it already done so with other civilizations?

The Zoo hypothesis was proposed in 1973 by Harvard astrophysicist John Ball. He stated that, "Extraterrestrial intelligent life may be almost ubiquitous. The apparent failure of such life to interact with us may be understood in terms of the hypothesis that they have set us aside as part of a wilderness area or zoo."[14] Perhaps he garnered this concept from the famous science fiction show of the late 1960s, *Star Trek*. A key philosophy was the Prime Directive, which was often mentioned in the original series as well as the later versions such as *Star Trek: The Next Generation*, *Star Trek: Voyager*, and *Star Trek: Enterprise*. The Prime Directive espoused that there could be no interference with the natural development of lower technology cultures. The Prime Directive is the antithesis of the history of human development, which has involved the assimilation and/or conquering of lower technology cultures. John Ball argued that the Zoo hypothesis predicts that we shall never find ET because they do not want to be found and they have the technological ability to ensure this. This hypothesis explains the difficulty in establishing the existence of ET. It does not explain the many reports of individuals seeing UAP up close, which for a *Star Trek* aficionado is a clear violation of the Prime Directive.

Another hypothesis that I will propose is a combination of the Great Filter and Zoo hypotheses. It can be called the Benevolent Life hypothesis. The assumption made is that as intelligent life develops, its benevolent nature improves. The only example that we can use to base this assumption is the development of life here on Earth.

A relationship between benevolence and a species' mental and social development can be seen in the animal kingdom. Some of the higher orders of life have shown empathy for their own kind. Primates, elephants, mice, dogs, and dolphins have demonstrated empathy.[15] Concern for others of their own species as well as lower species is most developed in humans, arguably the highest developed species on this planet. One can make the claim that our empathy for each other has improved as society and civilization have advanced over the last 2,000 years. Certainly, this is the moral direction that most major religions state that humankind must undertake. Yet our malevolent nature is still very much alive. Watch the evening news and it is difficult to see much of our benevolence.

As an intelligent species develops it may achieve pure benevolence in its social norms given sufficient time. The barrier to this achievement is whether a species destroys itself before achieving that level. This is the Great Filter. Will we destroy ourselves before humankind reaches a more benevolent state of existence? If the answer is yes, then we do not need to worry about ET or whether we will achieve interstellar travel. But if we can avoid that calamity, then we may make it to the stars and we would be a much more peaceful race as we encounter other civilizations out in the cosmos. The same may be said about ET. If an ET civilization has survived the Great Filter, then it is likely to be peaceful, caring, and thoughtful toward other civilizations that it encounters.

It can be argued that such an ET civilization would not only be peaceful but would be considerate of how their interaction with a lower civilization could be detrimental. Humankind is not likely to fare well if it encounters an advanced civilization, even if benevolent. The realization that our civilization is inferior and at the mercy of another civilization could cause a collective existential crisis for humanity. Humanity might question the purpose of its existence and whether any of our achievements were meaningful. And what would we do with technology that we might learn? Today, we would likely improve our weapons of war and mass destruction. That won't end well. How would our scientific community react to the knowledge that any developments were in vain, as they had already been achieved and could be provided by ET? It is therefore possible that an encounter with an advanced race could severely impact humankind's advancement. ET likely realizes the negative effects of an encounter with a lower-level species. The reaction that we might expect from a benevolent ET might be similar to the Zoo hypothesis. There would not be direct contact. ET might observe and study us, but with minimal interaction. We should not expect a landing on the White House lawn.

The Benevolent Life hypothesis fits well with the reported behaviors in UAP sightings. There are signs of intelligent control of the craft but very little attempt at overt contact. There have been some reports of what individuals consider direct contact but these interactions, if they occurred, are not sufficient to impact human society. If this hypothesis is correct, then humanity should not expect contact with ET in the near future. Instead, this hypothesis argues that part of the search for ET should include that we concentrate our efforts on improving our own benevolence. Otherwise, we may never have the opportunity to meet ET and answer Carl Sagan's question, "Is mankind alone in the universe?" We should remember Sagan's words as he showed us a photograph that *Voyager I* took of the Earth from four billion miles away and it showed a small blue dot. Sagan's words should make us pause and contemplate both the insignificance and the wonderful uniqueness of our world. "Look again at that dot. That's here. That's home. That's us. On it everyone you love, everyone you know, everyone you ever heard of, every human being who ever was, lived out their lives."

Chapter Eleven

What's Next

We have come a long way as a civilization since the modern Foo Fighter/ flying saucer/UFO/UAP reports that began in 1942. Aircraft have advanced from propeller to jet propulsion to space craft that have explored our solar system. Computer technology has gone from a computer that fills a room to a computer that fits in the palm of your hand with 10,000 times more memory than the computers aboard our space shuttles of the 1980s. Communications have improved from using wire to carry phone signals to the wireless technologies of today and the internet upon which so much depends. We have also developed the ability to destroy most if not all life on our planet. Yet our understanding of UAP has hardly changed.

Eighty years of off-and-on military investigations have led to no solid conclusions. Military concerns related to UAP have been tied to national security implications. The U.S. Air Force stated that there were no national security concerns with UAP during the 1950s–1970s. The Air Force publicly ignored the UAP subject for the remainder of the twentieth century. All inquiries were met with a statement that the Air Force stopped investigating the subject in 1970. The Navy and the DoD took the lead with investigations of UAP in the twenty-first century. National security concerns were made prominent again after UAP sightings over our military facilities were reported. Nonetheless, there are no indications that the military will be any more successful in solving this enigma than they have been for the last eighty years.

Understanding of UAP must come from the scientific community. Ongoing investigative work should not exclusively fall under the auspices of DoD, which has a different set of fundamental interests that do not include open data and public science. The scientific community must have openness if it is to flourish in its analysis of any subject matter.

This scientific openness must also exist within the scientific community itself. Discussions of how to solve the UAP issue should extend beyond discussions between two scientists in a café, which abruptly cease when other colleagues draw near. The subject must be approached with the same level of scientific openness as any other topic. Genuine scientific inquiry does not investigate a subject solely based on prevailing social norms.

NASA is the most appropriate scientific body to lead an investigation of UAP, especially if it turns out that a percentage of UAP are controlled by an unknown non-human intelligence. NASA's mission includes the search for life in the cosmos.[1] There could not be a more appropriate organization to define what constitutes proof of extraterrestrial intelligent life. The rest of the scientific community can join the endeavor with NASA at the helm. NASA had already indicated their willingness to take on such a role when they held a press conference on the UAP subject in May 2023.[2] However, to ensure the success of these investigations, both NASA and the scientific community will require sufficient financial support.

Congress must take the initiative to provide funding specifically to NASA and the scientific community. Congress has already shown a desire to investigate the UAP subject based on extensive language that they have placed in the National Defense Authorization Acts of 2022, 2023, and 2024. This responsibility goes beyond Congress. It is also the public's responsibility to indicate to their congressional representatives that they appreciate the work done by Congress and that the public wants more effort focused on investigating UAP. This is best achieved through campaigns to push the public to write and call their congressional representatives. With public support, Congress will respond. For those readers so inclined, there now exists a website designed specifically to allow the public to send their UAP concerns to their representatives: https://declassifyuap.org/.

Congress has the power to provide specific funding to a NASA UAP project as well as funding for the broader scientific community through the National Science Foundation (NSF), an independent agency of the government that supports fundamental research and education in science and engineering. Congress should provide specific directives to the NSF, through the appropriations process. It can pass legislation that allocates funding to the NSF for the specific purpose of studying UAP. It is important that Congress specify a certain amount of minimal NSF funding that will be allocated for UAP research. The same stigma that has permeated the UAP subject will also exist in some of the NSF individuals when deciding between a UAP-related grant as compared to a grant related to a more established scientific subject. A mandatory minimal funding of UAP projects will help eliminate any prejudicial disapproval of grants related to UAP.

The amount of funding needed will be several hundred million dollars per year. Some of those funds should be awarded directly to NASA by Congress for the creation of a full-time scientific investigative body within NASA. Without access to military equipment, NASA will need to spend considerable amounts of money to procure equipment capable of capturing objects moving at extreme speeds through the atmosphere. They will need high-frame-rate automated camera systems, dedicated satellite systems, military grade infra-red sensors, hyperspectral spectrometers, and phase array radar systems. All these systems are expensive, but it is feasible. The NSF budget for 2024 is estimated to be $11.3 billion. It would only require 1 to 2 percent of that budget for the study of UAP.

Congress should also provide a directive to the FAA to provide open coop-eration to NASA. Although the FAA is also a federal agency, they have closed their door to openness in their recent alignments with the military and the Department of Homeland Security. Their role is to provide civilian air safety, and there is no reason why they cannot share data related to UAP with NASA and the scientific community.

NASA's role will be critical. Already, NASA has a program to look at how we can identify intelligent life by looking at technosignatures.[3] Technosigna-tures are signs of an advanced civilization by looking at distant electromag-netic emissions, atmospheric pollutants, night-time light emissions, and other indications of intelligence. NASA can take the lead by extending the study of technosignatures to any indications of ET in our solar system, near Earth, or in our atmosphere.

One of NASA's first steps will be to identify and agree upon characteristics that are an indicator of technosignatures of extraterrestrial intelligence. Here is an example. When you hear someone say, "We have seen no evidence to indicate that UAP are of extraterrestrial origin," you probably take that at face value. You shouldn't. You should ask the question, "What characteristics would you need to measure to establish that a UAP was extraterrestrial?" This is the question that needs to be answered before anyone can claim that they have or have not detected an object that is extraterrestrial. The answer is not easy, and it requires careful thought from a collegiate body of scientists who can evaluate characteristics such as acceleration, velocity, interaction with the atmosphere, and then define what is proof of ET. Once this is done, then there will be a basis upon which to answer the question, "Is there evidence of ET?" Whenever the day comes that we encounter ET, we will need those criteria. Why not develop those criteria now?

NASA should also consider making intentional attempts to communicate with UAP. There are no significant drawbacks to such an endeavor, and it is much less expensive than the detection of the characteristics of an unknown craft. Communication signals could be sent across multiple EM frequencies such as radio, microwave, and optical. Given the apparent attraction of UAP to nuclear facilities, conducting these communication attempts in close proximity to such sites would enhance the probability of success. The challenge lies in sending signals to extraterrestrial civilizations with entirely different languages. Linguistic experts and astrobiologists could develop diverse communication signals capable of being detected and potentially eliciting a response. Someday humanity may encounter ET and will need protocols on how to attempt communication. Those protocols should be developed now.

NASA will also be able to bring in cooperation from the rest of the world's space agencies. NASA has partners with the space programs of all the major nations of the world.[4] The study of UAP is a worldwide issue and is not unique to the United States. The entire world should be involved. This effort can help bring the nations of the world together in peace, just as NASA has done with the International Space Station. This cooperation is needed for the day that humanity encounters the first extraterrestrial civilization. Humanity should be seen as a single united race that lives on planet Earth and not as many different warring nation-states. NASA's study of UAP can help be the catalyst for this change.

The first step in this journey is to relinquish our anthropocentric view of the universe around us. We must fully divorce ourselves from the pre-Copernican view that everything revolves around us and that we must always be in control. Most scientists believe that there are civilizations in our galaxy, much more advanced than our own. Logic dictates that those civilizations will find us long before we find them. We should try and detect any such potential contact. It makes sense to devote resources to searching for ET, as such an eventual encounter will likely be one of the most significant events in the history of human development. We also need to realize that we will not be in control of such an encounter. It is much more likely that it will be ET that decides when any encounter will take place. We are not at the top of the totem pole, and we need to be comfortable with that concept both as a society and as individuals. Perhaps that realization will also help us treat those less fortunate than ourselves more humanely and humbly.

Often, it is science fiction that helps lead us forward. And, on occasion, science fiction seems to mold our future. Arguably, few science fiction stories have influenced our science and our society as much as Gene Roddenberry's TV series, *Star Trek*, broadcast in the late 1960s. Roddenberry chose the name of the spaceship in his famous TV series as a tribute to the first U.S. Navy nuclear-powered aircraft carrier, the USS *Enterprise*. NASA chose the name of its very first space shuttle built in 1976 on the USS *Enterprise* of *Star Trek* fame. *Star Trek* did more than ensure the continuance of the name of its spaceship. It highlighted scientific inventions decades before they had ever been conceived.

Roddenberry's *Star Trek* predicted many of our current and past products at a time when such technologies were not on the horizon. The flip-phones of the early 2000s bore a striking resemblance to the standard mode of communication on *Star Trek*, a show produced in an era when phones were wall-mounted contraptions with wires connected between telephone poles. No one had thought of wireless communication. Lt. Uhura, the spaceship's communication officer, would touch a device placed in her ear to communicate. This was the precursor to the modern Bluetooth headset. Siri was already envisioned back in the 1960s. *Star Trek*'s crew gave verbal commands to a computer and would hear a reply from a computerized female voice. This was envisioned in an era when the personal computer had yet to be invented. Dr. McCoy, the doctor on board the spaceship *Enterprise*, used what he called a medical tricorder to scan a patient and diagnose their illness. These types of hand-held medical devices are now under development. Replicators on board the spaceship *Enterprise* were used to provide food and drink on command. Already, this is beginning to become a reality with 3D printers. These are only half of the technological predictions that the *Star Trek* TV series brought us. Just as important were the societal breakthroughs and predictions made on the show.

Star Trek forecasted the way our society would need to change if we were ever to become a spacefaring people. The *Star Trek* crew represented a single world and no individual nation-states. Beyond the iconic Capt. Kirk, there was the ship's helmsman, Hikaru Sulu, who was of Asian descent. Filmed during the heart of the Cold War, the ship's navigator, Pavel Chekov, was Russian-born. These men represented the lack of ethnic and cultural prejudices that Roddenberry projected for our future.

Roddenberry's predictions for our future included race relations. The communication officer, Lt. Nyota Uhura, was a Black female and she played a major role in the show. In one episode of *Star Trek*, the first Black–White kiss on American network television occurred between Capt. Kirk and Lt. Uhura. This was during an era when it was illegal in some states for Black–White marriages. Roddenberry was ahead of his time, and he believed that this was the route that humanity must take if we were to venture to the stars as one race. The iconic Mr. Spock even represented our unity with other intelligent species.

Along with these social changes was the concept of the Prime Directive—the directive that we would need to respect any extraterrestrial civilizations that were less advanced by not interfering with their development. Roddenberry believed that to travel to the stars we would do so not as different nation-states but as one people. Our differences became our strength, embodying the essence of humanity on Earth.

We can reach the stars. Interstellar travel is within our grasp. The technological hurdles are immense, but they can be achieved with time and effort. Just as daunting are the societal hurdles we will need to transcend to ensure our survival here on Earth long enough to become an interstellar species. This process is often referred to as universalization, and it describes the transition from nation-states to a single human race that journeys to the stars.

The universalization process needs to begin here on Earth. We can seize the UAP enigma as a unique opportunity, utilizing it to refine the essential skills required for potential encounters with intelligent extraterrestrial life. More importantly, it is also an opportunity to better ourselves. We are one human race, and this is the message that we should send out to the cosmos. This little blue dot is us.

Appendix

UFO Sighting Questionnaire Interview

Date of interview: _____

Date of sighting: _____

WITNESS INFORMATION

Witness Name: _____ Current Age _____

Address: _____ Phone: _____

Email: _____ Education: _____

Occupation: _____

At Time of Sighting:

Vision: _____ Hearing: _____ Health: _____

WITNESS SIGHTING

Describe what you were doing before the event and what you saw once the event began.

_____

_____

_____

_____

_____

_____

_____

_____

_____

_____

_____

_____

_____

_____

_____

_____

_____

_____

WITNESS SIGHTING: SPECIFIC QUESTIONS

Location of the sighting along with latitude/longitude values if known

_____

_____

Date and time when you saw the object

_____

_____

Description of the object at various angles

_____

_____

How do you know what the time was?

_____

_____

For how long did you observe the object?

_____

_____

What made you first notice the object?

_____

_____

What did you think the object was when you first noticed it?

_____

_____

Time, direction, and elevation in which the object was first seen?

_____

_____

Relative size of object at arm's length; first seen.

_____

_____

Time, direction, and elevation in which the object was closest?

_____

_____

Relative size of object at arm's length; at its closest approach.

_____

_____

Time, direction, and elevation in which the object was last seen?

_____

_____

Relative size of object at arm's length; last seen.

_____

_____

How did you lose sight of the object?

_____

_____

What were the weather and sky/star conditions?

_____

_____

Were there any notable astronomical objects or man-made objects in the sky near the object? If yes, indicate the approx. time, object's relationship in the sky to the known object, brightness comparison, size comparison, etc.

_____

_____

Brightness of the object. Choose one: (a) brighter than the sun (b) brighter than the moon (c) bright(er) than a particular star/planet (example: It was about as bright as Jupiter) (d) brighter than the sky background but no lights (e) same darkness as the sky (f) darker than the sky (g) other (explain)

_____

_____

Lumination of the object. Choose one. Was the object(s): (a) self-luminous (b) dull finish (c) reflecting (d) transparent (e) other (explain)

_____

_____

Color of the object.

_____

_____

Was the object "fuzzy," "sharply outlined," or "like a bright star"?

_____

_____

Did the object move in front of or behind anything?

_____

_____

Description of speed.

_____

_____

Any sound, heat, or smell?

_____

_____

Any other aircraft in the area?

_____

_____

Any effect before or after on electronic products?

_____

_____

Any animal reactions?

_____

_____

If only lights were seen, did the lights maintain fixed positions?

_____

_____

Do you remember if background stars were ever blocked out?

_____

Please provide a detailed sketch of the object(s), including color, lights, and surface features or texture.

Please give names and contact information for any other witnesses.

_____

_____

Have any other groups or individuals interviewed you? _____

If yes, then provide names and date of interview.

_____

_____

Other comments.

_____

_____

_____

_____

_____

_____

_____

_____

_____

Previous sightings? _____

If yes, then fill out a second form describing that occurrence.

_____

_____

What were your thoughts regarding UFOs prior to your sighting?

_____

_____

QUESTIONS TO USE IF A WITNESS HAS AN ELECTROMAGNETIC ISSUE WITH A DEVICE SUCH AS A CELL PHONE, CAMERA, TV, AUTOMOBILE, ETC.

Model of affected equipment.

How long has witness owned equipment?

How often does the witness charge the equipment's battery?

If applicable, did the equipment lose a signal?

Did the equipment power go down?

Did equipment retain power, but some apps shut down or failed to work? (list)

Did equipment get warm or hot to the touch?

If a call was made was there any effect on sound quality (for example, buzzing, hiss, popping, reverb, wowing, hearing other calls)? If "yes," was the sound quality affected by whomever was being called?

Did equipment function normally after the encounter?

Have any specific apps stopped working correctly? (list)

If available, measure the equipment for any electrical or magnetic traces using an EM meter. Take measurements at varied distances from the equipment until the signal fades. Provide a drawing. Measure distances in all directions along with readout values. Measure a similar unaffected piece of equipment to use as a control.

Has the battery life changed?

Has any data been corrupted (saved photos, vids, music lost, apps dropped, etc.)?

If equipment doesn't work anymore would the witness consider giving it to you for analysis?

Check with the owners of all nearby cell equipment towers and determine if any equipment outages occurred during the time frame in question.

If any other witnesses were in the area, check the operation of their equipment even if they were not using their equipment and were not aware that there had been any equipment failure.

Notes

CHAPTER ONE

1. Keith Chester, *Strange Company: Military Encounters with UFOs in World War II* (San Antonio: Anomalist Books, 2007), pp. 284–96.

2. Chester, *Strange Company*, p. 130.

3. Michael D. Swords and Robert Powell et al., *UFOs and Government: A Historical Inquiry* (San Antonio: Anomalist Books, 2012), p. 44, pp. 48–50.

4. Swords and Powell, *UFOs and Government*, p. 65.

5. United States Air Force, *Project Blue Book and Project SIGN*, microfilm, card file 1948.11, 6387703, National Archives and Records Administration, Washington, D.C., Andrews AFB, MD.

6. Edward Ruppelt, *The Report on Unidentified Flying Objects* (New York: Doubleday and Co., 1956), p. 43.

7. United States Air Force, *Project Blue Book and Project SIGN*, review of all card files for 1949.

8. Ruppelt, *The Report on Unidentified Flying Objects*, p. 48.

9. United States Air Force, *Project Blue Book and Project SIGN*, review of all card files for 1950.

10. United States Air Force, *Project Blue Book and Project SIGN*, review of all card files for June and July 1952.

11. Ruppelt, *The Report on Unidentified Flying Objects*, p. 99.

12. Roy Craig audiotape interview of Jay Nogle, location of interview at Malmstrom AFB, Montana, October 19, 1967, Roy Craig files at Cushing Archival Library, Texas A&M University.

13. Capt. Edward Ruppelt extensively quoted in "15% of Saucer Reports Are Labeled Mystery," United Press news story, dateline: Dayton, Ohio, July 18, 1952.

14. Associated Press news story, dateline: Albuquerque, New Mexico, July 19, 1952.

15. Ruppelt, *The Report on Unidentified Flying Objects*, pp. 116–17.

16. Ibid.

17. Ibid., 118.

18. Swords and Powell, *UFOs and Government*, p. 160.

19. Chadwell, H. Marshall, memorandum to Director of Central Intelligence, subject: "Flying Saucers," September 17, 1952. Freedom of Information Request.

20. Swords and Powell, *UFOs and Government*, pp. 175–97.

21. Robertson Panel, *Report of Scientific Advisory Panel on Unidentified Flying Objects,* convened by Office of Scientific Intelligence, CIA, January 14–18, 1953.

22. Thornton Page to James L. Klotz, October 3, 1992; and Page's notes on his talk to the Society for Scientific Exploration, May 30, 1987.

23. Jerome Clark, *The UFO Book: Encyclopedia of the Extraterrestrial* (Michigan: Visible Ink Press, 1998), p. 305.

24. Carl Sagan and Thornton Page, *UFO's: A Scientific Debate* (London: Cornell University Press, 1972), pp. 56–70.

25. Clark, *The UFO Encyclopedia*, pp. 953–1001.

26. Antonio F. Rullán, "The Levelland Sightings of 1957." Center for UFO Studies, Chicago, IL, October 1999.

27. United States Air Force, *Project Blue Book and Project SIGN*, review of all card files for November 1957.

28. Swords and Powell, *UFOs and Government*, pp. 276–78.

29. United States Air Force, *Project Blue Book and Project SIGN*, review of all card files for 1959–1966.

30. United States Air Force, *Project Blue Book and Project SIGN*, card file 1966.03, 8671584, Dexter and Hillsdale, MI.

31. News Release, Congressman Gerald R. Ford, House Republican Leader, March 25, 1966, Gerald Ford Presidential Library, University of Michigan.

32. J. Allen Hynek and Jacques Vallee, *The Edge of Reality: A Progress Report on Unidentified Flying Objects* (Quality Books, 1975).

33. Swords and Powell, *UFOs and Government*, p. 307.

34. Robert Low to E. James Archer and Thurston E. Manning, memo, August 9, 1966, American Philosophical Library archives, Philadelphia, PA.

35. "Condon to Head UFO Study," *Science* 154, no. 3746 (October 14, 1966): p. 244.

36. Swords and Powell, *UFOs and Government*, pp. 312–32.

37. Edward Condon, *Final Report of the Scientific Study of Unidentified Flying Objects.* (E. P. Dutton & Co., 1969).

38. Thornton Page, "Book Review," *American Journal of Physics* 37, no. 10 (October 1969): pp. 1071–72.

39. "Unidentified Flying Objects and Air Force Project Blue Book," *United States Air Force*, accessed August 8, 2022, https://www.af.mil/About-Us/Fact-Sheets/Display/Article/104590/unidentified-flying-objects-and-air-force-project-blue-book/.

40. Michael D. Swords, "Research Note: Delphos, Kansas, Soil Analysis," *Journal of UFO Studies*, New Series 3 (1991): pp. 116–37.

41. Erol A. Faruk, "The Delphos CE2 Case: A New Appraisal of the Data," *SCU*, November 2021, accessed August 9, 2022, https://www.explorescu.org/post/a-new -appraisal-of-the-data-of-the-delphos-ce2-1971-case.

42. Jennie Zeidman, "A Helicopter-UFO Encounter Over Ohio," *Center for UFO Studies*, 1979.

43. Barry Greenwood and Lawrence Fawcett, *Clear Intent: The Government Coverup of the UFO Experience* (Englewood Cliffs: Prentice-Hall, Inc., 1984).

44. "Iran, Reported UFO Sighting," document 6 846 0139 76, *U.S. Defense Intelligence Agency* (September 1976), obtained by FOIA. https://www.dia.mil/FOIA /FOIA-Electronic-Reading-Room/.

45. Capt. Henry S. Shields, "Now You See It, Now You Don't," *Meaconing, Interference, Jamming, and Intrusion Quarterly* (October 1978).

46. Bruce Maccabee, "The Fantastic Flight of JAL1628," *International UFO Reporter* 12, no. 2 (March/April 1987), accessed August 12, 2022, http://brumac.mysite. com/JAL1628/JL1628.html.

47. Richard F. Haines et al., "Report of an Unidentified Aerial Phenomenon and Its Safety Implications at O'Hare International Airport on November 7, 2006," Case 18, March 9, 2007, Richard F. Haines Ufology papers, Woodson Research Center, Rice University, Houston, TX.

48. Robert Powell and Glenn Schulze, "Stephenville Lights: A Comprehensive Radar and Witness Report Study Regarding the Events of January 8, 2008," December 18, 2010, *SCU*, accessed August 14, 2022, https://www.explorescu.org/post /stephenville-lights-a-comprehensive-radar-and-witness-report-study.

49. Robert Powell and Carl Paulson et al., "2013 Aguadilla Puerto Rico: The Detailed Analysis of an Unidentified Anomalous Phenomenon Captured by the Department of Homeland Security," August 10, 2015, *SCU*, accessed August 14, 2022, https://www.explorescu.org/post/2013-aguadilla-puerto-rico-uap-incident-report-a -detailed-analysis.

50. Ralph Blumenthal and Helene Cooper, "Are U.F.O.s Real?: Secret Pentagon Unit Tried to Find Out," *New York Times*, December 17, 2017, accessed August 14, 2022, https://www.nytimes.com/2017/12/16/us/politics/pentagon-program-ufo-harry -reid.html.

51. Swords and Powell, *UFOs and Government*, pp. 361–67.

52. Aime Michel, *Flying Saucers and the Straight-Line Mystery Hardcover* (New York: S. G. Phillips, 1958).

53. Robert Roussel and F. Buchi, "UFO, the End of the Secret," *Rhedae Magazine*, 1976, French to English translation of an interview of Lt. Colonel Alexis by Francine Buchi, accessed August 15, 2022, https://rr0.org/time/1/9/7/6/Alexis_Interview/.

54. "GEIPAN: Its History," *CNES-GEIPAN*, accessed August 15, 2022, https:// www.cnes-geipan.fr/en/histoire-du-geipan.

55. Centre National D'Études Spatiales, "No. 16 Technical Report, Trace Analysis" (Toulouse, March 1, 1983).

56. Centre National D'Etudes Spatiales, "No. 17 Technical Report, L'Amarante" (Toulouse, March 21, 1983).

57. Ministry of Defence (United Kingdom), "Unidentified Flying Objects Report of Sighting, Rendlesham Forest, December 1980," British National Archives, Kew, Richmond, United Kingdom.

58. Maj. Gen. Wilfred de Brouwer, "The Belgian UFO Wave," *MUFON 39th International Symposium Proceedings* (July 2008): pp. 140–42.

59. Marie-Therese de Brosses, "A UFO on the F16's Radar," *Paris-Match*, July 5, 1990, French to English translation of an interview of Colonel Wilfred de Brouwer made by Robert Durant.

60. Leslie Kean, *UFOs: Generals, Pilots and Government Officials Go on the Record* (New York: Crown Archetype, 2010), pp. 93–98.

CHAPTER TWO

1. United States Air Force, *Project Blue Book and Project SIGN*, microfilm, card file 1957.10, 6972968, N. Luffenham, England, National Archives and Records Administration, Washington, D.C., Andrews AFB, MD.

2. United States Air Force, *Project Blue Book and Project SIGN*, card file 1957.12, 6970187, Chitose-Hokkaido, Misawa Air Base, Japan.

3. "During the Investigative Interview (Part I)," *Solutions Risque*, accessed September 3, 2022, https://www.solutionsrisque.com/using-open-ended-questions -investigative-interview-part-1/.

4. "Special Report 14: Analysis of Reports of Unidentified Aerial Objects," by Battelle Memorial Institute, *United States Air Force*, Project No. 10073, May 5, 1955.

5. U.S. Food and Drug Administration, "Statistical Review and Evaluation, Clinical Studies," NDA #21-647, VIOX," May 27, 2003, p. 6.

6. "Unidentified Flying Objects and Air Force Project Blue Book," *United States Air Force*, accessed September 4, 2022, https://www.af.mil/About-Us/Fact-Sheets /Display/Article/104590/unidentified-flying-objects-and-air-force-project-blue-book/.

7. Allan Hendry, *The UFO Handbook: A Guide to Investigating, Evaluating, and Reporting UFO Sightings*, First Edition (New York: Doubleday, 1979).

8. AE Cano Basave et al., "A Weakly Supervised Bayesian Model for Violence Detection in Social Media," *Proceedings of the Sixth International Joint Conference on Natural Language Processing* (Nagoya, Japan, 2013) pp. 109–17, accessed September 4, 2022, https://aclanthology.org/I13-1013.pdf.

9. Carl Sagan and Thornton Page, *UFOs: A Scientific Debate* (Cornell: Cornell University Press), pp. 15–16, January 1, 1996.

10. Michael D. Swords and Robert Powell et al., *UFOs and Government: A Historical Inquiry* (San Antonio: Anomalist Books, 2012), pp. 3–7.

11. Sagan and Page, *UFOs: A Scientific Debate*, p. 116.

12. "Dozens Report UFO Over Texas Town," *CBS News*, January 15, 2008, accessed September 25, 2022, https://www.cbsnews.com/news/dozens-report-ufo-over -texas-town/.

13. Robert Powell and Glenn Schulze, "Stephenville Lights: A Comprehensive Radar and Witness Report Study Regarding the Events of January 8, 2008," De-

cember 18, 2010, SCU, accessed August 14, 2022, https://www.explorescu.org/post /stephenville-lights-a-comprehensive-radar-and-witness-report-study.

14. United States Air Force, *Project Blue Book and Project SIGN*, review of card files for April 1951 through April 1953.

15. United States Air Force, *Project Blue Book and Project SIGN*, microfilm, review of card files for April 1, 1952, through April 7, 1952.

16. Edward Ruppelt, *The Report on Unidentified Flying Objects* (New York: Doubleday, 1956), pp. 111–18.

17. *International News Service*, July 28, 1952.

18. Motion Picture Films from the Army Library Copy Collection 1964–1980, Records Group 111, Maj. Gen. John A. Samford's statement on "Flying Saucers," Pentagon, Washington, D.C., July 31, 1952, National Archives at College Park, MD, accessed September 27, 2022. https://catalog.archives.gov/id/25738.

19. Swords and Powell, *UFOs and Government*, pp. 252–55.

20. United States Air Force, *Project Blue Book and Project SIGN*, microfilm, card file 1957.11, 7228923, White Sands, NM.

21. Coral Lorenzen, "The New Mexico Story," *APRO Bulletin*, November 1957, pp. 1, 5.

22. United States Air Force, *Project Blue Book and Project SIGN*, microfilm, review of card files for November 1, 1957, through November 6, 1957.

23. "NICAP: The Chronos," *NICAP*, accessed September 22, 2022, http://nicap .org/chronos.

24. "1960 Census of Population, Final Population Counts for States," *United States Census Bureau*, accessed September 29, 2022, https://www.census.gov/library/publi cations/1960/dec/population-pc-a1.html.

CHAPTER THREE

1. J. Allen Hynek, *The UFO Experience: A Scientific Inquiry* (New York: Ballantine Books, 1972), pp. 25–35.

2. Paul R. Hill, *Unconventional Flying Objects: A Scientific Analysis* (Charlottesville, VA: Hampton Roads Publishing, 1995), p. 15.

3. United States Air Force, *Project Blue Book and Project SIGN*, microfilm, card file 1952.03, Report IR-23-52, Misawa AFB, Japan, National Archives and Records Administration, Washington, D.C., Andrews AFB, MD.

4. Delbert E. Anderson, "A Compelling Patrol," *Ohio UFO Notebook* 11 (1996): p. 15.

5. Devlin Rugne and Robert Powell, "MUFON Case 41298 Revisited," MUFON Case Management System, case 41298, May 18, 2013.

6. United States Air Force, *Project Blue Book and Project SIGN*, card file 1952.06, Report 52-139, Kimpo AFB, Korea.

7. United States Air Force, *Project Blue Book and Project SIGN*, card file 1952.07, Report WGINT 3–52.

8. Edward Moran and James Clarkson, "MUFON Case 49005," July 15, 2013.

9. United States Air Force, *Project Blue Book and Project SIGN*, card file 1950.07, 9615244, Peril Strait, Alaska.

10. J. H. Kirkpatrick, letter to Dr. James McDonald, May 16, 1969, Papers of James McDonald, University of Arizona Archives, Tucson, Arizona.

11. "MUFON Case 9118," July 1979

12. "MUFON Case 76852," June 1992.

13. Phil Leech, "MUFON Case 74282," August 2013.

14. Michael D. Swords, *Grassroots UFOs: Case Reports from the Center for UFO Studies* (San Antonio: Anomalist Books, 2005), pp. 18–21, 169–74.

15. Patrick Reilly, "Several Recent UFO Sightings Reported by Pilots over the Pacific Ocean," *New York Post*, October 22, 2022, accessed October 24, 2022, https://nypost.com/2022/10/20/multiple-recent-ufo-sightings-reported-by-pilots-over-the-pacific-ocean/.

16. Harley D. Rutledge, *Project Identification: The First Scientific Field Study of UFO Phenomena* (Englewood Cliffs: Prentice-Hall, 1981), p. 4.

17. Rutledge, *Project Identification*, pp. 28–38, 66–67.

18. "Laser Microphones, and Long Distance Listening Becomes Reality," *Endoacustica Europe*, November 1, 2010, accessed October 25, 2022, https://www.endoacustica.com/blogen/2010/11/01/laser-microphones-and-long-distance-listening-becomes-reality/.

19. Pieter R. Roelfsema, Damiaan Denys, and P. Christiaan Klink, "Mind Reading and Writing: The Future of Neurotechnology," *Trends in Cognitive Sciences* 22, no. 7 (July 1, 2018): pp. 298–610. https://doi.org/10.1016/j.tics.2018.04.001.

CHAPTER FOUR

1. Keith Chester, *Strange Company: Military Encounters with UFOs in World War II* (San Antonio: Anomalist Books, 2007), p. 89.

2. Chester, *Strange Company*, p. 142.

3. United States Air Force, *Project Blue Book and Project SIGN*, microfilm, card file 1948.04, CX 59769, National Archives and Records Administration, Washington, D.C., Andrews AFB, MD.

4. United States Air Force, *Project Blue Book and Project SIGN*, card file 1952.05, 9614426.

5. Edward Condon, *Final Report of the Scientific Study of Unidentified Flying Objects* (E. P. Dutton, 1969), pp. 188–89.

6. Richard H. Hall, *The UFO Evidence* (New York: Barnes and Noble Books, 1997), p. 71.

7. Raymond E. Fowler, *Casebook of a UFO Investigator: A Personal Memoir* (Englewood Cliffs, NJ: Prentice-Hall, 1981), p. 31.

8. United States Air Force, *Project Blue Book and Project SIGN*, card file 1965.09, 9372331.

9. Bill Chalker, "The UFO Connection: Startling Implications for North West Cape and Australia's Security," *Omega Science Digest*, March 1985.

10. Bob Pratt files, MUFON. Interviews with patrolmen Troy Todd, Jerry Jeter, Forrest Bartlett, Michael Davidson, and John Birdsong, *National Enquirer*, June 13, 1978.

11. *"UFO INVESTIGATOR,"* October 1977, p. 4.

12. Hall, *The UFO Evidence*, p. 46.

13. Ibid, p. 40.

14. Linda Revis, "MUFON Case OH_US_0703-1988-0002," March 7, 1989.

15. The Cometa Report, "UFOs and Defense: What Should We Prepare For?" (Monaco: Éditions du Rocher, July 1999), p. 28, accessed November 20, 2022, https://translate.google.com/website?sl=fr&tl=en&hl=en&prev=search&u=https://static.blog4ever.com/2013/11/755757/cometa.pdf.

16. Amanda Perthen, "Pilots Tell of Cockpit Close Encounters," *London Daily Star*, July 16, 1993.

17. Robert Spearing, "MUFON Case 62960," MUFON Case Management System, case 62960, January 29, 2015.

18. Interviewee Brian Tietje (in person), interviewer Robert Powell, February 10, 2007.

19. Gary Neitzel, "MUFON Case 36765," March 26, 2012.

20. David Kreiter, "MUFON Case 69105," August 8, 2015.

21. United States Air Force, *Project Blue Book and Project SIGN*, card file 1952.05, Report IR-23-52.

22. United States Air Force, *Project Blue Book and Project SIGN*, card file 1968.10, 7170577 and 6981875.

23. Thomas Tulien, "A Narrative of UFO Events at Minot Air Force Base," October 24, 1968—Minot AFB, North Dakota, accessed November 24, 2022, https://minotb52ufo.com/.

24. Claude Poher, "Analysis of Radar and Air-Visual UFO Observations on October 24, 1968 at Minot AFB, North Dakota, USA," August 2005, accessed November 25, 2022, https://www.explorescu.org/post/analysis-of-radar-and-air-visual-ufo-observations-on-24-october-1968-at-minot-afb-north-dakota-usa/.

25. Robert Powell, "July 1975: F-4 Phantom Jets vs. Otherworldly Craft," *SCU Review*, 2.3, no. [6] (July 2021): p. 10, accessed November 13, 2022, https://www.explorescu.org/post/scu-review-volume-2-3.

26. Michael Kalloniatis and Charles Luu, "Visual Acuity," Webvision, June 5, 2007, accessed November 26, 2022, https://webvision.med.utah.edu/book/part-viii-psychophysics-of-vision/visual-acuity/.

27. Robert Powell et al., "A Forensic Analysis of Navy Carrier Strike Group Eleven's Encounter with an Anomalous Aerial Vehicle," March 2019, accessed November 28, 2022, https://www.explorescu.org/post/2004-uss-nimitz-strike-navy-group-incident-report/.

28. Powell, "A Forensic Analysis of Navy Carrier Strike Group Eleven's Encounter with an Anomalous Aerial Vehicle," pp. 196–225.

29. Salvatore Pais, "Inertial Mass Reduction Device: Navy Case PAX 205," 2000, accessed November 29, 2022, https://www.navair.navy.mil/foia/sites/g/files/jejdrs566/files/document/%5Bfilename%5D/2021-003244%20FINAL%20VERSION%20PAX%20205%20-%20INERTIAL%20MASS%20REDUCTION%20DEVICE.pdf.

30. Harold White, "Warp Field Mechanics 101," NASA Johnson Space Center, September 2011, accessed November 29, 2022, https://ntrs.nasa.gov/api/cita tions/20110015936/downloads/20110015936.pdf.

CHAPTER FIVE

1. Mark Rodeghier, "UFO Reports Involving Vehicle Interference: A Catalogue and Data Analysis," *Center for UFO Studies*, October 1981, accessed December 14, 2022. http://www.cufos.org/books/UFO_REPORTS_INVOLVING_VEHICLE_IN TERFERENCE.pdf.

2. Leonard Stringfield, *Civilian Research, Interplanetary Flying Objects Newsletter*, January 7, 1955.

3. United States Air Force, *Project Blue Book and Project SIGN*, card file 1949.07, 6310669, National Archives and Records Administration, Washington, D.C., Andrews AFB, MD.

4. Coral E. Lorenzen, *The Great Flying Saucer Hoax: The UFO Facts and Their Interpretation* (New York: William-Frederick Press, January 1962), pp. 17–23.

5. Kenju Terauchi (Captain with Japan Air Lines) [statement to the FAA] translation by Sayoko Mimoto, November 17, 1986. https://www.theblackvault.com/docu mentarchive/ufo-case-japanese-airlines-jal1628-november-17-1986/.

6. Beverly Trout, "MUFON Case 70430," MUFON Case Management System, case 70430, July 2004.

7. Robert Powell, "MUFON Case 50042," August 21, 2013.

8. United States Air Force, *Project Blue Book and Project SIGN*, file 24–411.

9. Rodeghier, "UFO Reports Involving Vehicle Interference," pp. 2–5.

10. Ibid., pp. 8–13.

11. Ibid.

12. Chuck Modlin, "MUFON Case 20706," November 25, 2009.

13. Brad Sparks, "Comprehensive Catalog of 1,700 Project Blue Book UFO Unknowns: Database Catalog," December 20, 2016, accessed December 23, 2022. https://www.pdfdrive.com/comprehensive-catalog-of-1700-project-blue-book-ufo -unknowns-e30734801.html.

14. Telephone interview of Lt. Col. Howard Wright by Dr. James McDonald, May 16, 1970, Series 1, Box 15, Wright, Col. Howard T.: B-25 Texas case 1/16/57, Papers of James E. McDonald, University of Arizona Archives, University of Arizona, Tucson, Arizona.

15. United States Air Force, *Project Blue Book and Project SIGN*, card file 1957.01, 6786486.

16. Carl Sagan and Thornton Page, *UFO's: A Scientific Debate* (London: Cornell University Press, 1972), pp. 56–70.

17. Edward Condon, *Final Report of the Scientific Study of Unidentified Flying Objects* (Boston: E. P. Dutton & Co., 1969), pp. 204–7.

18. United States Air Force, *Project Blue Book and Project SIGN*, card file 1957.07, 6961742.

19. United States Air Force, *Project Blue Book and Project SIGN*, card file 1957.07, 6962862.

20. United States Air Force, *Project Blue Book and Project SIGN*, card file 1957.07, 6966211.

21. United States Air Force, *Project Blue Book and Project SIGN*, card file 1957.07, 6964142.

22. United States Air Force, *Project Blue Book and Project SIGN*, card file 1964.11, 8721949.

23. Ibid.

24. Office of the Director of National Intelligence, "Preliminary Assessment: Unidentified Aerial Phenomena," June 25, 2001, accessed December 25, 2022. https://www.dni.gov/files/ODNI/documents/assessments/Prelimary-Assessment-UAP-20210625.pdf.

CHAPTER SIX

1. Dave Keel, "MUFON Case 13112," MUFON Case Management System, case 13112, October 20, 2008.

2. Dan Wright, "MUFON Case 1414," MUFON Case Management System, case 1414, December 7, 2001.

3. George Hoenig, "MUFON Case 930703E," MUFON UFO report evaluation, July 12, 1993.

4. W. L. Garner, "MUFON Case 930824C," MUFON UFO report evaluation, August 24, 1993.

5. *Melbourne Sun*, April 12, 1966.

6. "The Case of the Diverted Headlight Beams—What Caused This Phenomenon," *Maryborough Advertiser*, April 13, 1966, p. 5.

7. Bill Chalker, "The Bent Headlight Beam Case Revisited," *UFO Research Australia Newsletter*, May–June 1984, pp. 17–30.

8. United States Air Force, Project Blue Book and Project SIGN, card file 1968.11, 7170923, National Archives and Records Administration, Washington, D.C., Andrews AFB, MD.

9. Erling Jensen, "The UFO near Haderslev," *The Scandinavian UFO Information Newsletter*, September–October 1970.

10. Leslie Harris, "UFOs and Solid Light Phenomena," *Flying Saucer Review* 23, no. 4 (January 1978): pp. 3–6.

11. Auguste Meessen, "The Belgian Wave and the Photos of Ramillies," 2011, pp. 6–7, Belgian Committee for the Study of Space Phenomena, accessed January 17, 2023, http://www.cobeps.org/pdf/Ramillies.pdf.

12. Melvin Podell, "MUFON Case 18743," MUFON Case Management System, case 18743, August 2009.

13. Keith Basterfield, "Boyup Brook Revisited," *UFO Research Australia Newsletter*, September–October 1983, pp. 3–6.

14. National UFO Reporting Center, Hesperia, Michigan, accessed January 21, 2023, https://nuforc.org/webreports/reports/067/S67734.html.

15. Laurie Mustard, "This Was One Weird Close Encounter," *Winnipeg SUN*, October 4, 2002.

CHAPTER SEVEN

1. National UFO Reporting Center, accessed February 12, 2023, https://nuforc .org/webreports/ndxloc.html.

2. Mutual UFO Network, accessed February 12, 2023, https://mufoncms.com /last_20_report_public.html.

3. U.S. Air Force, "Unidentified Flying Objects and Air Force Project Blue Book," accessed February 12, 2023, https://www.af.mil/About-Us/Fact-Sheets /Display/Article/104590/unidentified-flying-objects-and-air-force-project-blue-book/.

4. Michael D. Swords and Robert Powell et al., *UFOs and Government: A Historical Inquiry* (San Antonio: Anomalist Books, 2012), pp. 177–200.

5. Carl Bernstein, "The CIA and the Media," *Rolling Stone*, October 20, 1977, pp. 55–67.

6. Terry Hansen, "Psychological Operations," *The Missing Times: News Media Complicity in the UFO Cover-up*, 2nd ed. (Self-published: Terry Hansen, 2012), pp. 235–43.

7. Ryan Smith, "O'Hare UFO Sighting in 2006 One of the Most Famous Reported," *Chicago Tribune*, March 20, 2013, accessed February 21, 2023, https://www .chicagotribune.com/redeye/ct-redeye-xpm-2013-03-20-37880251-story.html.

8. Office of the Director of National Intelligence, "Fiscal Year 2019 Annual Report on Security Clearance Determinations," April 2020, accessed February 20, 2023, https://fas.org/sgp/othergov/intel/clear-2019-nocontract.pdf.

9. Swords and Powell, *UFOs and Government*, pp. 100–3, pp. 500–2.

10. 654th Aircraft Control and Warning Squadron Grenier Air Force Base, Manchester, New Hampshire, Unit History, April to June 1950.

11. Larry Auldridge, "Jets on 24-Hour Alert to Shoot Down 'Saucers'," *The San Francisco Examiner*, July 29, 1952, p. 2.

12. Gen. William Garland interview by Robert Ginna of *Life* magazine, "Memorandum for the Record, Flying Saucers," February 28, 1952.

13. Edward Ruppelt, *The Report on Unidentified Flying Objects* (New York: Doubleday, 1956), pp. 1–3.

14. USAF Academy, *Introductory Space Science, Volume II*, Chapter 33, 1970.

15. Peter Griffiths, "U.S. Pilot Was Ordered to Shoot Down UFO," Reuters (London), October 20, 2008, accessed February 21, 2023, https://www.reuters.com/article /uk-britain-ufo/u-s-pilot-was-ordered-to-shoot-down-ufo-idUKTRE49J1P620081020.

16. Victor Rodriguez, "MUFON Case 74787," MUFON Case Management System, case 74787, February 26, 2016.

17. Robert Powell and Peter Reali et al., "A Forensic Analysis of Navy Carrier Strike Group Eleven's Encounter with an Anomalous Aerial Vehicle," March 2019,

pp. 6–7, accessed February 22, 2023, https://www.explorescu.org/post/2004-uss -nimitz-strike-navy-group-incident-report.

18. Derrick Taylor, "A Timeline of the U.F.O.s That Were Shot Down," *New York Times*, February 21, 2023, accessed February 23, 2023, https://www.nytimes.com /article/ufo-object-balloon-shot-down.html.

19. Katie Rogers, "Inside the Hunt for U.F.O.s at the End of the World," *New York Times*, February 20, 2023, accessed February 23, 2023, https://www.nytimes .com/2023/02/20/us/politics/ufos-alaska-deadhorse.html.

20. Ed Kilgore, "Jimmy Carter Saw a UFO on This Day in 1973," *Intelligencer*, September 18, 2019, accessed February 24, 2023, https://nymag.com/intel ligencer/2019/09/jimmy-carter-saw-a-ufo-on-this-day-in-1973.html.

21. Steve Brusk, "Kucinich: I Saw a UFO," CNN, October 31, 2007, accessed February 25, 2023, https://politicalticker.blogs.cnn.com/2007/10/31/kucinich-i-saw -a-ufo/.

22. Barack Obama, *Late Late Show with James Corden*, question by Reggie Watts, May 19, 2021, accessed February 25, 2023, https://www.cnn.com/videos/me dia/2021/05/19/barack-obama-talks-ufos-late-late-show-int-orig-bdk.cnn.

23. NASA—Climate Science Investigations, "Why Must Scientists Be Skeptics," accessed February 26, 2023, http://www.ces.fau.edu/nasa/introduction/scientific -inquiry/why-must-scientists-be-skeptics.php.

24. Pew Research Center, "Public and Scientists' Views on Science and Society," January 29, 2015, accessed February 27, 2023, https://www.pewresearch.org/sci ence/2015/01/29/public-and-scientists-views-on-science-and-society/.

25. Peter Sturrock, "Report on a Survey of the Membership of the American Astronomical Society Concerning the UFO Problem," *Journal of Scientific Exploration* 8, no. 1, 1994, pp. 1–45.

26. James McDonald, "Science in Default: Twenty-Two Years of Inadequate UFO Investigations," American Association for the Advancement of Science, 134th Meeting, December 27, 1969.

CHAPTER EIGHT

1. Seth Shostak, "The Drake Equation," SETI Institute, July 2021, accessed March 11, 2023, https://www.seti.org/drake-equation-index.

2. A. Wolszczan and D. A. Frail, "A Planetary System around the Millisecond Pulsar PSR1257 + 12," *Nature* (1992).

3. NASA Exoplanet Archive, NASA, accessed March 14, 2023, https://exoplanet archive.ipac.caltech.edu/index.html.

4. The Habitable Exoplanets Catalog, The Planetary Habitability Laboratory of the University of Puerto Rico at Arecibo, accessed March 14, 2023, https://phl.upr .edu/projects/habitable-exoplanets-catalog.

5. Cornell University, "Astronomers Discover a Huge Chemical 'Factory' in Interstellar Space, Suggesting Origin of Water in Solar System," *ScienceDaily*, accessed March 13, 2023, www.sciencedaily.com/releases/1998/04/980410102358.htm.

6. Colin Stuart, "Water on Earth Might Predate the Solar System," *Sky and Telescope*, March 13, 2023, accessed March 15, 2023, https://skyandtelescope.org /astronomy-news/water-earth-predates-solar-system/.

7. Heidi Newberg, "Diffractive Interfero Coronagraph Exoplanet Resolver (DICER): Detecting and Characterizing All Earth-Like Exoplanets Orbiting Sun-Like Stars Within 10 pc," NASA, January 9, 2023, accessed March 20, 2023, https://www .nasa.gov/directorates/spacetech/niac/2023/Diffractive_Interfero_Coronagraph_Exo planet_Resolver/.

8. Paco Chierici, "There I Was: The X-Files Edition," *Fighter Sweep*, March 14, 2015, accessed August 8, 2018, https://fightersweep.com/1460/x-files-edition/.

9. Robert Powell and Peter Reali et al., "A Forensic Analysis of Navy Carrier Strike Group Eleven's Encounter with an Anomalous Aerial Vehicle," March 2019, pp. 28–93, accessed March 16, 2023, https://www.explorescu.org/post/2004-uss-nim itz-strike-navy-group-incident-report.

10. Leslie Kean, Ralph Blumenthal, and Helene Cooper, "Real U.F.O.s? Pentagon Unit Tried to Know," *New York Times*, December 17, 2017, p. 1.

11. Chris Mellon, personal notes, email to the author, July 13, 2023.

12. Kean, Blumenthal, and Cooper, "'Wow, What Is That?' Navy Pilots Report Unexplained Flying Objects," *New York Times*, May 26, 2019.

13. Helene Cooper and Julian E. Barnes, "U.S. Finds No Evidence of Alien Technology in Flying Objects, but Can't Rule It Out, Either," *New York Times*, June 3, 2021.

14. *Late Late Show with James Corden*, Question by Reggie Watts, May 19, 2021, accessed February 25, 2023, https://www.cnn.com/videos/media/2021/05/19/barack -obama-talks-ufos-late-late-show-int-orig-bdk.cnn.

15. Courtney Kennedy and Arnold Lau, "Most Americans Believe in Intelligent Life beyond Earth; Few See UFOs as a Major National Security Threat," Pew Research Center, June 30, 2021, accessed March 20, 2023, https://www.pewresearch.org/fact -tank/2021/06/30/most-americans-believe-in-intelligent-life-beyond-earth-few-see -ufos-as-a-major-national-security-threat/.

16. Edward Ruppelt, *The Report on Unidentified Flying Objects* (New York: Doubleday, 1956).

17. John "Jay" Stratton, personal notes, email to the author, September 2, 2023.

18. John Stratton, "The Pentagon's Top UFO Hunter–Guest : John 'Jay' Stratton," Audacy Podcast, interview of John Stratton by George Knapp, February 7, 2023, accessed March 22, 2023, https://www.audacy.com/podcast/weaponized-with-jeremy -corbell-george-knapp-6d09d/episodes/the-pentagons-top-ufo-hunter-guest-john-jay -stratton-4c145.

19. Ryan Graves, "We Have a Real UFO Problem. And It's Not Balloons," *Politico*, February 28, 2023, accessed March 24, 2023, https://www.politico.com/news /magazine/2023/02/28/ufo-uap-navy-intelligence-00084537.

20. Adam Goldsack, "They're Not Going to Hide It," UAP Media UK, August 29, 2022, accessed March 24, 2023, https://www.uapmedia.uk/articles/sengillibrand.

21. Jake Tapper, "Romney on UFOs: 'I Guess All Things Are Possible'," *CNN Politics*, June 27, 2021, accessed March 24, 2023, https://www.cnn.com/videos/poli tics/2021/06/27/sotu-romney-on-ufos.cnn.

22. Dan Robitzski, "Senator 'Can't Imagine' UFOs Came from Anywhere on Earth," The_Byte, May 21, 2021, accessed March 24, 2023, https://futurism.com/the-byte/senator-ufos-earth.

23. "H.R.7900—National Defense Authorization Act for Fiscal Year 2023," 117th Congress (2021–2022), pp. 1432–1435, 2882–2903, accessed March 24, 2023, https://www.congress.gov/bill/117th-congress/house-bill/7900.

24. Scientific Coalition for UAP Studies, accessed March 26, 2023, https://www.explorescu.org/.

25. Harvard University, The Galileo Project, accessed March 26, 2023, https://projects.iq.harvard.edu/galileo.

26. "Solar System Exploration: Our Galactic Neighborhood, Oumuamua," NASA, accessed March 26, 2023, https://solarsystem.nasa.gov/asteroids-comets-and-meteors/comets/oumuamua/in-depth/.

27. "Preliminary Assessment: Unidentified Aerial Phenomena," Office of the Director of National Intelligence, June 25, 2021, accessed March 21, 2023, https://www.dni.gov/files/ODNI/documents/assessments/Prelimary-Assessment-UAP-20210625.pdf.

28. University of Würzburg, "Detecting Unknown Anomalies: Artificial Intelligence for Space," *SciTechDaily*, April 15, 2021, accessed March 28, 2023, https://scitechdaily.com/detecting-unknown-anomalies-artificial-intelligence-for-space/.

29. NASA Science: Space Place, NASA, accessed March 28, 2023, https://spaceplace.nasa.gov/science/en/.

CHAPTER NINE

1. Thomas S. Kuhn, *The Structure of Scientific Revolutions* (Chicago: The University of Chicago Press, 1962), p. 37.

2. Harley D. Rutledge, *Project Identification: The First Scientific Study of UFO Phenomena* (Englewood Cliffs, New Jersey: Prentice-Hall, 1981).

3. Matthew Szenher et al., "A Hardware and Software Platform for Aerial Object Localization," *Journal of Astronomical Instrumentation* 12, no. 1 (2023). DOI: 10.1142/S2251171723400020.

4. National Reconnaissance Office, "Recent Sentient Highlights, May 6, 2021, "Freedom of Information Request, Approved for Release: 2022/06/02 C05136331, accessed April 17, 2023, https://documents3.theblackvault.com/documents/nro/C05136334.pdf.

5. Office of the Director of National Intelligence, "Preliminary Assessment: Unidentified Aerial Phenomena," June 25, 2021, accessed April 14, 2023, https://www.dni.gov/files/ODNI/documents/assessments/Prelimary-Assessment-UAP-20210625.pdf.

6. The Black Vault, "June 2021 Classified UAP / UFO Report Given to Congress Partially Released," Freedom of Information Request, March 23, 2022, accessed April 14, 2023, https://www.theblackvault.com/documentarchive/june-2021-classified-uap-ufo-report-given-to-congress-partially-released/.

7. Sean Kirkpatrick, "Subcommittee on Emerging Threats and Capabilities Hearing Status Open/Closed: To Receive Testimony on the Mission, Activities, Oversight,

and Budget of the All-Domain Anomaly Resolution Office," April 19, 2023, audio and video, 2hr:11min:47sec to 2hr:11min:53sec, https://www.armed-services.senate .gov/hearings/to-receive-testimony-on-the-mission-activities-oversight-and-budget -of-the-all-domain-anomaly-resolution-office-

8. United States Air Force, *Project Blue Book and Project SIGN*, microfilm, card file 1957.11, National Archives and Records Administration, Washington, D.C., Andrews AFB, MD.

9. United States Air Force, *Project Blue Book and Project SIGN*, card file 1959.06, 8406927, Papua, New Guinea.

10. Walter Sheets, "MUFON Case 1473," MUFON Case Management System, case 1473, September 8, 2001.

11. Jennifer Chu, "E.T., We're Home," MIT News Office, April 1, 1936, http:// www.macleans.ca/archives/what-was-the-price-of-vimy-ridge/.

12. "F-4 Phantom Fighter Bomber," U.S. Air Force, June 25, 2012, accessed April 30, 2023, https://www.airforce-technology.com/projects/f-4-phantom-fighter -bomber/.

13. "F-15 Eagle," U.S. Air Force, April 2019, accessed April 30, 2023, https:// www.af.mil/About-Us/Fact-Sheets/Display/Article/104501/f-15-eagle/.

14. "Texas Instruments Model 99/4A Personal Computer," Smithsonian National Museum of American History, accessed April 30, 2023, https://americanhistory.si .edu/collections/search/object/nmah_1064832.

CHAPTER TEN

1. Giuseppe Cocconi and Philip Morrison, "Searching for Interstellar Communi- cations," *Nature* 184, no. 4690 (September 19, 1959): pp. 844–46.

2. Seth Shostak, "UFOs," SETI Institute, accessed May 29, 2023, https://www .seti.org/ufos.

3. Noam Levin et al., "Remote Sensing of Night Lights: A Review and an Out- look for the Future," *Remote Sensing of Environment* 237 (February 2020).

4. National Space Society, "Development of Interstellar Travel and Settlement," accessed May 29, 2023, https://space.nss.org/nss-roadmap-to-space-settlement-3rd -edition-2018-part-6/#milestone30

5. Dirk Schulze-Makuch, "The 100-Year Starship Symposium—A Historic Meet- ing?," *Astrobiology* 12, issue 1 (January 23, 2012).

6. Harold White et al., "Eagleworks Laboratories: Advanced Propulsion Phys- ics Research," December 5, 2011. Joint Propulsion Meeting, December 5–9, 2011, Huntsville, Alabama.

7. Breakthrough Initiatives, "News," accessed May 29, 2023, https://breakthrough initiatives.org/news/4.

8. John Wenz, "Exclusive: NASA Has Begun Plans for a 2069 Interstellar Mis- sion," *New Scientist*, December 19, 2017, accessed May 30, 2023, https://www .newscientist.com/article/mg23631576-000-exclusive-nasa-has-begun-plans-for-a -2069-interstellar-mission/.

9. Ryan Finnerty, "Adjusted Radar Settings Likely behind Rash of Unknown Object Detections," *FlightGlobal*, February 13, 2023, accessed June 4, 2023, https://www.flightglobal.com/military-uavs/adjusted-radar-settings-likely-behind-rash-of-usas-unknown-object-detections/152026.article.

10. Kevin H. Knuth, Robert M. Powell, and Peter A. Reali, "Estimating Flight Characteristics of Anomalous Unidentified Aerial Vehicles," *Entropy* 21, no. 10 (October 2019), https://doi.org/10.3390/e21100939.

11. Lockheed Martin, "Cleared for Takeoff: The Hypersonic Flight Era," July 30, 2019, accessed June 6, 2023, https://www.lockheedmartin.com/en-us/news/features/2019-features/cleared-for-takeoff-hypersonic-flight.html.

12. Eric M. Jones, "Where Is Everybody?," An account of Fermi's question from a collection of letters by those at the luncheon (1985), doi:10.2172/5746675, accessed June 10, 2023, https://www.osti.gov/servlets/purl/5746675.

13. Michael H. Hart, "Explanation for the Absence of Extraterrestrials on Earth," *Quarterly Journal of the Royal Astronomical Society* 16 (1975): pp. 128–35.

14. John A. Ball, "The Zoo Hypothesis," *Icarus* 19 (1973): pp. 347–49.

15. Iasmina Hornoiu, "Animals Are More Than We Think: Empathy and Social Intelligence in Animals," *Finding Neuron*, January 26, 2021, accessed June 15, 2023, https://finding-neuron.com/2021/01/06/empathy-and-social-intelligence-in-animals/.

CHAPTER ELEVEN

1. NASA, "Are We Alone in the Universe? NASA Calls for New Framework," October 27, 2021, accessed June 20, 2023, https://www.nasa.gov/feature/are-we-alone-in-the-universe-nasa-calls-for-new-framework.

2. NASA, "Public Meeting on Unidentified Anomalous Phenomena (Official NASA Broadcast)," May 31, 2023, accessed June 20, 2023, https://www.youtube.com/watch?v=bQo08JRY0iM&t=12109s.

3. Marc Kaufman, NASA, "Technosignatures and the Search for Extraterrestrial Intelligence," October 18, 2018, updated June 22, 2023, accessed June 24, 2023, https://astrobiology.nasa.gov/news/technosignatures-and-the-search-for-extraterrestrial-intelligence/.

4. NASA, "NASA Partners Worldwide," August 24, 2021, accessed June 23, 2023, https://www.nasa.gov/oiir/nasa-partners-worldwide.

Index

Page references for figures are italicized.

About the Author

Robert Powell is a founding board member of the Scientific Coalition for UAP Studies (SCU), a 280-member organization with the mission of bringing science to the investigation of UFOs. He was the director of research at MUFON from 2007–2017 and created MUFON's Science Review Board in 2012. Powell is one of two authors of the detailed radar/witness report on the "Stephenville Lights" as well as the SCU report "UAP: 2013 Aguadilla, Puerto Rico." He is the primary author on the recently published paper, "A Forensic Analysis of Navy Carrier Strike Group Eleven's Encounter with an Anomalous Aerial Vehicle" and a secondary author of a paper published in the journal *Entropy* entitled, "Estimating Flight Characteristics of Anomalous Unidentified Aerial Vehicles." Powell is a member of the Society for Scientific Exploration, the UFODATA project, and the National Space Society. He is a coauthor of a book published in July 2012: *UFOs and Government: A Historical Inquiry* and the author of a book designed for children published in November 2020 entitled *The Truth About UFOs: A Scientific Perspective.*

Powell has a BS in chemistry and is a former collegiate debater. He has twenty-eight years of experience in engineering management in the semiconductor industry. He helped Advanced Micro Devices develop its first flash memory technology that is used in today's flash cards for cameras, PCs, video cameras, and other products. His experience includes managing a state-of-the-art chemistry laboratory and managing a research and development group that worked on nanotechnology using atomic force microscopes, near-field optical microscopy, and other techniques. Powell is also a coholder of four patents related to nanotechnology. He currently resides in Austin, Texas.

Milton Keynes UK
Ingram Content Group UK Ltd.
UKHW022012210324
439914UK00004BA/27